MW01195620

FIGHTING FOR CITIZENSHIP

CIVIL WAR AMERICA

PETER S. CARMICHAEL, CAROLINE E. JANNEY,
AND AARON SHEEHAN-DEAN, EDITORS

This landmark series interprets broadly the history and culture of the Civil War era through the long nineteenth century and beyond. Drawing on diverse approaches and methods, the series publishes historical works that explore all aspects of the war, biographies of leading commanders, and tactical and campaign studies, along with select editions of primary sources. Together, these books shed new light on an era that remains central to our understanding of American and world history.

FIGHTING FOR CITIZENSHIP

BLACK NORTHERNERS AND THE DEBATE OVER MILITARY SERVICE IN THE CIVIL WAR

Brian Taylor

THE UNIVERSITY OF NORTH CAROLINA PRESS

CHAPEL HILL

Designed by April Leidig

Set in Miller by Copperline Book Services

Manufactured in the United States of America

The University of North Carolina Press has been a member
of the Green Press Initiative since 2003.

Library of Congress Cataloging-in-Publication Data

Names: Taylor, Brian (Brian M.), author.

Title: Fighting for citizenship : black Northerners and the debate over
military service in the Civil War / Brian Taylor.

Other titles: Civil War America (Series)

Description: Chapel Hill : The University of North Carolina Press, 2020. |
Series: Civil War America | Includes bibliographical references and index.

Identifiers: LCCN 2020004162 | ISBN 9781469659763 (cloth) |
ISBN 9781469659770 (pbk. : alk. paper) | ISBN 9781469659787 (ebook)

Subjects: LCSH: Citizenship—United States—History. | African American
soldiers—History—19th century. | African Americans—United States—
History—19th century. | United States—History—Civil War,
1861–1865—African Americans.

Classification: LCC E540.N3 T29 2020 | DDC 973.7/415—dc23

LC record available at https://lccn.loc.gov/2020004162

For my father, Steve, for letting me take his history
books off the shelf to look at the pictures;

my mother, Lois, for teaching me to write
despite my best efforts to the contrary;

my sister, Jenny, for putting up with
the cannon fire down the hall;

my wife, Diane, for her unwavering love and support and
for letting me turn that shoe rack into a bookshelf;

my son, Steve, for allowing me to practice my lectures
during our walks around the neighborhood;

and my mentor and friend Chandra Manning for
teaching me about the craft of history and for looking past
potentially problematic sports allegiances.

"Some things you will remember;
some things stay sweet forever."
—JOHN DARNIELLE

CONTENTS

ACKNOWLEDGMENTS

MY FIRST THANKS GO to the staff of the University of North Carolina Press and the editorial board of the press's Civil War America series, especially Mark Simpson-Vos, Jessica Newman, Caroline Janney, Jay Mazzocchi, and Elizabeth Crowder. For the past three years, the UNC Press staff and the Civil War America board have given their time, attention, and expertise to my project. They have helped me sharpen my argument, address questions left unanswered in my original manuscript, and refine my prose. When I have needed extra time for revisions or responses to readers' comments, they have been patient and understanding. Their assistance has improved this project immeasurably. Thanks are due to the staffs at the following archives: Commonwealth of Massachusetts Archives, Historical Society of Pennsylvania, Library of Congress, Massachusetts Historical Society, and Moorland-Springarn Research Center at Howard University. Thanks are also due to the staff of Georgetown's Lauinger Library, especially Maura Seale and Scott Taylor.

During the time I have spent working on this project, I have had the opportunity to teach at three wonderful schools: Georgetown University, the University of Maryland, Baltimore County, and the Universities at Shady Grove. At Georgetown, I benefited from the opportunity to learn from and work alongside Katie Benton-Cohen, Maurice Jackson, Michael Kazin, Amy Leonard, Joseph McCartin, Meredith McKittrick, David Painter, Aviel Roshwald, Erika Seamon, and James Shedel. Special thanks go to Adam Rothman for the time and attention he devoted to this project; I have learned a great deal about writing, interpreting sources, and coming up with titles from Adam. Special thanks also to Stephen Kantrowitz, for his attention to this manuscript. At UMBC and Shady Grove, I am grateful to Amy Froide, Anne Sarah Rubin, and Andrew Nolan for their time, advice and support. Gratitude is also due to Djuana Shields, Jan Liverance, and Jessica Knoll for their patience and assistance.

Over the past few years, I have cherished the opportunity to work with engaged, enthusiastic, motivated undergraduate students like Kat Ball, Jack

Bennett, Shannon Burke, Maggie Chaquette, Matt Costas, Sian Davies, Megan Howell, Rob Kasper, Aidan Kenney, Peter Kentz, Casey Kuhns, Brynne Long, Devinie Lye, Maria Marshall, Read Masino, Andrew Meshnick, Casey Nolan, Aidan Poling, John Reilly, Jack Romine, Nick Simon, Emma Thompson, and Philip Tsien. You have inspired me with your intellectual curiosity and challenged me to look at the past in new ways. Thanks are also due to those who signed their names a couple of years ago; it means more than you can know. I am humbled to think that my teaching may have had a positive impact on your lives. Thank you.

Three students from my Georgetown years made significant contributions to this manuscript. Viviana DeSantis, Catherine Hanlon, and Andreas Paraskevopolous assisted me with this project by combing through the digital archives of black and abolitionist newspapers. Their research was an invaluable aid to me as I revised the early chapters of this work, and their enthusiasm for and dedication to this project helped me immeasurably. Andreas, Catherine, and Viviana, words cannot adequately express my gratitude for the contributions you made to this project. Thank you.

During my graduate studies, I was lucky enough to connect with some fellow travelers whose expertise and friendship I have benefited from to no end. These include Anthony Eames, Graham Hough-Cornwell, Jeff Reger, Kate Stier, and Cory Young. Thanks are due to Elena Abbott for weeknights at Paradiso and for real talk during our first year teaching; to my friend and coauthor Tom Foley—anyone who has heard me lecture knows that I got many of my best ideas from conversations I had with Tom while walking to the Metro in the fall of 2015; and to Jordan Smith, another regular at Paradiso, for his steadfast friendship and for always giving me a place to stay in Philly.

I would be remiss not to thank the many good people I worked with at the National Museum of American History during the course of completing this project. During my time at NMAH, I was fortunate enough to work with Terry Averill—who plays the best John Brown you'll ever see—Xavier Carnegie, Katie Hardy, Julia Imbriaco, Elisabeth Kilday, Brianna Kosowitz, Tory Martin, Susan Evans McClure, and Chris Wilson. Thanks are also due to the staff of Politics and Prose, in particular Bob Attardi, as well as Nick Day and Sandra Palacios-Casado.

Before coming to D.C., I learned about history from Clayton Black, Marc Gallicchio, Judith Giesberg, Charlene Mires, Paul Rosier, Father Joseph Ryan, Janet Sorrentino, and Carol Wilson; about writing and politics from Christine Wade; and about the greatest speeches in U.S. history from Michele Volansky. Thank you all.

I would not have completed this project without the following people, friends I met outside the worlds of academia and public history who have supported me at every turn: Josh and Shannon Arnie, Dan and Lauren Beadell, Anthony and Elizabeth Capone, Wayne and Jane Carey, Natalie Eder, Erick Kuhlmann and Olivia Pyanoe, Kevin and Laura McGarry, Carlos and Susan Miranda, Chris Reese, Steve and Ally Reuter, Mandy and Shawn Spencer, Arlene and Tony Urbanski, Adam and Caralynn Walters, and Cathy Zomlefer. Special thanks are due to Brandon and Liz Becker—Brandon always offered me a sympathetic ear during the years we were both in grad school, and Brandon and Liz brought me a stopwatch once, which was really nice of them. I also owe particular thanks to Tom Knox, a fellow member of Team Stay Positive, one hell of a center fielder, and a friend "of life"; and to Tony Lopiano, a fellow academic whose support and commiseration has been invaluable, and who is a reliable ally when the pit turns rough. Further gratitude goes to and Eddie and Kristen Raleigh—Eddie was my partner in crime during my first year in D.C., while I was starting this project. Thanks to all members of Hal's Angels, past and present; all members of QIMP, past and present, especially Dom Lopiano; and everyone from Pub Quiz at Quarry House. You all always made Sundays something to look forward to.

Throughout the process of completing this project, I have been buoyed by the relentless support of my extended family. Thanks are due to Betty and Buck Caudill, Lane Swenson, Paul Swenson and Kiera McNamara, Kathy Taylor and Teri Weston. Special thanks are owed to Diane Lane, a constant source of encouragement whom I have often turned to for advice during the process of completing this project, and Tom Lawler, the best father-in-law a guy could ask for and a tireless champion of my work. I also extend gratitude to Holly, Jackie and Archie, who, he would like it known, should be listed as a coauthor of this work.

Thanks are due some people who have no earthly idea who I am but whose work has inspired me: John Darnielle, Brian Fallon, Craig Finn, Dave Hause, John K. Samson, Bruce Springsteen, Patrick Stickles, Joe Strummer, Dan Yemin—your music was the soundtrack to this project. Thanks also to Nick Foles, Brandon Graham, Malcolm Jenkins, Jason Kelce, and the entire 2017–18 Philadelphia Eagles—all we got, all we need.

I am grateful to some friends and family who never got to see this project completed. Morgan West was a gentle giant gone too soon. Ed Langrall was one of the most selfless men I've ever met. Uncle Bill, I would've loved to see this book in your library. Deborah Lawler was a steadfast supporter of my work and of the life Diane and I built together. I love and miss you all.

Eagle-eyed readers of this book's front matter will notice that the following people were already mentioned in the dedication; I think that if you write a book, you get to thank people twice if that's what you want to do. Chandra Manning has seen this project through from front to back and is the best mentor I could've hoped for, an incredibly warm, generous soul to whom I am eternally grateful. My parents and sister have never given me anything but love, support, and encouragement; there is no *Fighting for Citizenship* without Steve, Lois, and Jenny Taylor. I am writing this on October 6, 2019, seven years to the day since I married my wife, Diane; from the jump, she believed in me and my ability to complete this project, and she has had my back the whole way. Like the song says, "You were the only one who understood me then; you're the only one who will." Our son, Steve, is sleeping upstairs; maybe he'll write a book someday, or maybe he won't. Whatever he does, I hope he is lucky enough to have the support of a group of colleagues, friends, and family as wonderful as the group I've just thanked. Once more, thank you.

INTRODUCTION

"**O** HEAVENLY FATHER, we want you to let our folks know that we died facing the enemy! We want 'em to know that we went down standing up! Amongst those that are fighting against our oppression. We want 'em to know, Heavenly Father, that we died for freedom!" John Rawlins, a fictional black soldier played by Morgan Freeman, speaks these words as he and other members of his regiment gather around a campfire on the eve of battle in a memorable scene from the 1989 Hollywood film *Glory*. The film is the primary basis for many Americans' knowledge of black soldiers' participation in the Civil War and, overall, it serves as a good introduction to the topic. The film takes misleading and seemingly inexplicable liberties with the history of the Fifty-Fourth Massachusetts Regiment, but it serves an important function in replacing the moonlight-and-magnolias romanticizing of films like *Gone with the Wind* with the "courageous image of black soldiers and their white officers that prevailed in the North during the latter war years and the early postwar decades."[1]

Glory concludes with the Fifty-Fourth's failed assault on Fort Wagner in Charleston Harbor on July 18, 1863. Its final shot features Confederate soldiers dumping the lifeless bodies of Colonel Robert Gould Shaw, played by Matthew Broderick, and Silas Trip, a fugitive slave turned soldier played by Denzel Washington, into a mass grave. Their bodies sink together, and the scene symbolizes the film's integrationist, optimistic bent: Trip has taken his freedom and proved his worth by fighting, and his death brings a tragic sort of progress; in death he wins the equality denied him in life. The scene encapsulates the film's interpretation of the war as a struggle that saw black men fight to win freedom.

There is much validity in this interpretation, but it oversimplifies the motivations, hopes, fears, and frustrations that animated black soldiers' Civil War service, as well as the war's impact on African Americans' struggle for justice. In fact, black soldiers' thinking about their participation in the Union war effort is better encapsulated in an earlier scene, in which Shaw asks Trip to serve as the regiment's color-bearer. Trip refuses. "I ain't fightin' this war for you, sir," he tells Shaw. Despite Shaw's persistence, Trip remains steadfast: "I still don't wanna carry your flag." Trip's reluctance to carry this symbol of state authority—of white authority—is true to black men's purpose in fighting: for them the war was never about maintaining a government that had previously existed. Black Americans saw in the war an opportunity to create an entirely new nation, a United States that would live up to the principles proclaimed in the Declaration of Independence. African Americans focused on the questions Trip asks Shaw as the two consider the war's meaning and outcome: "What about us? What do we get?" They hoped the answer to Trip's second question would be a new Union, one purified of slavery and racism.[2]

Later in the film, during the climactic assault on Fort Wagner, Trip sees Shaw killed at the head of the regiment, and races to pick up a fallen United States flag. Trip is then killed moving the flag forward. He sees in the Union cause a chance to move the nation forward and accomplishes that task symbolically by moving its foremost symbol up Fort Wagner's parapet. That he dies in the attempt, though, suggests that while the war provides an opportunity for black men to prove their equality, military service may prove an imperfect, uncertain vehicle for winning lasting gains. The film clearly intends to present a positive interpretation of the war and its impact on black Americans, but when we focus on Trip and his meditations on black men's reasons for fighting, it tells a more troubling story truer to the war's impact.[3]

Over the past several decades, historians have chronicled black soldiers' military experience but paid little attention to how these men got into the Union army in the first place. Most historians have ignored the question of why black men enlisted, assuming that they would eagerly grab the first chance to battle the Confederacy. Some did. But for many the decision to join the Union army was neither quick nor uncomplicated. One can understand why an enslaved black Southerner, choosing between continued bondage or flight and enlistment, would think it in *his* best interest to enlist—a chance to fight, and perhaps die, for freedom might convince him to make the difficult, courageous decision to flee for Union lines. Black Northerners were already free, however, and they knew that black service in previous American wars had availed African Americans little. In the aftermath of the American Revolution and the War of 1812, slavery and discriminatory laws had expanded. Considering the United States' history of betraying black soldiers, black Northerners faced powerful arguments against donning Union blue and helping to bring the slaveholding South back into the Union. How could they *ensure* that, if they fought, their service would fundamentally change the United States and its treatment of African Americans? What strategy should they follow to make the opportunity presented by the war bear fruit?

From the war's first shots African Americans considered these questions at community meetings and in the pages of black newspapers, developing what this study terms a "politics of service." Although white Northerners loudly proclaimed their intention to keep the developing conflict a "white man's war," black Northerners familiar with American history knew white officials would seek to enlist black soldiers at some point. Black Northerners also understood that they needed to view the war and military service as political issues. They possessed interests different from the masses of white Northerners who rushed to enlist in 1861 motivated by a desire to restore the Union. How to use their service to achieve a new Union was a key political question facing black Northerners during wartime. As the war progressed, many of them responded to this question by recommending that, when white officials allowed them to enlist, black men should withhold their service until the federal government met black demands. Black Northerners' "politics of service" represented their recognition that they needed to view the war as an opportunity to use black military service to win gains—abolition, equal rights, citizenship—that had long eluded them. They developed this politics from the war's earliest days and altered it to fit changing circumstances as the war progressed.

This study focuses on black Northerners' strategic approach to the war and the debate over enlistment that consumed black communities in the North from 1861 through mid-1863. It demonstrates that these individuals' discussions about the war and enlistment influenced the process of black military enrollment, the course of black service, and the postwar change it helped achieve. In particular, this study concentrates on black Northerners' drive to use military service to win government recognition of African American citizenship. In insisting that their service bring them full status as Americans, black soldiers and activists pushed U.S. law forward, forcing government officials and legislators to clarify who counted as an American and what that meant. Black Northerners' debate over service and citizenship played a crucial, if long unrecognized, role in the development of American citizenship. It did not, however, create a citizenship whose rights and privileges all African Americans could enjoy; despite the fact that black soldiers won formal citizenship for African Americans through their service, as both the Civil Rights Act of 1866 and the Fourteenth Amendment defined black men and women born in the United States as citizens, in the Civil War's aftermath many African Americans endured discrimination that branded them as second-class citizens. As a result, African Americans facing the prospect of serving their country in later wars have asked the same question some black Northerners asked in 1861: "Why should we fight for the United States?"

This study contributes to the literature on black military service by considering

the process by which black men entered the Union army and the way in which
their goals and rhetoric influenced the war and its outcome. Black Civil War
service is by now a well-covered topic; following the lead of pioneering black historians like William Wells Brown and W. E. B. Du Bois, authors since the 1950s
like Benjamin Quarles, James M. McPherson, Dudley T. Cornish, John David
Smith, and the scholars of the Freedmen and Southern Society Project have produced first-rate studies of the black military experience.[4] They have illuminated
the Lincoln administration's decision to employ black soldiers, black troops' battlefield performance, and black men's experiences in the army. Previous scholars
have tended, however, to treat black enlistment as a nearly automatic outcome.
Some have acknowledged that black Northerners debated joining the military,
but no one has comprehensively traced this debate or examined its implications.[5]

In his recent, otherwise excellent study of the Lincoln administration and
black service, John David Smith claims that "during the first two years of the
war, northern black communities had little interest in and impact on [Union]
war policy."[6] In truth, black Northerners debated the war and U.S. policy constantly following the Union's rejection of black volunteers in April 1861. Some
historians have recognized that black soldiers did not see preserving the antebellum Union as a particularly important goal; Chandra Manning, for instance, has written that black troops fought not to preserve the Union but to
"make the American Revolution live up to its promises."[7] This study builds on
this insight and gives African Americans' thinking about the concept of Union
more sustained attention than it has previously received.

In addition to forging a new Union, black Northerners wanted to use service to validate black manhood and win black citizenship. Historians have
long recognized that black soldiers associated their service with manhood:
Dudley T. Cornish's 1966 study of black service concludes with this observation: "The Negro soldier proved that the slave could become a man."[8] This
study recognizes black men's association of service with manhood and en-
dorses the work of scholars who have attended to this topic, but it does not
take black manhood as its central concern.[9] Rather, this book joins the work of
academics who have since the 1970s concentrated on the connection between
black military service and citizenship. Scholars like Mary Frances Berry, Joseph P. Reidy, Christian Samito, and Stephen Kantrowitz have deepened our
understanding of the way in which black men sought to use service to achieve
citizenship and the results of their campaign. As of yet, however, no one has
paid extended attention to black Northerners' debates over enlistment or explained how they influenced African Americans' thinking and conduct during
and beyond the war.[10] This study seeks to fill this historiographical gap by

considering the process by which black men entered the Union army and the influence of their goals and rhetoric on the war and its outcome.

Black service was a nonlinear, uneven process with irregular results. Understanding black Northerners' debate over service is fundamental to understanding how this process unfolded and what it accomplished. Today it may seem inevitable that black men would volunteer to fight the Confederacy as soon as white officials adopted black enlistment as policy, but we must not let our knowledge of the war's course distort our ability to see it as African Americans saw it in 1861.

From 1861 black Americans enslaved and free discussed the war and its potential impact all over the United States. Yet black Northerners' dialogue was distinctive in its public character. Following the Northern states' slow postrevolutionary emancipations, black men and women living in the North had built communities and civil-society institutions that served as forums for public discussion.[11] Black Northerners debated service within these institutions: black churches hosted "war meetings," black debating societies considered the war's meaning for African Americans, and black newspapers published editorials and letters on the topic of black service. In the pages of organs like Philadelphia's *Christian Recorder*, run by the African Methodist Episcopal (AME) Church, and New York's *Weekly Anglo-African*, black Northerners could feel part of an "imagined community," a "black North" in which the common consumption of black newspapers overcame geographical isolation.[12] Black newspapers provide an excellent window into black Northerners' thinking about the war and military service. A careful perusal of the development of black Northerners' wartime debate over strategy and the relationship between military service, rights, and citizenship as it developed in the pages of black and abolitionist newspapers—supplemented by engagement with letter collections associated with prominent black activists, abolitionists, and Republican politicians, as well as published primary sources—serves as this study's primary basis.[13]

This methodology, of course, privileges some voices over others. Black Northerners play an outsized role in this manuscript relative to their percentage of the wartime black population. Although they had a unique ability to discuss the war publicly, the individuals on which this study focuses represent a minority of the African American population of the Civil War–era United States. On the eve of the Civil War, nearly 4 million enslaved blacks and nearly 500,000 free blacks lived in the United States. Most of these free African Americans lived outside the South; of this population, more than 70 percent of black men ages eighteen to forty-five living in states in which slavery had been abolished prior to the Civil War served in the Union army.[14] Black

Northerners, however, accounted for a relatively small percentage of the total number of black Union troops: of the 178,975 black men who served in the Union army, only 32,732—roughly 18.2 percent of the total—hailed from the Northern free states. Another 41,719 black men from the slaveholding Border States Kentucky, Maryland, Delaware, and Missouri served the Union as soldiers. The majority of black men who served the U.S. cause were enslaved in Confederate states when the war began. This study thus focuses on a minority of the wartime black population, which accounted for a minority of black troops' presence in the Union army.[15]

This study also privileges the voices of established black professionals like Henry Highland Garnet, Frederick Douglass, and Henry McNeal Turner who regularly published items in black newspapers and played leadership roles at the meetings of local black communities. Moreover, this work establishes the existence of substantial opposition within the Northern black community to the proposition that black men ought to enlist in the Union army at the first possible opportunity. Yet that opposition has oftentimes been preserved not in the voices of those who initially articulated it, but in the voices of black leaders reporting on the progress and outcome of "war meetings" or recruitment drives.

Furthermore, this study privileges the voices of men, who authored the majority of items concerning the debate over enlistment and the war that appeared in the pages of black newspapers. This ranks as a significant issue, as it is clear that black women attended and participated in community meetings where the war and military service were discussed.[16] Black women's voices appear in this book, but they are underrepresented; the comprehensive analysis of black women's part in developing and articulating the politics of service remains to be written. Most obviously, in its desire to examine the contours of a debate too long ignored or only tangentially acknowledged in the literature on black military service, this work privileges the voices of those who dissented. Yet a perusal of the wartime debate over enlistment and service suggests that at any given point in the war, it is likely that more black Northerners supported than opposed the proposition that black men should fight for the United States at the first chance.

Moreover, black Northerners eventually decided against waiting to enlist until their demands had been met. Despite having articulated a politics of service that contemplated joining the military only after the government had honored their requests, black Northerners enlisted en masse in a Union army that treated them unequally. They fought for a nation in which slavery and discrimination continued, and they did so despite the fact that they had received no guarantee of further change. Does this result negate the politics of service's importance? Why pay attention, one might ask, to a political position that was ultimately disregarded?

First, attention to the politics of service helps us understand how black service happened. Large-scale black service resulted from white officials' decision to allow black men to enlist, but it also owed to careful, contentious debate and black men's individual *decisions* that fighting would benefit African Americans. This was a contingent process whose result was not preordained. The politics of service highlighted black Northerners' sense of self-worth and determination to be treated fairly, convictions that influenced their service and that they surely imparted to the ex-slave soldiers with whom they interacted. Understanding the politics of service and the opposition to immediate enlistment it inspired allows for an accurate picture of the historical moment in which black men entered the Union army in large numbers to emerge.

Additionally, prominent black Northerners like George T. Downing and Frederick Douglass, intimately familiar with the debate over black service, had access to the highest offices of government during the Civil War. Before the war, black leaders had established ties with Republican leaders like Charles Sumner, who developed a close working relationship with Abraham Lincoln.[17] African Americans enjoyed "unprecedented access" to the White House, finding in Lincoln the first president willing to listen to their concerns. "African American leaders, abolitionists and Radical Republicans," Manisha Sinha has written, "played a crucial role in pushing the president" on a range of issues including black rights, citizenship, and equality.[18]

Black Northerners' access to the White House translated into access to other government departments as well. In the summer of 1863, a dissatisfied Frederick Douglass possessed the clout necessary to secure a face-to-face meeting with Secretary of War Edwin Stanton on the subject of black enlistment, during which he bluntly informed Stanton of the policies to which he objected.[19] Thus Douglass and other black leaders made top Union officials aware of African Americans' grievances and goals. In this way, white Northerners became aware of discussions about enlistment that black Northerners conducted in their churches, debating societies, and newspapers. White leaders knew they needed to address African Americans' concerns. Black Northerners' thinking about the war influenced the manner in which their white counterparts encouraged black men to enlist, and it is possible that Union officials possessed enough familiarity with black Northerners' debate over service to know that an affirmation of black citizenship would help convince them to join the military. This is but one way in which Civil War–era African Americans pushed federal officials to clarify and codify the content of American citizenship.

This last point highlights the importance to Union victory of the North's

comparatively open and developed civil society.[20] Black Northerners had built
public institutions that fostered discussions about bringing black war aims
in line with Union war aims.[21] These discussions helped white Northerners
construct conceptual frameworks of what black service might look like and
what might inspire black men to enlist, contributing to the process by which
African Americans became an element of Northern military strength. In articulating their politics of service, black Northerners advanced the causes of
abolition, black rights, and black citizenship. No matter how much promise
went unfulfilled in the wake of Union victory, a stalemate or Union defeat
would have been far worse. Seen in this light, black Northerners' politics of
service emerges as a vital contribution to the Union war effort.

Nor did the politics of service disappear once black troops entered the
army. The politics of service concerned African Americans' relationship to
the United States, and that topic remained relevant after black men started
to fight and die in the Union army. When they stopped arguing about enlistment, black Northerners shifted their politics' focus and began to use the service black troops *were* providing to push for immediate change, arguing that
the terms under which they served mattered as much for the citizenship they
sought to win as the fact that they were serving at all. Black Northerners who
did not enlist saw that they too needed to agitate for the change they sought.
As Cincinnati's *Colored Citizen* argued, while black troops were fighting, black
civilians on the Northern home front needed to remain "jealous of [these servicemen's] honor, and . . . zealous for [their] rights."[22] Black Northerners' recognition that those who did not join the military had a vital part to play in
ensuring that black service fulfilled its transformative potential inspired their
late-war protests against discrimination in the Union army and on the home
front. Moreover, the politics of service remained influential into the postwar
period, as black service became the linchpin in black activists' push for citizenship, equality before the law, and the vote.

The historical actors on whom this study focuses might have lacked numerical strength, but the debate they sparked carried significance disproportionate
to their numbers. This circumstance owed to the reasons articulated above,
and to the fact that the first public and clearly government-sanctioned efforts
to recruit black regiments happened in the North. As Douglas Egerton has
written, despite the fact that scattered quasi-official movements to arm black
troops had occurred in Louisiana, Kansas, and the Carolinas in 1862, "virtually all Americans" understood that the Northern black regiments recruited in
1863 "were to serve as a test case" for the policy of black enlistment.[23] When in
1863 Massachusetts governor John Andrew received authorization for his state
to recruit a black regiment—what became the Fifty-Fourth Massachusetts—

he recognized that it was "perhaps the most important corps to be organized during the whole war," and that the success or failure of this regiment would "go far to elevate or to depress the Estimation in which the character of the Colored Americans [would] be held throughout the World."[24]

Looking back from the vantage point of 1865, the *New York Tribune* concurred, describing what would have happened if the Fifty-Fourth Massachusetts had faltered: "Two Hundred Thousand Colored Troops, for whom it was a pioneer, would never have been put into the field, or would not have been put in for another year, which would have been equivalent to protracting the war into 1866."[25] When 1863 opened, however, it was no sure thing that black men from the North would rush to arms. To understand why they might have hesitated and why they ultimately enlisted, one must understand the wartime debate in which black Northerners engaged, and its impact on the course of black service and the war itself.

One must also understand the citizenship black Northerners sought to use military service to win. In its commentary on the subject, this study draws inspiration from the challenge presented by Chandra Manning and Martha Jones to rethink citizenship's meaning in light of the day-to-day relationships of power that determine one's ability to enjoy the rights and privileges associated with being an American. In recent works, both Jones and Manning have shown that, at different times in U.S. history, African Americans' ability to exercise citizenship rights in practice has mattered as much as what laws have said or failed to say regarding black citizenship. In her recent work on antebellum Baltimore, Jones has demonstrated that, although many whites sought to define them as outside the bounds of citizenship, African Americans exploited both the uncertainty surrounding their status and local and state courts' willingness to hear their claims. In so doing, they were able to "secure through their performance" rights that citizens claimed —to sue and be sued, to travel between states, to hold property. Through their access to local levers of justice, antebellum African Americans at times "appeared to be like citizens." In defiance of *Dred Scott* and other white attempts to define them as lacking citizenship, black Americans acted out a vision of birthright citizenship that had yet to be enacted in constitutional law.[26]

Similarly, in her 2016 study *Troubled Refuge*, Chandra Manning offers a new definition of citizenship as experienced by Civil War–era African Americans. She recognizes that the things that mattered most to African Americans emerging from bondage—freedom from slavery's violence and control over their lives and families—did not flow from access to suffrage or other rights associated with citizenship, but from "direct access to the power of the federal government." Manning defines the citizenship African Americans claimed during the

Civil War period as "an alliance between former slaves and the national government, which freedpeople could call on to protect their rights to things that mattered to them."[27] Along with the work of Evelyn Nakano Glenn on the difference between formal and substantive citizenship—a key point of departure for this study—Jones's and Manning's works challenge us to reconsider the relationship between the formal possession of citizenship and access to the levers of state power necessary to the enjoyment of rights and privileges flowing from citizenship. Their scholarship especially informs this study's latter portions, which argue that black service achieved formal rather than substantive citizenship, a reality that has in the decades since the Civil War left many African Americans unable to enjoy in practice the rights and privileges they possess in theory.

When they talked of the citizenship they sought, antebellum and Civil War-era black Northerners often refrained from enumerating the rights and privileges they saw as integral to its possession. Black Northerners' nonspecificity as to citizenship's content grew out of a general nineteenth-century confusion about what precisely American citizenship entailed. This status had no concrete definition prior to the Fourteenth Amendment. Today, for many Americans citizenship implies a universality of rights and privileges and equality among citizens. But scholars like Rogers Smith and Judith Shklar have seen that a key paradox lies at the heart of American citizenship: the United States is in theory a republic devoted to equality, but the history of American citizenship reads largely as a story in which some Americans have denied citizenship to others based on ascriptive qualities like race, ethnicity, and gender.[28] "The tension between an acknowledged ideology of equal political rights and a deep and common desire to exclude and reject large groups of human beings from citizenship has marked every stage of the history of American democracy," Shklar writes.[29]

William Novak has shown that in the antebellum United States, an individual's possession of citizenship and entitlement to an array of privileges and immunities depended on status markers like residence, occupation, and organizational membership, as well as ascriptive qualities like race and gender.[30] Given this context, it is perhaps not surprising that black Northerners tended not to articulate a consistent set of rights and privileges without which one did not enjoy citizenship.[31]

Black Northerners did tend to associate full status as an American with suffrage and legal equality, although they did not consistently specify whether they saw these rights as flowing from citizenship, or as complementary to citizenship but necessary to its full enjoyment. If we cannot know precisely how they conceived of the relationship between citizenship, suffrage, and legal equality, we can see why they associated these concepts closely with citizenship.[32] Shklar has convincingly argued that Americans' preoccupation with suffrage derived from that right's denial to slaves.[33] "The denial of the suffrage to large groups of Americans . . . made the right to vote . . . a mark of social standing. To be refused the right to vote was to be almost a slave," she writes. Anxious to remove this mark of bondage, disenfranchised Americans have clamored for the vote.[34] Because of the history of slavery and Americans' unequal enjoyment of citizenship, whatever citizenship laws say, Americans only *feel* like citizens when markers of their inferiority have been removed. Antebellum black Americans understood the degradation implied in their disenfranchisement and felt it keenly as the white male electorate expanded; it is not surprising, then, that black Northerners associated the vote with citizenship. The Constitution did not—and does not—confer a right to vote or tie suffrage to citizenship, but Civil War–era African Americans did not feel that black citizenship had been truly recognized while black men, at least, could not vote.

Shklar's insight regarding the connection between voting and citizenship illuminates black Northerners' connection of legal equality to citizenship as well, as it surely derived from their experience of life in the antebellum North. By statute and custom, Northern states regularly restricted the rights, privileges, and opportunities available to free black men and women. Black Northerners remained sensitive to the sting of these restrictions and identified their removal as key to making black citizenship a reality. Antebellum black agitators, Stephen Kantrowitz has observed, wanted to achieve more than inclusion within a citizenship defined as a common set of rights and obligations; their political activity was animated by "a vision of solidarity, regard, and even love that continued to reverberate for generations to come."[35] Black Americans desired legal change, but they also sought a sense of acceptance within American society. A crucial part of this acceptance could only derive from a feeling of equal standing, and this feeling would only come when black Americans possessed the same array of rights as white Americans. Achieving legal equality was a way for black Americans to gain the feelings of equal citizenship and acceptance they sought.

That black Americans wanted citizenship and associated it with suffrage and legal equality in their wartime and postwar debates is clear; less clear is that citizenship was really worth fighting and dying for. Scholars like Shklar, Michael Vorenberg, and Kate Masur have highlighted citizenship's often disappointing practical results. Officials who determine citizenship's bounds have generally described it in ascriptive terms and thus limited individual rights in discriminatory ways.[36] American officials' tendency to see citizenship in ascriptive terms has often made the Fourteenth Amendment a poor guarantor of citizens' rights; its language is too vague to prevent states, private entities, and individuals from discriminating against African

Americans and members of other groups. It is certainly desirable that every-one enjoy citizenship, suffrage, and legal equality, but given the harsh realities of modern capitalism, American social organization, and American politics, none of these can by itself allow marginalized groups to alter their collective material circumstances.[37] Given these constraints on citizenship as a historical reality, when one sees that black Americans wanted their military service to win citizenship, one might conclude sadly that the end was not worth the sacrifice.

Such a conclusion places too much emphasis on legal and material status and too little on individual self-worth. Had, as Vorenberg suggests, the framers of the postwar amendments passed a civil rights measure with expansive language about freedom rights rather than the Fourteenth Amendment's vague language of citizens' privileges and immunities, they likely would have encoded in the Constitution a more effective bulwark for citizens' rights than the Fourteenth Amendment has proved to be. But like it or not, while citizenship's meaning has changed profoundly over the course of American history, the concept has been meaningful and will in all likelihood remain so for Americans when they think about their place in their nation. In this context, the feeling that one is a citizen has value.

In October 1868, roughly a year and a half before the Fifteenth Amendment's ratification, Iowa enfranchised black men. An anonymous black Iowan described his reaction to his enfranchisement to the *Davenport Gazette*:

I'm a *man*; I have enjoyed citizenship two days out of forty years, and from the fullness of a grateful heart, I beg leave to thank the legal voters in our young State for the substantial test they have given of their sympathy for freedom, by extending to the colored man the right of suffrage. I, in common with my people, felt proud of Iowa last Tuesday. . . . When the sun broke in upon the world last Tuesday morning, what hopes, born years before in the curse of slavery, and carried through its blight— encouraged by its death, fluttered half with fear for a realization; but that day with its contending brilliancy went into night, and left a brilliant record never to be effaced. The Fatherhood of God, the brotherhood of man, was vindicated, a burden was rolled from the shoulders of oppression, and a glad *Te Deum* went up to the God of *all men*. Jefferson's "all men are created equal" appeared with a deeper significance, and Iowa was proud of what she had done. One of the first in this noble work, we feel proud of her. We see the Stars and Stripes and feel that it is our flag. The same old bunting that in childish years we gazed at through a mist of slavery, now purged of its stain, its brilliant stripes are broader, and its glittering stars increased in number.[38]

Unfortunately, San Francisco's black newspaper the *Elevator* reprinted this portion of this letter without indicating its author or the date on which it was written or published. Still, the correspondent clearly composed it just days after gaining the suffrage, and his enfranchisement could hardly have allowed him or other black Iowans to change their material circumstances in that short time. Yet things had changed for this man. The stain of disenfranchisement removed, he felt that not only had his place in the American polity improved, but also that of black Americans generally. It is important to focus on the limitations inherent to key elements of American political life like citizenship, but it is equally important to remember that they serve purposes that may not be easy to quantify. In a society founded on the principle of republican equality, in which every person's citizenship supposedly makes that person equal to every other citizen, feeling that one is a citizen has value that cannot be quantified or measured.[39]

Whatever citizenship, and the yardsticks of suffrage and legal equality that they used to measure their possession of citizenship, failed to do for African Americans in a collective socioeconomic and political sense, we must not forget the lesson of this unnamed black Iowan: that historical events work changes both tangible and intangible. They came to mean far too little in reality for far too many African Americans, but black citizenship, manhood suffrage, and legal equality were momentous departures from the United States' history of slavery and state-sanctioned blatant discrimination. Despite Reconstruction's failures, the fact that black soldiers forced the United States to recognize black citizenship, rights, and equality meant something to black Americans of the Civil War generation and their descendants. And it likely gave at least some hope that they could win further change. Citizenship, suffrage, and legal equality have not always justified the lofty terms in which Americans have spoken of these concepts. But they are not nothing, either. To brand black soldiers' efforts tragic or naïve because they resulted in an imperfect citizenship misses this point.

FINALLY, IN CONSIDERING the relationship between black service and black citizenship, one must also grapple with the troubling reality that black men *had* to kill and die in large numbers to win citizenship. As W. E. B. Du Bois noted, white Americans saw nothing laudable in the refusal to fight and kill, believing that those who would not fight deserved neither emancipation nor citizenship. "The ability and willingness to take human life has always been, even in the minds of liberal men, a proof of manhood," Du Bois wrote, and only black service "made emancipation possible. . . . Nothing else made Negro citizenship conceivable, but the record of the Negro soldier as a fighter."[40] Recently, Carole Emberton has elaborated on this point, highlighting the limitations of citizenship won at the point of a bayonet. Black soldiers, she notes, seemed threatening to whites who saw black men as bestial and uncontrollable, and uncomfortable whites relied on various racist rationales to accommodate themselves to black service.[41] Du Bois and Emberton have recognized that the tensions inherent in forcing men to fight for their rights limited the extent to which black Americans could enjoy the political rights their service helped win. Their insights leave historians to ask, in Emberton's phrase, "not *if* military service made blacks into citizens but instead what *kind* of citizens it made."[42] This study seeks to address her question by assessing the degree of citizenship available to black Americans in the postwar world.

In his 2013 study of Lincoln and the United States Colored Troops, John David Smith observes that, at times, historians have "romanticize[d] and exaggerate[d]" black soldiers' martial abilities, "embellishing assessments of their combat with notions of heroism." Trying to counter this trend, Smith weighs the evidence and finds that black troops "discharged their duties more or less like all soldiers, irrespective of time, race or place."[43] Many Americans, quite naturally, admire black soldiers who fought to make the United States live up to its founding promises, and we want them all to have fought heroically, fulfilling our highest aspirations. But the reality is that while many black soldiers fought bravely and performed truly heroic deeds, others skulked and ran, as with any other group of soldiers in human history. There was a time when the American public needed heroic accounts of black service. But it is time now to take a hard look at what it meant that black men had to fight to earn citizenship, and to evaluate the citizenship their struggle helped produce. This study shows that black Americans strategized about how to use military service in the Civil War to fundamentally transform the nation and served with an eye toward using their service to confirm black citizenship. Although they were ultimately unable to create a nation that lived up to their highest aspirations, black soldiers' service helped transform American life, law, and citizenship in momentous, complex ways that can be fully appreciated when we consider the scope of their thinking about the war, the Union, military service, and citizenship.

1

IF WE ARE NOT CITIZENS, THEN WHAT ARE WE?

TO 1861

IN THE WINTER OF 1856, black Californians convened in the African Methodist Episcopal Church on Seventh Street in Sacramento, where their young state's legislature had started meeting just two years earlier. These were the delegates to the Second Annual State Convention of Colored Citizens. They addressed numerous concerns, chief among them their drive to repeal the statewide ban on black testimony. On the meeting's second day, however, the convention was brought to a halt by delegate William H. Newby's comments on black military service and patriotism. Born free in Virginia in 1828, Newby had grown up in Philadelphia, migrated to California in the wake of the Gold Rush, and become an influential figure in California's growing black community. He edited the *Mirror of the Times*, a black newspaper started in San Francisco in the mid-1850s, and served as corresponding secretary of San Francisco's Athenaeum Institute, a black literary and debating society. He also became a regular contributor to *Frederick Douglass' Paper* and apparently developed significant international contacts—the next year, Newby would leave California for a position in Haiti as the personal secretary to the French consul general.[1]

Newby opposed a resolution pledging black men to "cast [their] lot in the fortunes of battle, to protect [the United States] from foreign invasion," claiming that he would welcome a foreign army if "that army provided liberty to [him] and [his] people in bondage." White Americans, he said, would feel the same way if asked to fight for a country that systematically oppressed them. Why, Newby asked, should black men fight for the United States? Their forefathers had fought for the country and been rewarded with "chains and oppression." Newby argued that black men ought to refuse to fight until whites "put away their prejudice, and do a just part by [African Americans]."[2] Other delegates shared his objections to the resolution proclaiming black men's willingness to fight, and it failed.

William H. Newby articulated a compelling critique of the United States' failure to reward black service in the wars of the early republic and suggested that this failure ought to color black men's attitudes toward service in future American wars. African Americans, he suggested, would feel allegiance to a United States that treated them fairly; they did not, as matters stood, owe the country allegiance. Newby's interpretation of American history depicted black veterans as victims of bad faith, warriors who had answered their country's call and reaped betrayal. Until white Americans rectified this injustice, he concluded, black men should refuse to fight.

Whether or not they agreed with Newby's conclusion, most black Northerners shared the frustrations that inspired it and joined him in contesting the myriad forms of oppression they encountered. Prior to the Civil War, federal and state laws restricted black rights and defined African Americans as second-class citizens or noncitizens. These individuals faced overwhelming social prejudice that touched seemingly every facet of their everyday lives. Finally, the American republic had incubated an expanding, aggressive Southern empire built on the unrequited toil of black men and women. To combat these evils, disenfranchised black Northerners took to the public sphere, asserting their citizenship and equality and launching state-level campaigns for rights and citizenship. They frequently anchored their claims on their ancestors' service and, as a result, discussed black service often. Black Northerners also talked about the nation they hoped would emerge from their struggle: a nation whose laws reflected the ideals proclaimed in the Declaration of Independence. They sought to forge a new United States, a nation that would fulfill the promise of its founding principles.

Their efforts bore some fruit. From the early 1830s onward, black Northerners found willing allies among white abolitionists dedicated to slavery's immediate destruction. Indeed, in many Northern states black rights improved from the 1830s through the late antebellum years.[3] Moreover, as Martha Jones has shown, despite antebellum white officials' desire to define African Americans as outside the bounds of citizenship and restrict black rights, free black Northerners were able at times to claim rights and privileges associated with citizenship.[4] Still, when the Civil War began most black Northerners remained disenfranchised, and all struggled against discrimination. Moreover, they had watched a slew of frightening national developments in the 1850s that culminated in the infamous *Dred Scott* decision, which asserted that African Americans could not be American citizens. Black Northerners knew they faced a crisis, and they considered a range of responses. As sectional war loomed, some embraced emigration to foreign countries, others advocated the government's destruction, and others still followed William H. Newby in denying allegiance to the United States.

When war came in 1861, black Northerners found themselves at a crossroads. They wanted a nation in which they could enjoy the supposedly unalienable rights of the Declaration of Independence, but they did not agree about how to achieve it. Nor was there consensus about whether fighting for the United States would help their cause. Black Northerners' dissent had achieved some success and helped sustain their communities, but it had failed in its larger goals, and this mixed record left black leaders divided as to how to proceed. The prewar history of black Northerners' protest and politics shows that it was no foregone conclusion that black men would fight for the United States in the Civil War.

———

BY 1861, THE PROSPECT of African Americans bearing arms would have seemed unthinkable to many white Americans, but black Americans had amassed a long record of military service, having served in colonial militias since the sixteenth century. Arming black soldiers, though, made white colonists nervous, as they recognized that black service undermined evolving notions of racial inferiority. Whites also feared that slaves might turn weapons on their masters. Nevertheless, concerns over manpower won out, and black soldiers served in Indian wars up and down the Atlantic Seaboard as well as in larger conflicts like the French and Indian War.[5] But black service did not mean black equality. During the colonial period, law codes restricted black rights, and slavery remained the dominant status for black colonists. Nevertheless, the patchwork nature of colonial legislation meant that black freemen in certain colonies could exercise some of the same rights as whites, and British subjecthood law suggested that some black men might possess the rights of British subjects.[6]

However white colonists conceived of their black counterparts' civic status, free and enslaved blacks occupied an undeniably central role in the colonial economy. This was the case both on Southern plantations and in large Northern cities, where many black men worked as sailors and stevedores along wharves and waterfronts. In these urban environments, African Americans joined in the popular unrest that preceded the American Revolution. Crispus Attucks, an escaped slave who had for twenty years worked as a sailor and rope maker in Boston, figured prominently in the mob whose harassment of

British soldiers on the night of March 5, 1770, precipitated the Boston Massacre. Black colonists like Attucks participated in the ideological ferment and street violence of the early 1770s and in the open warfare that followed. Black men fought at Lexington and Concord and at Bunker Hill, carried George Washington's army to safety after it met disaster at Manhattan, and manned the fleet that ferried the general across the Delaware River to make his Christmas attack at Trenton.[7]

Black service in the Revolution did not happen without controversy. Though black soldiers had fought since the start of the conflict, the Continental Congress declared black men ineligible to serve in 1775. However, when Congress imposed troop quotas on the states in 1777, many began to enlist black men. Military necessity won out, and African American soldiers served in infantry units from all states except Georgia and South Carolina and in naval units from every state.[8] Black troops were more likely than their white counterparts to be given non-arms-bearing roles, yet on land and sea, free and enslaved black men fought alongside white troops in integrated units. Historians have generally put the number of black men who served the patriot cause at 5,000, though recently historian Alan Gilbert has argued that this number is too low.[9]

African Americans also fought against the American Revolution. Historian Sylvia Frey has estimated that somewhere between 80,000 and 100,000 slaves fled their masters over the course of the war, and many made their way to British Army camps. Enticed by promises of freedom, enslaved black Southerners served the British Army in a variety of functions. Like the patriots, the British often relegated black soldiers to support roles, and many bondsmen who reached British lines were eventually reenslaved or sold into British Caribbean slavery. Nonetheless, many did find lasting freedom. British officers like Guy Carleton saw they owed a debt to the African Americans who had served their cause, and when the British evacuated New York and other strongholds at the war's end, thousands of former slaves went with them, defying the revolutionaries' insistence on recovering these runaways. Enslaved Americans' recognition that freedom lay with the British highlighted the contradiction at the heart of the American Revolution, a war for liberty waged by slaveholders.[10]

A similar dynamic unfolded during the War of 1812. Congress barred black men from militia service in 1792, and the secretaries of the army and navy later barred black men from the navy and marines. Yet white Americans remained willing as ever to take black help when they found themselves in a tight spot. Black men thus served under Oliver Hazard Perry on the Great

Lakes, volunteered to defend Northern cities when British invasion looked imminent in the summer of 1814, and fought at New Orleans alongside Andrew Jackson. Just as in the Revolution, however, the British offered freedom to American slaves, and black troops also accompanied the British Army as it burned Washington and fought with the British Navy on Chesapeake Bay and the Great Lakes.[11] In all likelihood, as the proslavery attorney Francis Scott Key sat aboard a British prison ship during the Battle of Baltimore and composed his paean to American liberty, enslaved Marylanders were attempting to seize their liberty by reaching the British fleet.

African American participation in the wars of the early republic did not kill slavery or win black citizenship, but the Revolution's emphasis on liberty and equality carried obvious antislavery implications. As such, it was perhaps not a surprise that some developments during the revolutionary era boded well for the cause of black rights. In 1778, the Continental Congress rejected South Carolina's proposal to amend the proposed Articles of Confederation's comity clause—which guaranteed that citizens of one state would be treated as citizens in any other state to which they traveled—to include whites only. The clause defined slaves and the indigent as outside the bounds of citizenship, implicitly suggesting that black freemen could be citizens. In later decades, black Northerners often referred to this comity-clause debate as proof that white Americans of the founding generation had considered African Americans citizens. As Northern states wrote new constitutions, many refrained from outlawing black voting. African American men possessing the requisite property could vote in Maryland, North Carolina, and several federal territories that later became slave states. Most importantly, the Confederation Congress passed the Northwest Ordinance of 1787 banning slavery in the territories of the Old Northwest and conferring rights on those territories' inhabitants without reference to race or color. Slavery and discriminatory legislation persisted across the United States, but these enactments signaled that some revolutionary-era white Americans were willing to recognize some African Americans as citizens.[12]

The Constitution that replaced the Articles of Confederation, however, contained troubling provisions and ambiguities around slavery and black citizenship. The document failed to define citizenship or any rights, privileges, or immunities it might entail. Still, the framers' decision not to link citizenship to whiteness suggested that African Americans could retain the citizenship that had been recognized in various ways under the Articles of Confederation. Article IV, Section II also seemed to offer hope to African Americans recognized as citizens within their states of residence, as it forbade states from abridging the privileges and immunities of other states' citizens. However, this clause's promise would be dimmed in the coming decades by Southern-endorsed narrow constructions. Regarding slavery, the Constitution was famously ambiguous; the framers omitted the distasteful words "slave" and "slavery" but provided the institution with key supports, including the Fugitive Slave Clause and the Three-Fifths Clause. In truth, the framers harbored no single intention toward slavery. Some felt the document put slavery on a path to eventual extinction; others rejoiced in the protections it gave to slaveholders. What can be said with certainty is that the Constitution did not explicitly nationalize the gradual emancipationist sentiments that animated much of the North during the revolutionary era and that convinced many Americans that slavery had begun an inevitable gradual decline.[13]

Americans who believed slavery was faltering were badly mistaken. From the early 1790s on, the institution grew in economic importance and scope as its center of gravity shifted westward from the Atlantic Seaboard to the Old Southwest. Slave-grown agriculture remained immensely profitable for those wealthy enough to accumulate sufficient land and labor. The expansion of textile production associated with the Industrial Revolution—first in Great Britain and later in the United States—caused the demand for cotton to rise rapidly and remain high generally. White cotton planters could feed this demand thanks to improvements in cotton-gin technology that made it profitable to grow short-staple cotton farther inland than coastal Georgia and South Carolina, where cotton production had previously been concentrated. Following the Louisiana Purchase, Southerners moved west to join the cotton boom, buying slaves from older states like Virginia and Maryland whose economies had shifted from tobacco production to less labor-intensive grains. The profits and powerful social and psychological benefits to be reaped from slavery gave white Southerners compelling economic motivations to oppose antislavery measures.[14]

As Southern slavery grew, substantial free black communities took root in major Northern cities, where black populations swelled around the turn of the nineteenth century thanks to revolutionary-era manumissions and migrations. Philadelphia's black population quadrupled between 1790 and 1810, and by 1820 over 12,000 African Americans called the city home, accounting for over 10 percent of its population. Black Northerners flocked to urban environments because they provided job opportunities, sociability, and strength in numbers. White racism, though, sharply limited black Northerners' ability to find good-paying jobs; James and Lois Horton have estimated that, prior to the Civil War, between two-thirds and three-fourths of black Northerners worked at menial occupations. Still, a black middle class developed that included ministers like the former slave Richard Allen, entrepreneurs like the sailmaker and Revolutionary War veteran James Forten, and professionals like the doctor James McCune Smith. Yet while prominent black men like Allen, Forten, and Smith attained comparative wealth and status and exercised considerable influence within the black community, they constituted a mere 2 percent of the black Northern population. The nineteenth century brought a type of freedom to most black Northerners that entailed scant socioeconomic or occupational mobility.[15]

Nor did this freedom entail equal rights or citizenship. In 1848, at a national convention of black leaders, a committee headed by Frederick Douglass described black Northerners as "slaves of the community."[16] Born a slave in Maryland, Douglass escaped to the North in 1838 and befriended influential white abolitionists; by 1841, he was lecturing publicly about his life as a slave, the start of a long career that saw him become black America's foremost spokesman.[17] Douglass was in a unique position to compare treatment of African Americans in the North and the South, and the difference he described was one of degree rather than kind.

Northern states generally afforded their black residents basic legal protections against bodily harm, allowed for redress of grievances, and recognized black property rights, but a hodgepodge of discriminatory laws and practices prevailed from state to state. Five states in the North barred black testimony in cases to which a white person was a party. Informal custom barred most black Northerners from jury service, placing clear practical limits on their legal protections. As new states carved out of the Northwest Territory entered the Union, they often barred black immigrants or placed onerous entrance requirements on them. Informal prejudice governed public accommodations, as segregation generally reigned in public transportation, theaters, hotels, restaurants, hospitals, and cemeteries. Lastly, many Northern states denied black men the ballot. In states like Pennsylvania where black men had voted for decades, new state constitutions outlawed black voting, and between Maine's admission to statehood in 1820 and the Civil War, no new state permitted black voting. The 1820s and 1830s, often hailed as an era of democratic expansion, really witnessed the expansion of a master race, or Herrenvolk, democracy that saw black men disenfranchised as the white electorate expanded.[18]

State and federal authorities typically defined these disenfranchised but free African Americans as second-class citizens at best.[19] State judges North and South tended to refrain from denying black citizenship outright, but they withheld its full benefits, a delicate balancing act that produced tortured legal reasoning. Federal officials denied black citizenship more consistently. Several early Congressional acts—such as a 1790 restriction of naturalization to whites or the 1792 law barring black service—undermined black citizenship, and attorneys general denied the existence of black citizenship through various legal formulas. Even at the federal level some ambiguity persisted: in their speeches during the Missouri Crisis, many Northern congressmen recognized that at least some African Americans were citizens. The general trend in pre-Civil War citizenship law, however, was to deny black citizenship's existence or severely circumscribe black citizens' rights and privileges.[20]

The U.S. State Department's policy in issuing passports to African Americans offered a particularly revealing window into federal officials' attitudes toward black citizenship. Usually, department officials declined to issue black travelers full-fledged passports asserting their bearers' citizenship.[21] Instead, they gave free black travelers special certificates acknowledging a relationship between the bearers and the U.S. government. State Department policy was not consistent—officials issued black sailors "seamen's protection certificates" that *did* state their bearers' citizenship—and in the mid-nineteenth century many Americans thought of passports primarily as travel documents establishing identity rather than signifiers of citizenship. Secretaries of state, however, wanted to equate possession of a passport with citizenship. Black activists were aware of the State Department's desire to link passports to citizenship, and many black passport applicants were motivated by a need to highlight the inconsistencies in American citizenship law. Like state judges who denied black citizenship but acknowledged that African Americans possessed membership in the political community, the State Department saw black men and women as persons outside the bounds of citizenship who yet possessed a relationship to the federal government. "The claim to birth while not grounds for 'full' citizenship," Craig Robertson has written, "did apparently entitle individuals to protection regardless of their skin color," and the State Department contemplated black Americans as residents, not citizens.[22]

Most states barred free black men from their militias, membership in which had long been connected with full citizenship. The 1790 statute that organized the federal army lacked a color clause because, historically, armies could be augmented by manpower drawn from any rank of society as circumstances dictated. Americans saw the militia as a permanent body whose members were upstanding, respectable community stewards; permanent militia membership carried connotations of citizenship and community standing, and Congress limited it to whites. In organizing their units, most states followed the federal standard. Only Louisiana, with its wealthy community of free *gens de couleur*, permitted black men to serve. Black Northerners recognized that whites-only militia laws stemmed from white Americans' desire to deny citizenship to African Americans, and in the 1850s black men petitioned the New York and Massachusetts legislatures to permit black militia service. Both campaigns, however, failed. Black men might have taken cold comfort from the fact that Congress did not exclude them from American military life entirely, as John C. Calhoun's 1842 effort to bar black troops from all branches of federal service failed. Nevertheless, American military law clearly showed African Americans that whites considered them less than citizens, undesirables fit only for naval service or enlistment in time of crisis.[23]

Black Northerners confronted persistent attempts by whites to deny them the benefits of citizenship and faced economic, social, and political obstacles to the full enjoyment of their freedom, but they did not have to fear reenslavement as a consequence of protesting their treatment. Thus they developed a rich tradition of protest and political activism.[24] Led by ministers, middle-class professionals, and slaves turned public lecturers like Frederick Douglass, black Northerners pressed for equal rights and full citizenship. Black activists drew on the institutions African American Northerners had built during the early nineteenth century, which proved critical to the coalescence of free black communities: these included churches, mutual-aid societies and, from 1827 onward, the black press.

Starting in 1830, black Northerners held national and state conventions; the first national convention met in Philadelphia at Richard Allen's Mother Bethel AME Church that year. These gatherings allowed delegates representing local black communities and organizations to search for solutions to the common problems black Americans faced. Through civil-society gatherings such as these, black Northerners developed a politics that targeted discrimination in their region as well as slavery in the South. Many black Northerners had recently emerged from slavery, or they had been born to parents who had escaped slavery; in addition, many had friends and relatives still enslaved in the South. If African Americans in the North were slaves of the community as Frederick Douglass suggested, they used the tools at their disposal, and the relative freedom from reprisal they enjoyed, to contest the terms of their bondage.[25]

Black Northerners frequently held public protest meetings at which they based claims to rights and citizenship on military service in previous American wars, hoping that the magnitude of the black contribution to the nation's independence would move whites to justice. These activists demanded to know whether white Americans could in good conscience deny the fruits of victory to descendants of black soldiers who had fought to achieve it. In 1838, black Pennsylvanians petitioned their state's constitutional convention, asking, "When called on by our Country in an hour of danger, were we ever found wanting?" Reminding the white delegates that some black Revolutionary War veterans yet lived, they inquired pointedly, "Are [black veterans] to be torn from the citizenship of the commonwealth and disowned?"[26]

Robert Purvis led this petition drive, which aimed to prevent black disenfranchisement. He was a freeborn, college-educated black abolitionist and author who as president of the Philadelphia Vigilance Committee assisted fugitive slaves on their way north. Was it their fate, he inquired, "to be looked for in the 'hour of danger,' [only to] be trampled under foot in the time of peace?"[27] Antebellum black agitators like Purvis insisted that because African American soldiers had served the United States in the wars of its infancy, the country owed them more than disenfranchisement and discrimination. Unmoved by this appeal, Pennsylvania legislators denied Purvis and his brethren the franchise.

Black Northerners knew that, in the popular mind and early histories of the Revolutionary War, the black role in achieving independence was suppressed, and they tried to force white Americans to remember black veterans' service. They frequently read white officials' recognitions of black service into the minutes of state and national conventions; black authors, orators, and conventiongoers invoked Andrew Jackson's proclamations to the black Louisianans who fought at New Orleans so frequently that historian Benjamin Quarles has called them "the two most widely quoted documents in antebellum black historiography."[28] In 1854, a correspondent of *Frederick Douglass' Paper* quoted from Jackson's declaration and asked indignantly, "If we are not citizens, then what are we?"[29]

Boston's William C. Nell, a black abolitionist and author, became black soldiers' chief antebellum historian. Seeking to prove that the nation's wars had been "signalized by the devotion and bravery of colored Americans," Nell published a short pamphlet in 1851 detailing these servicemen's efforts, followed by a mammoth 400-page work in 1855.[30] In the wake of the 1857 *Dred Scott* decision, he redoubled his efforts, organizing annual Crispus Attucks Day celebrations in Boston on the anniversary of the Boston Massacre. By invoking military service as a primary basis for black citizenship, black Northerners testified to their faith that they could rhetorically parlay their ancestors' service into rights and citizenship.[31]

During the antebellum period this strategy failed, but this setback does not mean that black Northerners' faith in their ability to use military service to claim citizenship was misplaced. Throughout American history, individual black men reaped substantial gains from their time in the armed forces. Many slaves who fought in the wars with Great Britain won their freedom, and black service during the Revolution helped push Northern states toward emancipation. During Rhode Island's 1841–42 Dorr War, a revolt by disenfranchised white Rhode Islanders who sought to wrest power from the state's mercantile elite, black Rhode Islanders sided with the victorious ruling faction, which rewarded their loyalty with suffrage. These precedents suggested that, if white Americans again called on black assistance in time of war, black Northerners could use that occasion to insist that their service be rewarded with rights and citizenship. Such changes would come in this scenario as a next logical step since black freedom, at least in the North, had already been established. During this theoretical conflict, black leaders would have an advantage they had lacked during the Revolution: institutional platforms backed by large free black communities from which to make their appeals for proper rewards.[32]

Black Northerners' appropriation of the rhetoric and example of the Revolutionary War generation involved a deep acceptance of American principles rather than a search for alternative solutions to the problems of slavery and prejudice, and black Northerners acknowledged as much.[33] At the 1853 Colored National Convention, a committee headed by Frederick Douglass and George B. Vashon, a Syracuse-based lawyer, educator, newspaperman, and Vigilance Committee member, confessed that black Northerners had not discovered "any new principles adapted to ameliorate the condition of mankind." The "great truths of moral and political science, upon which we rely," they said in a published address to white Americans, "have been evolved and enunciated by you. We point to your principles, your wisdom, and to your great example as the full justification of our course this day."[34]

Black Americans believed in the principles the founding generation had proclaimed but failed to enact; they believed that by steady agitation and good conduct, and by the cultivation of a middle-class respectability that would prove black Americans' equality with whites, they could force white Americans to live up to the nation's founding principles. William Wells Brown, a Kentucky-born slave who escaped and became a prominent abolitionist lecturer, declared in 1854 that when black freedom came, "the revolution that was commenced in 1776 would . . . be finished, and the glorious sentiments of the Declaration of Independence . . . would be realized, and our government . . . would really be the LAND OF THE FREE AND THE HOME OF THE BRAVE."[35]

Black Northerners' faith in their white counterparts' fidelity to American tenets may seem naïve to modern readers familiar with white Americans'

willingness to sacrifice the country's principles for the tangible and psychological benefits of white supremacy. But knowledge of later events should not
color one's attitude toward earlier modes of protest. When William Wells
Brown proclaimed his faith in American founding values, Reconstruction's
failures lay in the future. Viewed in the context of the time, black Americans'
belief in the applicability of American founding principles to their struggle
and in these principles' efficacy as rhetorical bases for their claims was not
without merit.

For black Northerners, the ideals and rhetoric of the revolutionary generation were not created equal. One document, the Declaration of Independence,
and the human equality and natural rights whose existence it proclaimed, was
central to their protest thought. The declaration defined black Northerners'
conception of what an America cleansed of discrimination and slavery would
look like. In pamphlets, speeches, resolutions, and editorials, black Northerners affirmed the document's centrality to their vision. As early as 1791, the black
scientist Benjamin Banneker told the Declaration's author, Secretary of State
Thomas Jefferson, in a personal letter that it was "pitiable" that Jefferson had
been "fully convinced of the benevolence of the Father of Mankind, and of his
equal and impartial distribution of . . . rights and privileges," and yet continued to hold slaves.[36] Black Northerners cited the Declaration of Independence
to demand that white Americans bring state and national legislation in line
with their nation's founding principles. In 1799, Philadelphia ministers Richard Allen and Absalom Jones secured seventy-three signatures on a petition to
the president and Congress asserting that, "if the Bill of Rights, or the Declaration of Congress [were] of any validity," African Americans would be "admitted
to partake of the liberties and unalienable rights therein held forth."[37]

In appealing to the Declaration of Independence's equality clause, black
leaders of the early 1800s were ahead of their time; prior to the 1820s, Americans tended to ignore this proviso and focus on the Declaration's assertion of
American sovereignty.[38] Banneker, Allen, and others like them, though, knew
that pointing to the equality clause was a savvy rhetorical strategy. As in the
1830s the first generation of free black Northern leaders passed from the scene
and a new, less deferential group of orators, authors, and agitators took their
place, the Declaration's provision became even more central to black protest
rhetoric. In the thirty years before the Civil War, rarely did black delegates
convene without invoking the Declaration of Independence. In 1843, a Michigan black convention proclaimed the document "the text-book of this nation"
and complained that compelling African Americans to obey state laws they
had no voice in framing violated the Declaration of Independence and the

Constitution.[39] Whatever its understanding of the literal meaning of Jefferson's equality clause, the Continental Congress had proclaimed human equality in unabashedly universalistic terms, and black Americans insisted on their inclusion in that equality. "Our fathers of the revolution . . . proclaimed—'all men' not a part of men—but 'ALL men are created equal, endowed by their Creator with certain inalienable rights, among which are life, liberty and the pursuit of happiness,'" announced black Ohioans in 1851.[40]

To highlight the contradictions between American principle and practice, black Northerners held "counter–July Fourth celebrations," sometimes on July 5, rather than celebrate the Fourth of July alongside whites. When Frederick Douglass in 1852 asked, "What to the American slave is your Fourth of July?," he was putting a new, particularly eloquent spin on an old tactic.[41] Black Northerners in New Haven held such a July 5 event in 1832 at which the minister Peter Osborne stated, "On account of the misfortune of our color, our fourth of July comes on the fifth. . . . When the Declaration of Independence is fully executed, which declares that all men, without respect to person, were born free and equal, we may have our fourth of July on the fourth."[42] As black New Yorkers put it in 1831, "[We believe the time will] come when the Declaration of Independence will be felt in the heart, as well as uttered from the mouth, and when the rights of all shall be properly acknowledged and appreciated."[43] The declaration was the key to antebellum black Northerners' thinking about the type of country they wanted to emerge from their successful protest struggle, and their belief in its principles provided them a critical source of unity.[44]

Unity was often in short supply in the black North, especially during the late antebellum period. Always, more united than divided black Northerners; nevertheless, because the species of oppression they suffered varied from place to place, they developed different solutions to the problems they faced. Several issues, often pitting principle against pragmatism, proved divisive at antebellum state and national conventions. Should black Northerners advance their struggle through black-only institutions or on principle oppose all color-based restrictions? Should they try to force the United States to live up to its professed ideals or seek freedom and citizenship by emigrating, perhaps to Canada or Sierra Leone? Beginning in the 1830s with the rise of a new, aggressive white abolitionist movement dedicated to immediate abolition, black reformers' close ties with white activists caused additional difficulties.[45]

Black Northerners involved in abolitionist or antislavery activity sensed that their white friends regarded them at a distance. White abolitionists in Boston, historian Stephen Kantrowitz has written, lacked much "feeling for the lives, work or experiences of the black members of their alliance," and their contacts with black men and women "remained tentative, self-conscious and symbolic." Theoretically integrated, antislavery or abolitionist organizations often contained a predominance of white members leavened by a smatter-ing of black men and women; some organizations, like Boston's Female Anti-Slavery Society, required segregated seating at their meetings. Black activists sometimes charged their white counterparts with racism and chafed at their seeming assumption that they would command antislavery efforts. In 1857, Frederick Douglass expressed the frustration black activists felt toward their well-meaning but aloof associates, and presaged black Northerners' wartime objections to the Union army's insistence on staffing black regiments with white officers.[46] Referring to a certain "class of Abolitionists" that did not sup-port black-run institutions, Douglass observed, "In some quarters the efforts of colored people meet with very little encouragement. We may fight, but we must fight like the Seapoys of India, under white officers."[47]

White abolitionists often battled over ideological purity and morally correct tactics, and their schisms presented black activists with a series of dilem-mas. How should they respond to white abolitionists who focused narrowly on abolition to the neglect of black rights and citizenship? Should they follow the lead of William Lloyd Garrison and his American Anti-Slavery Society and "come out" of all institutions that supported slavery, including churches and political parties? Should they adopt the Garrisonian program of transform-ing society totally, or was it better to focus on the issues that mattered most to their lives? Should they join the Garrisonians in abstaining from politics, instead relying on moral suasion to effect change? If black activists entered politics, were they bound to support the Liberty Party, founded in 1840 by non-Garrisonian abolitionists, or could they ally with ideologically unsound but viable antislavery parties like the Republicans of the mid-1850s? When black leaders debated these controversial questions, differences of opinion could harden into animosity; at an 1860 meeting in New York's Zion Church, verbal disagreements over black emigration degenerated into violence. Black Northerners agreed that they wanted to realize the promise of the Declara-tion of Independence, but they disagreed about how to accomplish this task. Despite their common devotion to bettering life for black Americans, Jane and William Pease have written, black Northerners' prewar conventions were "weakened by the divisiveness of ideological controversy and the shattering consequences of personal rivalry."[48]

Class tensions divided black Northerners as well. African American lead-ers imbibed and helped fabricate the middle-class ideals of their evolving market-capitalist society, and their class perspectives sometimes angered black nonelites. Prominent individuals sincerely believed that achieving personal and community respectability—by practicing middle-class virtues like thrift, sobriety, economy, pluck, and independence—could erode white prejudice.[49] In service of this goal, Patrick Rael has written, well-to-do black Northerners directed a "veritable flood of advice . . . to the black non-elite—virtues to cultivate and influence to shun, behaviors to avoid and habits to embrace." Sometimes this advice provoked direct conflicts between the black professional class and black nonelites. At the 1848 national convention, the "lesser lights" who were familiar with the harsh realities of survival and obstacles to occupational mobility defeated a resolution imploring black men to spurn menial trades and seek respectable employment. Such incidents were relatively rare, but it is likely that lower-class black Northerners resented, to some degree, their better-off brethren's habit of preaching middle-class virtues. These class tensions might have contributed to black leaders' frequent antebellum complaints that they lacked followers. The burdens of daily life accounted for much of the political apathy black leaders like Douglass detected among black Northerners, but as Jane and William Pease have speculated, black nonelites' resentment of these leaders' class-infused rhetoric likely also played a role.[50]

These divisions aside, black Northerners were reminded frequently of their common predicament during the late antebellum years, when new laws and court rulings threatened black rights and facilitated slavery's expansion. In 1850, Congress authorized a controversial new Fugitive Slave Law that trampled African Americans' constitutional rights and required all Northerners to assist in recapturing fugitive slaves.[51] In 1854, Congress approved the Kansas-Nebraska Act, which repealed the prohibition on slavery in the northern reaches of the Louisiana Purchase that had governed westward expansion since the 1820s. Finally, in 1857 Chief Justice Roger Taney held in *Dred Scott v. Sandford* that Congress could not bar slavery from any federal territory. Politicians who opposed slavery's expansion, like the Illinois Republican Abraham Lincoln, characterized Taney's ruling as the latest in a series of conspiratorial acts by the so-called Slave Power, a cabal of federal officials and proslavery politicians bent on nationalizing slavery.[52]

Incensed by Taney's ruling on this count, black Northerners were more outraged by his assertion that they were not American citizens. Taney found that two classes of Americans existed: those holding state citizenship and those holding federal and state citizenship. He repeated Southern judges' frequent contentions that African Americans owed their country allegiance as community members but did not possess a sufficient array of rights to qualify for federal citizenship. What rights *were* necessary to federal citizenship he did not specify. Taney justified his finding by erroneously claiming that no African Americans had been considered state or federal citizens at the time of the Constitution's adoption. For black Northerners, it mattered little that the chief justice had been led into bad history by his desire to ensure slaveholders' property rights; what mattered was that the highest court in the land had ruled that black men and women were not citizens of the nation black soldiers had helped establish and defend.[53] "I stand at the threshold of the Supreme Court and ask for justice, simple justice," despaired Frances Ellen Watkins Harper in 1857. Harper was a well-known antislavery lecturer, author, and women's rights advocate who would found the National Association of Colored Women in 1896. She continued, "Upon my tortured heart is the thrown the mocking words, 'You are a negro; you have no rights which white men are bound to respect!'"[54]

Black Northerners were frightened and angered by the events of the 1850s. Setbacks like the *Dred Scott* decision came on the heels of two decades of collaboration with white abolitionists and antislavery politicians. Peaceful political agitation seemed increasingly ineffective, and black Northerners looked for alternatives. Some began to wonder if African Americans ever could enjoy equal rights or citizenship in the United States. The late 1850s saw the proliferation of several black- and abolitionist-led colonizationist movements involving Haiti, South America, and Africa. These causes also involved prominent leaders like Martin Delany, a Pittsburgh-based newspaper editor, doctor, and author, and Henry Highland Garnet, an escaped Maryland slave who had become an influential orator and minister in New York.[55] Delany went so far as to travel to West Africa in 1858 to scout locations for black colonies, exploring the Niger River region and negotiating treaties with local leaders.

Many black Northerners shared the conviction that the time had come to flee; in the wake of the Fugitive Slave Law, thousands of black men, women, and children, many of them former fugitives resettled in the North, fled to Canada. Other black Northerners thought domestically as they grew more radical. Frederick Douglass, formerly a Garrisonian pacifist, embraced violence. Throughout the decade, he met with the white abolitionist John Brown, who had told Douglass as early as 1848 of his violent plans, and by the mid-1850s Douglass was publicly absolving murderers of slave catchers from guilt and preaching slave rebellion. Henry Highland Garnet had embraced violence as early as 1843, when at that year's national convention his militant rhetoric proved so controversial the delegates refused to publish it, and by 1854 William Wells Brown also openly spoke of slave rebellion. Black Northerners' turn to emigration and violence stemmed from their reactions to developments they deplored and could do little to halt.[56]

The Fugitive Slave Law also inspired black Northerners to embrace military preparedness by forming their own militia companies. African Americans in the North had long collaborated for self-defense purposes. By the 1830s, most major Northern cities had Vigilance Committees like the one Robert Purvis presided over in Pennsylvania. These predominantly black committees helped runaway slaves establish themselves in new locations and defend their newly seized freedom. In the 1850s, black Northerners embraced an explicitly military style of organization, founding militia companies all over the region. New York City alone boasted the Attucks Guards, the Free Soil Guards, and the Hannibal Guards. Black Philadelphians organized the Frank Johnson Guards in the mid-1850s, and black Bostonians founded the Massasoit Guards in 1855 and the Liberty Guards in 1857. These outfits, and numerous others like them, represented black Northerners' independent response to the assault on their liberties contained in the new fugitive slave legislation.[57]

Antebellum black militia units, Benjamin Quarles has written, "were largely ceremonial, parading on August 1, or at the grand opening of a church or school."[58] They did not always wield weapons; some possessed firearms, and the Morris Grove Attic Guard featured sixteen axe-wielding members, but some marched with broomsticks. That these companies were not always heavily armed did not allay white fears, especially in the aftermath of John Brown's failed raid of October 1859. Two days after the raid's failure, Pennsylvania's adjutant general disarmed and disbanded a forty-man company of black men. Michigan authorities demobilized the black company that formed in the raid's wake, the Detroit Military Guards, and black Bostonians attributed Massachusetts officials' reluctance to repeal legislation barring black men from the state militia to the unsuccessful attack. State officials' desire to neutralize these black units derived from the wariness with which whites regarded armed black men as well as the heightened fear of black violence following the attack at Harpers Ferry. In the wake of Brown's incursion, which included five black participants and which, white Americans quickly learned, had received support from prominent abolitionists, state officials likely also doubted black loyalty. Their doubts might have been further fueled by some black leaders' arguments in the 1850s that the nation had forfeited African Americans' allegiance.

Black Northerners were committed to American founding ideals, but the idea that African Americans might not owe allegiance to the federal Union or might welcome its destruction had a long history in black protest thought.

This idea had appeared in David Walker's landmark 1829 *Appeal to the Colored Citizens of the World*. Walker was a used-clothing dealer who moved to Boston in the mid-1820s and became an outspoken abolitionist; his pamphlet outraged the white South, and he died under mysterious circumstances shortly after its publication.[59]

That Walker envisioned black Americans possessing allegiance to something other than the United States was apparent from his pamphlet's title, with its implicit description of black Americans as "colored citizens of the world." Walker argued against colonization and for African Americans' claim on the United States, yet he repeatedly used the term "American" to address whites exclusively. "God will not suffer [African Americans], always to be oppressed," he predicted. "Our sufferings will come to an *end*, in spite of all the Americans this side of *eternity*. . . . 'Every dog must have its day,' and the American's is coming to an end." Walker predicted calamity if the United States failed to cleanse itself of slavery and prejudice, and he counseled Americans to change for the sake of their own salvation: "Perhaps they will laugh at or make light of this; but I tell you Americans! that unless you speedily alter your course, *you* and your *Country are gone!!!!!!*"[60] His use of the term "American" suggested that the United States' treatment of African Americans had caused him to hesitate to identify with the nation. His prediction of divine judgment and national destruction demonstrated that black Americans could be pushed only so far by slavery and discrimination while maintaining their faith in their ability to find justice within the national framework. At some point, they would welcome the nation's destruction in the belief that a more just polity would take its place.[61]

Following Walker's lead, in the 1850s some black Northerners called for disunion and maintained that African Americans owed the United States no allegiance. By the latter part of the decade, disunionism—the proposition that Americans should refuse to participate in a federal Union with slaveholders— had long been a key tenet of Garrisonian dogma. The events of the 1850s, particularly the *Dred Scott* decision, gave new impetus to the anger and alienation felt by Garrison's black allies. Before a meeting of Garrison's American Anti-Slavery Society held in *Dred Scott*'s wake, Robert Purvis branded the American government "one of the basest, meanest, most atrocious despotisms that ever saw the face of the sun." He also reveled in the possibility that sectional tensions might destroy it: "And, I rejoice, sir, that there is a prospect of this atrocious government being overthrown, and a better one built up in its place."[62] A year later, the black abolitionist and orator Charles Lenox Remond affirmed the American Anti-Slavery Society's "earnest . . . purpose to dissolve the American Union and break into a thousand pieces the American Government," closing with the familiar Garrisonian cry "NO UNION WITH SLAVE-HOLDERS!"[63] On one level, Purvis and Remond simply articulated key principles of Garrisonian thought, but when Remond "boldly proclaimed himself a traitor to the government and the Union, so long as his rights were denied him for no fault of his own," he expressed frustrations born of his relegation to second-class citizenship.[64]

Black Northerners saw how incomplete their citizenship was and occasionally argued that their diminished status absolved them from national allegiance. In November 1859, as he prepared to leave for England ahead of the federal marshals who sought him in connection with John Brown's raid, Douglass lambasted the proposition that African Americans owed fealty to the U.S. government: "A government which refuses to acknowledge—nay, denies that I can be a citizen, or bring a suit into its courts of justice—in a word, brands me as an outlaw in virtue of my blood, now professes a wish to try me for being a traitor and an outlaw! . . . Allegiance and protection are said to go together, and depend upon each other. When one is withdrawn, the other ceases."[65] Douglass justified his association with Brown on the grounds that one who did not receive full protection from the government owed it no loyalty.[66] In 1858, a convention of black Ohioans resolved, "If the Dred Scott dictum be a true exposition of the law of the land . . . colored men are absolved from all allegiance to a government which withdraws all protection." This resolution was especially revealing because, a year earlier and prior to the *Dred Scott* ruling, black Ohioans had promised to fight for the United States in the event of foreign war.[67]

For decades, the idea that African Americans were citizens unjustly denied the fruits of citizenship had been an article of faith among black Northerners. The crises of the 1850s eroded this faith, inspiring some to embrace their lack of citizenship in justifying defiance of the law. The doctrine they developed as a result of this new analysis had far-reaching implications. In 1854, H. Ford Douglas, who had escaped from slavery eight years earlier and joined the convention movement in Illinois, proclaimed to a colonizationist meeting in Cleveland that he might fight with a foreign army, as the U.S. government had only ever treated him "as a stranger and an alien."[68] Alan Taylor has argued that American masters' brutal treatment of enslaved men and women created an "internal enemy," an enslaved population alienated from the American republic that would seek in wartime to aid the enemies of the United States, as American slaves did during the American Revolution and the War of 1812. Statements such as Douglas's suggest that oppression and discrimination could push free black Northerners to the point that they would abandon their belief in American principles and allegiance to the United States. Had war with a foreign power broken out in the late 1850s, it is possible that the United States would have had to deal with an "internal enemy" in the North as well.[69]

Indeed, during the antebellum decades, black Northerners sometimes debated whether they would become combatants for the United States in the event of war. In an 1833 lecture at the African Masonic Hall in Boston, the teacher, journalist, and abolitionist Maria Stewart asked whether the current generation of African Americans would fight for the United States as had their forefathers. "Can our 'brave soldiers' and 'fellow citizens,' as they were termed in time of calamity, condescend to defend the rights of whites and again be deprived of their own, or sent to Liberia in return?" she asked her audience. Stewart did not answer her rhetorical question, but the fact that she considered the issue a matter of debate showed the extent to which the nation's betrayal of black veterans had caused black activists to question their duty to America.[70]

In 1842, when war between the United States and Great Britain seemed possible, an unidentified black man considered the looming conflict in the *Colored People's Press*. Frustrated that black service had yielded little in terms of black rights and citizenship, he counseled black men to take no part in a foreign war until white Americans met black demands:

> There is no law in existence which can compel us to fight, and any fighting on our part, must be a VOLUNTARY ACT. The States in which we dwell have twice availed themselves of our *voluntary services*, and have repaid us with chains and slavery. Shall we a third time kiss the foot that crushes us? If so, we deserve our chains. No! let us maintain an organized neutrality, until the laws of the Union and of all the States have made us free and equal citizens.[71]

War with Great Britain never came, so black men did not have to answer the questions this author posed. That he asked them at all suggested that, for some black Northerners, bitterness over the betrayal of black veterans prevailed over national loyalty. Some of them might withhold their service to bargain for change in the event of a future war.

William H. Newby expanded on this idea in the 1850s; those who followed his regular missives in *Frederick Douglass' Paper*, published under the name "Nubia," would not have been surprised by the stance he assumed at black Californians' 1856 state convention. In a March 1855 letter, Newby commented on speculation that the United States might become involved in a foreign conflict.

He relished this possibility, for he saw that African Americans could turn this situation to their advantage by approaching it opportunistically:

All [the United States'] resources, physical, mental and financial, will be taxed to the utmost; and the colored people may yet be called upon for assistance, for their assistance would be no small item, when we reflect that they could muster a *hundred thousand* capable of bearing arms. I apprehend that the free colored people have learned a lesson since the last war. No promises, no flattery, no appeal to patriotism, will induce them to "fly to arms." The removal of all political disabilities, elevation to social equality, the same inducements to enlist that are held out to the whites, would be the terms demanded by them, before they would be willing to fight.[72]

Newby died in 1859, so it is impossible to know whether he would have maintained this attitude after the outbreak of hostilities in 1861.[73] Regardless, he injected debate over the question of black men's response to the outbreak of war into two of the most important civil-society institutions black Northerners possessed, the state convention movement and the black press, encouraging African Americans to consider how they might approach a future war strategically. Consideration of the proper response to the call to serve became, during the late antebellum period, a part of black politics.

Newby's thinking did not typify black Northerners' opinion on the question of service, especially during the late 1850s, when civil war seemed far more likely to erupt than a foreign conflict. Many still hoped that African Americans would find citizenship within the United States and insisted that black men would serve the nation in a future crisis. In 1859, the New York physician James McCune Smith took to Douglass's new monthly newspaper to proclaim black Americans citizens in spite of the *Dred Scott* ruling. His article was a telling comment on antebellum confusion over citizenship and what it entailed; Smith based his argument on his analysis of Roman citizenship, the rights of which he believed black Americans had enjoyed at one time or another. "Relying upon this basis for citizenship," he wrote, "we blacks may smile at the Dred Scott decision, and the various rulings of the minions of slaveholders ... [and] safely bide our time." The previous year, addressing a Crispus Attucks Day celebration in Boston, John Rock had predicted that war would soon come and that slaves would strike for freedom. Rock was a freeborn doctor, dentist, and lawyer who moved to Boston in the 1850s and became a prominent abolitionist orator; in 1865, he would become the first black lawyer to argue a case before the U.S. Supreme Court.[74] "Will the blacks fight?" he asked. "Of course they will. The black man will never be neutral. . . . Will he fight for his country right or wrong? This the common sense of every one answers; and when the time comes, and come it will, the black man will give an intelligent answer."[75]

Events, however, led Rock to reconsider this opinion, and two years later, at another Crispus Attucks gathering, he proclaimed that black Northerners would not repeat what he characterized as the mistakes of their forefathers. "Crispus Attucks was a brave man," Rock observed, "and he fought with our fathers in a good cause; but they were not victorious. They fought for liberty, but they got slavery. The white man was benefited, but the black man was in-jured." He desired to see all men free and prosperous, he said. But he added a stipulation: "By this I do not mean to imply, that, should our country be again situated as it was [at the time of the Revolutionary War], we would be willing to re-commit the errors of our Revolutionary fathers. The Scotch have a say-ing, 'When a man deceives me once, shame on *him*; but when he deceives me twice, shame on *me*.'"[76] Some black Northerners prepared to join a sectional war against slavery, but others vowed not to repeat previous mistakes by be-lieving that black military service could make white Americans live up to the nation's founding principles.[77]

When war erupted in 1861, it came in response to the election of a Republi-can president labeled a "moderate conservative on the spectrum of Republican thought" by one recent historian. This president opposed slavery's extension into the federal territories but stood pledged not to interfere with the institu-tion where it already existed.[78] He talked of gradual abolition—perhaps over the course of a hundred years—and had in 1858 announced himself "not in favor of negro citizenship," though he acknowledged its basic constitutionality in defiance of *Dred Scott*.[79] This war pitted a Confederate republic committed to maintaining slavery and white supremacy against an American republic that had steadfastly supported slaveholders' rights, contained four slave states and a host of other states that restricted black rights, and was controlled by a Republican Party whose antislavery convictions often failed to translate into support for black rights and equality. American history indicated that, even-tually, both sides would enlist black soldiers, but white racism had intensified over the course of the nineteenth century, as had white Southerners' commit-ment to slaveholding and white supremacy. Both of these trends suggested that white Americans might be more reluctant to enlist black troops than in earlier wars.

So did the pessimism that had overtaken some black Northerners' thinking regarding their future in the United States. Continuous setbacks and the depth of white prejudice had pushed some black leaders toward colonization; even Frederick Douglass, who had staunchly resisted colonization for years, had scheduled a trip to evaluate Haiti's suitability as a destination for black Americans. He canceled the journey only when hostilities commenced. Other black men had turned to violence against slavery, urging slave insurrection or joining in it themselves. Three free black Northerners and one black man from Canada had joined John Brown at Harpers Ferry, and evidence suggests that more might have joined had Brown clarified his intentions regarding the date of his raid.[80] Others advocated disunion, absolved themselves of national loyalty, and recoiled at the suggestion that black men would fight alongside whites as had their forefathers. The events of the 1850s led black Northerners to different conclusions about how to achieve the common end they sought: the birth of a new nation, one that would in practice honor the Declaration of Independence. Their differing assessments of the problems they faced would inform their analysis of how they should respond to the new national crisis. As war engulfed the nation, it was unclear what part black men would take in the coming conflict or how they would respond if asked to fight.

2

A WHITE MAN'S WAR?

APRIL 1861–DECEMBER 1862

S HORTLY AFTER Fort Sumter's fall in April 1861, *Douglass' Monthly* printed a letter from "Immaterial," a correspondent who, Frederick Douglass claimed, voiced the sentiments of "all thoughtful colored men of the North." Noting that slavery had caused the war, Immaterial also said, "[It is] extremely proper that the descendants of Africans should take a prominent part in [this] war which will eventually lead to a general emancipation of the race." Immaterial wanted to raise a regiment of black Northerners as a nucleus around which slaves, freed by the proclamation of emancipation he believed Lincoln would issue, could rally. He knew that whites opposed black enlistment, but he maintained that their objections would dwindle by war's end: "Every man, black or white, able and willing to carry a musket, will be wanted, and the Government will accept readily the services of all those who shall offer to bring down this infernal confederated rebellion to an end."[1]

With the benefit of hindsight, Immaterial looks downright prophetic. He sketched much of the basic outline of events that ended with slavery's destruction and nearly 200,000 black men fighting for the Union. Immaterial's scenario was only one, however, among many contemplated by black Northerners during the uncertain months after Sumter. Debate raged within black Northern communities about African Americans' proper attitude toward the conflict; Douglass's assertion that Immaterial spoke for all "thoughtful colored men of the North" was wishful thinking from one who wanted black men to rush to arms when permitted.[2]

Some black Northerners scorned enlistment. Weeks after Douglass ran Immaterial's letter, an anonymous correspondent assured New York's *Weekly Anglo-African* that black Baltimoreans had *not* tried to volunteer in Sumter's aftermath. Rumors circulated to the contrary, but, the correspondent observed, "[Only] two or three of our people who have enjoyed the good will of many of our leading white citizens [have actually tried to enlist]." The rest of black Baltimore was furious with these sycophants: their efforts were "by no means a representation of the true sentiment of the colored people of Baltimore or Maryland." These citizens' actions proved so unpopular that the correspondent stated, "Were it not for the exigent circumstances of the times, the cloud of indignant wrath that has brewed over them, from the breasts of our people, would soon put a stop to their career by ending their lives."[3] Black Baltimoreans' "indignant wrath" at the notion of fighting for the United States starkly contrasted with the enthusiasm for enlistment felt by Immaterial and Douglass.

Rebuffed in their efforts to volunteer in April 1861, black Northerners spent the next year and a half debating their proper response if Union officials allowed black men to serve. African Americans did not know quite what to make of the war in its earliest days, and no more than in antebellum times did they think with one mind. Historians have made sweeping statements about black Northerners' presumably unanimous desire to volunteer in Sumter's aftermath.[4] To be sure, many did want to enlist right away.[5] Others staked out a different stance, arguing that they should not serve until the government guaranteed change in return for their efforts. As early as April 1861, black Northerners began to insist that, if they enlisted, they would not fight merely to restore the political integrity of the antebellum United States. Echoing their prewar demand that the nation enact its founding principles, these prospective servicemen maintained that they would only fight if in subduing the Confederacy a new Union would be forged. They knew that for the war to create a new Union, it would have to prove lengthy and bloody; accordingly, they hoped for a long war and saw that early Confederate victories served their cause.[6] In their discussions of enlistment, the war, and their wartime objectives, black Northerners developed a politics of service, strategizing about how to seize on the opportunity the conflict brought. Mindful of the nation's history of betraying black veterans, African Americans in the North considered how they might make their service in this war *count* in a way their forefathers' contributions had not.

In the North, African Americans' thinking about enlistment evolved as 1861 turned to 1862, responding to shifting circumstances. Official pronouncements by politicians and commanders, personal experiences with white racism, and their changing analysis of events influenced black Northerners' thinking about their potential place in the Union war effort. Unable to know the conflict's ultimate course, these individuals contemplated a range of possible outcomes, and their knowledge of history encouraged some to assume that this newest crisis over slavery would end with a compromise, as others had.

Black Northerners trying to divine the direction of Union policy regarding slavery had neither the benefit of hindsight nor the ability to review relevant communications between generals and politicians. African Americans could only rely on their own analysis of the news, stories, and rumors that circulated in the wartime North to evaluate the war and Union policy toward the issues that mattered to them.

As black Northerners tried to determine where they fit into the Union war effort, many felt the signals they received were mixed. By the end of 1862, the Union's initial refusal of black service left African Americans in the North no more certain about their eventual enlistment than they had been in Sumter's immediate aftermath. The same was true of black Northerners' general uncertainty over Union policy toward their race and slavery, and of their analysis of their own treatment by white Americans. By the close of 1862, "the thoughtful colored men of the North" had not achieved consensus about where the war might go and what role they might play in it, although they shared a determination to bring the nation they had long envisioned into being.

———

AFTER FORT SUMTER'S FALL, influential black leaders and institutions urged black men to volunteer. Under the headline "Better Than Peace," Philadelphia's *Christian Recorder* declared, "There [was] no duty which the crisis may bring upon order-loving citizens . . . from which we would shrink."[7] In May, Frederick Douglass implored the government to enlist black men. "We lack nothing but your consent," he wrote. "We are ready and would go, counting ourselves happy in being permitted to serve and suffer for the cause of freedom and free institutions."[8] Philadelphia's Alfred M. Green, a well-known lecturer who had recently served a prison term for his role in a fugitive slave rescue, heartily endorsed black enlistment and corresponded with white officials about forming a black Home Guard unit.[9]

The *Recorder*, Douglass, and Green voiced a sentiment popular among black Northerners at the war's outbreak: because slavery had caused the war, the war might destroy slavery, and thus black men should fight at the first opportunity. Across the North, African American men responded enthusiastically to Abraham Lincoln's mid-April call for volunteers. Black Bostonians displayed particular enthusiasm. At a meeting in Boston's Twelfth Street Baptist Church, John Rock and Robert Morris urged enlistment. As one of the first black men to gain admission to the Massachusetts bar, and as justice of the peace in Suffolk County, Morris had long supported black military efforts; in the 1850s he had commanded Boston's Massasoit Guards and spearheaded efforts to gain state recognition of African American militia units.[10] If Massachusetts allowed black men to serve, he claimed, "there was not a man who would not leap for his knapsack and musket, and they would make it intolerably hot for Old Virginia."[11]

At a subsequent meeting, black Bostonians proposed forming a "Home Guard" unit. At this gathering, Rock proclaimed that black men would "not take advantage of the fact [that state law forbade their service] in this hour of our country's danger." Rather, he declared, "[We] will show even to our enemies that we have the best wishes for our country's prosperity." Wealthy hotelier and caterer George T. Downing and Lewis Hayden—a former fugitive and leading Vigilance Committee member—also spoke, and the meeting concluded with Captain Watkins of the city's Liberty Guards leading 125 volunteers in drill.[12] Similar enlistment movements took place in Washington, D.C., Pittsburgh, New Bedford, Philadelphia, Cleveland, Providence, Cincinnati, and New York City, among other places.[13]

White officials rejected these offers of service. New York's police chief informed black men that they must stop drilling or face mob violence.[14] Black Cincinnatians seeking to form a Home Guard unit met an especially harsh refusal. Police demanded the keys to a schoolhouse they had selected as a meeting site. The owner of one business to be used as a recruiting station was forced to remove an American flag from his premises, while police told the owners of another, "We want you d—d niggers to keep out of this; this is a white man's war." Amid rumors that a mob of white steamboat workers would attack black volunteers, black Cincinnatians halted their efforts. According to Peter Clark, the incident dampened their patriotism. Clark, the grandson of William Clark, Meriwether Lewis's famous companion, and his slave Betty, had by the mid-1850s become a prominent instructor in Cincinnati's black public school system, where he remained a fixture for decades.[15] When in 1862 local leaders sought black help to defend the city from an expected Confederate attack, Clark remembered that their appeals "fell upon the ears of colored men unheeded. They remembered their lesson."[16]

Despite these rebuffs, black Northerners discussed their potential place in the war, debating what they stood to gain from it, the course they hoped it would take, and their willingness to fight. Some black leaders continued to expect great things. Eminent black Northerners like Alfred M. Green, the philanthropist William P. Powell, and AME clergymen James Lynch, Jermain Loguen, and Thomas M. D. Ward continued to urge black men to enlist whenever permitted.[17] The government's initial refusal of black service, however, caused many other black Northerners to strategize about what kind of war they wanted to see and how their eventual participation might further their cause.

Black Northerners debated their place in the war in the pages of William Lloyd Garrison's *Liberator*, Frederick Douglass's monthly journal, Boston's *Pine & Palm*, Philadelphia's *Christian Recorder*, and New York City's *Weekly Anglo-African*. The *Anglo-African*, which had debuted in 1859, was managed by the brothers Robert and Thomas Hamilton. A book dealer and experienced newsman, Robert had worked on a series of black and abolitionist newspapers since the early 1840s. Amidst financial hardship, the brothers sold their organ to James Redpath, a white abolitionist, in early 1861. Redpath moved the operation to Boston, hired an editor who favored emigration to Haiti, and changed the periodical's name to the *Pine & Palm*. The sheet quickly fell on hard times, folding in 1862. Upset with his newspaper's rebirth as a proemigration organ, in July 1861 Robert resumed publication of the *Weekly Anglo-African*. The Hamilton brothers managed the revived paper, whose motto summarized their militant stance: "Man must be free; if not within the law, why then, above the law."[18]

Like the *Anglo-African*, Philadelphia's *Christian Recorder* provided black Northerners with a forum for discussing the war. Founded in 1852, the *Recorder* was an AME Church publication. In its early years it printed mainly religious items, but during the war it embraced the issues roiling the nation. AME minister Elisha Weaver edited the paper for most of the war. Born free in North Carolina, Weaver had studied at Oberlin College in Ohio, shepherded the development of Chicago's AME Church, and overseen the *Recorder*'s growth first in Indianapolis and then Philadelphia.[19] He broadened the periodical's coverage of secular issues, "turn[ing] the *Recorder* into a paper with a nationwide reach, that solicit[ed] and publish[ed] extensive coverage of the Civil War."[20] Though more parochial in its perspective, the *Recorder* joined the *Anglo-African* as a vital forum for discussion and debate. Both sheets helped unify a black population scattered across the Northern states by carrying letters, weekly reports, and transcripts of public gatherings.[21]

While many whites North and South predicted a short war and easy victory, black Northerners hoped for a long, arduous conflict, one sufficiently taxing to compel the federal government to enlist black soldiers and, as a concomitant, recognize black rights and citizenship. Speaking at the same meeting where Robert Morris had promised to make it "intolerably hot for old Virginia," William Wells Brown had declared that the time had not yet come for black volunteering because black men would not serve on terms of equality with white soldiers. "The only hope to-day for the colored man," Brown had insisted, "was in Jefferson Davis."[22] Brown expanded on this theme the following year. Speaking at a First of August celebration in Massachusetts, Brown explained the situation: "Everything . . . looks bright for us, while it looks dark for the Republic. If the rebellion had been crushed . . . and the Union as it was restored, the black man would have been left just where he was ten, fifteen or twenty years ago; but the war has gone on until there seems not to be a possibility of putting down the rebellion without giving the black man his freedom."[23]

Weeks after Sumter's fall, an anonymous correspondent of Boston's *Pine & Palm* made the same point. Northerners, the writer said, needed to be taught a lesson, and a Confederate invasion of Washington followed by the capture of Lincoln and his cabinet might provide it. Only when such calamities forced some Northern soul-searching could the country be saved: "The hopes of the country rest in Jeff. Davis, and the jubilant songs of freedom will arise when the armies of the Southern Confederacy sweep the Washington Cabinet into the Potomac."[24] Black Northerners saw that only a long, costly war would put the country in straits sufficiently dire to compel it to accept black service and improve black rights and status.[25]

Black Northerners' desire for a lengthy war was furthered by signs that seemed to indicate the Union was following a cautious, conservative policy toward slavery. In the spring of 1861, Union general Benjamin Butler had assured Marylanders that his troops would assist in quelling domestic insurrections, a statement widely read as a pledge to put down slave uprisings. George McClellan made a similar proclamation in western Virginia. Federal commanders returned fugitive slaves to their masters, even after federal laws directed otherwise. Lincoln revoked emancipatory proclamations made by two high-ranking commanders—John C. Fremont in Missouri in 1861, and David Hunter in the Department of the South in 1862—and replaced Secretary of War Simon Cameron, who had talked publicly of arming black soldiers, in early 1862. The president fired Cameron for his infamous corruption and inefficiency, but many black leaders read the move as further evidence of federal opposition to black service.[26] As late as August 1862, Lincoln publicly insisted that "his paramount object in this struggle [was] to save the Union . . . *not* to either save or destroy slavery."[27] Prominent Republicans, including Postmaster General Montgomery Blair, embraced colonization, and on multiple occasions Congress appropriated funds to deport emancipated slaves. Even Republicans' language stung; Republicans, especially in the Midwest, often denigrated African Americans while denouncing slavery.[28] "Every thing that [Republicans] do," cried the *Weekly Anglo-African* in January 1862, "indicates a disposition to save the country at the expense of the rights of man."[29]

Of course, even from the war's first summer, some developments suggested that it might take an antislavery course. As early as May 1861, Benjamin Butler developed his famous "contraband" doctrine allowing Union soldiers to refuse to return fugitive slaves who entered Union lines, and in August the First Confiscation Act essentially formalized this policy. Moreover, James Oakes has recently shown that by August 1861 events on the ground were moving in advance of the First Confiscation Act. Simon Cameron's implementation of the act barred Union soldiers from returning slaves who reached Union lines voluntarily. By a combination of slaves' initiative, federal legislation, and Cameron's orders, military emancipation was happening a year before Lincoln issued his preliminary Emancipation Proclamation. Oakes has even shown that actions usually seen as evidence of Northern hesitance to make war on slavery—such as Lincoln's revocation of Hunter's and Fremont's edicts—had nothing to with lack of antislavery zeal. Lincoln revoked the proclamations because he believed that Congress, not military commanders, had the authority to make permanent determinations regarding property rights, and because he wanted to ensure that military decrees conformed to the terms of congressional legislation.[30]

These insights are of tremendous value for the modern reader, and they suggest that Republicans put their commitment to destroying slavery into practice earlier than previously thought. To black Northerners who observed the war as it unfolded, however, many of the early signs of Republicans' antislavery intent would have been difficult to see. Most black Northerners did not travel with Union armies. On the home front, they could not witness the practical effects of the First Confiscation Act's implementation, and they did not receive correspondence from Cameron or Lincoln. They had only history, the war news they received, and their own analysis of the conflict to guide them as they searched for meaning.

Their anger at Union policies caused some black Northerners to withdraw their support from the U.S. war effort altogether; in early 1862, black newspaper correspondent George Stephens declined to "cheer at the success of any man or nation that sanctions human bondage."[31] Most black Northerners, however, saw that, no matter how offensive Union policies were, Union victory was preferable to the victory of a Southern Confederacy whose bedrock principle was slavery. They joined John Rock in "wish[ing] [the Union cause] that success which [it] will not deserve."[32]

If it did not cause most black Northerners to withdraw their support from the war effort, Union policy colored their attitudes toward enlistment. *Pine & Palm* correspondent "Bobb'n Around" linked his opposition to volunteering to the Union's position on slavery. The correspondent noted a problem with the proposal to join the military immediately: "[It would entail black soldiers serving under] such men as Gen. Butler, of Massachusetts, and Lieut. [Adam] Slemmer, of Fort Pickens; the first of whom has offered the services of the Massachusetts troops to suppress an insurrection in Maryland, and the latter, having already returned many poor slaves, who, through incredible hardships, had reached his strongholds."[33] The *Weekly Anglo-African* dramatically branded Lincoln's revocation of Fremont's proclamation "The Fatal Step Backward."[34] From the Colorado Territory, Wesley W. Tate described himself as a "disinterested spectator" to the war. He felt "much shame and indignation" at black volunteering efforts, and he was convinced that the war would end with slavery intact. Turning to ridicule, Tate directly addressed would-be black soldiers: "[I hope you have the] *honor* of marching in the *front* ranks to the next Bull Run or Lexington battle; so that while your patriotic names may be handed down to posterity in golden characters, on the pages of American history, your carcasses may be used by the Southern Traitors, to build up ramparts to defend their *peculiar institution*, for which cause you enlisted, bled, fought and died."[35]

Encounters with pervasive white racism dimmed black Northerners' hopes for the war. In August 1861 "Inquirer," a regular Philadelphia correspondent of the *Pine & Palm*, told of a federal recruiting party led by black musicians that was attacked by white volunteers who felt "aggrieved that colored men were used in drumming up recruits." Black Philadelphians seethed at their treatment. Several local black military companies, Inquirer continued, remained active, but he doubted they would enlist. "If there was any enthusiasm among us," he wrote, "we think a damper was put upon it at the outbreak of the present conflict, when several having offered their services, were contemptuously refused."[36]

N. B. Harris of Oberlin ruefully described his attempt to volunteer. Harris had heard that the local recruiting agent was enlisting black men, and he and a lighter-skinned friend tried to sign up. The agent refused Harris but accepted his friend. "What is this country coming to?" Harris asked. He knew that, were he a white foreigner, he could fight. Thus he lamented, "Because I am an American-born citizen, claiming all the rights as such, but granted none, I am not allowed to protect the Stars and Stripes."[37] Four years later, Richard McDaniel remembered telling a "white gentleman" of his desire to fight. The white man scoffed and predicted, "The rebels will have to spill the blood of all the white men in the North before a nigger can take up arms," then added that he would rather be "shot in the back" than "stand by the side of a black man and fight." McDaniel eventually served in the Eleventh United States Colored Troops (USCT) but remembered that, following this encounter, he thought he "never would enlist at all."[38] It is impossible to know how many times scenes like these played out during the war's first months. But when black men tried to volunteer and were refused, they felt angered and humiliated and often reassessed their desire to fight.

An incident that took place in Cincinnati in September 1862 perhaps best displays this dynamic. When the Confederate invasion of Kentucky threatened Ohio early in the month, Cincinnati officials deputized local Irish Americans to impress black men as laborers on city defenses. These newly minted deputies drove Cincinnati's black men through the streets like "beasts," pulling anyone who failed to present himself for duty from his home "at the point of the bayonet."[39] A "mobocracy" ruled, and Elisha Weaver, visiting the city at the time, reported that Irish American deputies would "take the bayonet off their guns, and ram it through [black families'] beds" when told that no black men were present. Cincinnatians impressed into their city's "Black Brigade" in later years took pride in the services they rendered the city in its time of need.[40] But in the moment this incident angered them, affecting their attitude toward the Union war effort.

City authorities had refused black men as volunteers in 1861 and violently impressed them the next year; this conduct was an insult. One black Cincinnatian wrote that the incident had "increased the tenacity of [his] self-respect" and changed his mind about black service. "I have been among those who desired the acceptance of our services in crushing the rebellion, but am changed now." He had wanted to fight for "equality before the law," but he had become convinced that, "having suffered with unexampled patience all [their] lives," black Americans "[did] not need additional suffering" to earn that equality. African American soldiers would only serve "as those in bondage do, involuntarily submitting to peremptory orders," and he opposed this menial service. Another black Cincinnatian relocated rather than support the Union war effort involuntarily. "I confess," he wrote, "I am not patriot enough to fight or dig trenches for 'the Union as it was,' 'the Constitution as it is,' and the negroes as they are; and so, for the time being, change my base of operation."[41]

Black Northerners saw the Cincinnati incident as a reflection of their inferior legal status. Elisha Weaver believed the affair proved that white immigrants possessed a more robust quality of citizenship than did native-born black Americans. City officials, he wrote, had impressed black Cincinnatians because the city's Irish population refused to serve unless black men did too. Weaver fumed, "In order to have [the Irish] go, who have all the rights of citizenship, it was necessary to pounce upon those who are deprived of all the laws and rights of citizenship in this country only on account of their color."[42] It was surely not lost on Weaver that these Irish Americans could, under the terms of 1862 legislation, obtain citizenship through enlistment, whereas African Americans had in 1857 been barred from citizenship by the land's highest court. If black Americans subject to state-sanctioned arbitrary violence possessed citizenship at all, it was inferior to that which whites enjoyed.

Black Northerners connected the white refusal to enlist black soldiers with white Americans' belief that African Americans were incapable of citizenship. In December 1861, Philadelphia's Rev. William Douglass argued that when the government had refused black service, it had merely acted in accordance with the *Dred Scott* decision. Thus "[people of color] had . . . [no] ground for complaint on that score." Black men might fight, but as any citizenship they enjoyed arose from their states of residence, they should only fight for those states; black men, that is, should only fight for political entities that recognized them as citizens.[43] At an October 1861 convention of black Baptists in New Bedford, Rev. William E. Walker read a series of resolutions drawn up by a "committee . . . on national affairs" that voiced black Northerners' frustration. The group commented on what it considered an "unjust and unwarranted" situation: "While the very foundations of the government are shaken . . . the national government still refuses to regard us as men and citizens, by not allowing men to take up arms in defence of free institutions." Though the committee saw federal enlistment policy as an affront to black manhood and citizenship, it did not withdraw its support from the Union war effort.[44]

These black Baptists possessed a degree of magnanimity not shared by all black Northerners; as the war ground on and the Union army still refused African American soldiers, some began to mock the Union war effort. In August, a black Chicagoan told the *Pine & Palm* of an incident in which a contingent of forty federal soldiers attacked a party of young black men and women attending a First of August celebration. The revelers drove off their white assailants, much to the delight of the anonymous correspondent, who lampooned the Union disaster at the First Battle of Bull Run the previous month: "African courage was at fever heat, and the morning papers had the melancholy duty to perform of recording another Bull Run."[45] When William J. Watkins, sojourning in Detroit, described that city's Military Guards, he, too, mocked the Union war effort. He joked that the Detroit Military Guards, who had volunteered at the outset of hostilities and been refused, included a talented band specializing in a piece called "Lincoln's Races, or Bull's Run Retreat." Earlier in the summer, Watkins had predicted that the war would kill slavery and that black men would fight.[46] As Union officials continued to spurn African American assistance, however, his zeal for enlistment faded. "Perhaps, before the war is over, [the Detroit Military Guards] *will be needed*, and *perhaps* they will have something else to attend to *then*," he warned. "*Now*, do your own fighting, Mr. Lincoln, from this time henceforth."[47]

It took Watkins several months to get to the point of making this declaration, but some black Northerners had opposed volunteering even as African American communities organized enlistment drives in April 1861. They counseled black men to use common sense and demonstrate awareness of their self-worth by refusing to serve the federal government. Perhaps black Northerners who opposed enlistment or advocated its delay did so after having supported the idea at first, changing their minds when they learned that black recruits had been rebuffed. Even if such a change of opinion occurred, however, the opposition to volunteering that some black Northerners expressed in the weeks and months following Sumter's fall proves that a vocal element within the African American community quickly recoiled from the idea. From the war's beginning, African Americans in the North disagreed loudly and profoundly about whether and under what circumstances black men should fight.

In Sumter's aftermath, a handful of black Northerners opposed volunteering outright. N. A. D. of Detroit catalogued for *Pine & Palm* various Southern slave codes and Northern discriminatory laws, concluding simply, "Catch me fighting for a country that perpetrates such outrages."[48] J. H. W. of Chillicothe, Ohio, believed that offers of service sent the wrong message. "If the colored people, under all the social and legal disabilities by which they are environed, are ever ready to defend the government that despoils them of their rights, it may be concluded that it is quite safe to oppress them," he argued. J. H. W. also linked his opposition to enlistment to the fact that African American service in previous wars had not bettered the race's condition: "The truth is, if in time of peace, the fact of our having bled in defense of the country when it was struggling desperately for independence, avails nothing, it is absurd to suppose that the fact of tendering our services in a domestic war when we know that our services will be contemptuously rejected, will procure a practical acknowledgment of our rights."[49]

Cincinnati's William Parham conducted frank correspondence concerning the war with his friend Jacob C. White Jr. of Philadelphia. Parham, the first black graduate of Cincinnati Law School, was a teacher who would become superintendent of the city's black schools. White, the scion of one of Philadelphia's leading black families, was an educator, a founding member of local black debating society the Banneker Institute, and a subscription agent for the *Weekly Anglo-African* and *Pine & Palm*.[50] Parham condemned black volunteering efforts, looking back scornfully on the days after Sumter. He described this time as follows: "[The] Northern heart was fired with indignation. . . . [and s]ome of our colored men thinking they were a part of this Northern heart alluded to, imagined themselves very indignant; and as all the rest of this heart was forming Home Guards &c concluded they must do likewise." Parham had refused to attend recruitment meetings, and the response would-be volunteers met only strengthened his conviction: black Ohioans were told that the war was a *"white men's fight, with which niggers had nothing to do."* Parham and White agreed that in October 1861, the time for black service had not come, but they disagreed about whether that time might come later. White thought it would, whereas Parham did not, "if Negro equality [was] to be its precursor." Parham believed that slavery would die as an unintended consequence of Northern victory, but he predicted that white prejudice would survive the war and dog African Americans' every step.[51]

In examining Parham and White's disagreement, a key development in black Northerners' thinking about enlistment emerges. Few African Americans in the region opposed black enlistment outright. Whites' reaction to black volunteering and government policy toward slavery and African Americans had dampened black men's enthusiasm for enlistment. But like White, most hoped these men might at some point find it in their interest to fight. Discussions about the part African American men might potentially play in the U.S. war effort remained central to Northern black politics despite the Union's refusal of black recruits. Black Northerners discussed the changes that might persuade them to join the fray, developing a politics of service that set the price of their enlistment following the government's rejection of black volunteers. This politics drew on the historical analysis African Americans had developed during the antebellum period, which lamented that the government had not properly rewarded their service in earlier American wars. Wanting to avoid a repeat of this outcome, black Northerners strategized about how to make this war different. This politics of service was frequently embedded within larger critiques of government policy, and it was often short on specifics. But it marked the beginning of black men's conceptualization of their military participation in the Union war effort.

The *Weekly Anglo-African* had discussed using black service strategically even before Fort Sumter's fall, arguing in March 1861 that black men should not fight unless given suffrage and other rights. On March 23, the newspaper made a suggestion to white Northerners: "[Before] prat[ing] of co-operation in the future, . . . recognise our just claims upon the inheritance which our past efforts aided . . . to secure[.] Before we [enlist] . . . we must have something better than flattery to convince us that after freely giving our blood to again build up the Union whose foot has bound us down for eighty-five years, that though free nominally, we shall not be as in the past, pariahs and outcasts." This commentary echoed William H. Newby's prewar suggestion that black men extract concessions from the United States prior to fighting for it again. "Messrs. Republicans," the influential publication demanded, "before you hand us *bullets* give us *ballots*. Ere you talk to us about instruments of war, give us those civic rights, those social privileges, for whose maintenance or defence only is war legitimate."[52]

Black Northerners developed their politics of service in Sumter's wake. On April 27, the *Christian Recorder* claimed in one piece that "there [was] no duty . . . from which [black men] would shrink," but in another it displayed a conditional approach to the war. In an article on "the Duty of Colored Americans to the Flag," the *Recorder* argued that while black men had been duty bound to fight in earlier wars, they were not in 1861, as laws and court decisions denied black humanity. For black men to volunteer under these circumstances would *"abandon self-respect,* and *invite insult,"* and the *Recorder* charged black men who had led volunteering efforts with "[betraying] that modest prudence which should always characterize a conscious manhood." Yet the *Recorder* also encouraged Northern blacks to pray that God might cause the government to "harmonize" itself toward them and prove worthy of African American assistance.[53] On the same day, the *Weekly Anglo-African* opposed black volunteering. Given the government's determination to "make this a white man's war," it asked, "is it wise to put [black men] in a position to have fresh contumely poured on them?" The newspaper urged black Northerners *"not* to fight for the Government" but to "hold [themselves] as Minute Men to *respond when the slave calls."*[54] These influential publications' comments prove that, within two weeks of Sumter's fall, the debate over black enlistment included those who advocated delaying military service until African Americans' demands were met.

The crucial aspect of black Northerners' politics of service was the set of conditions they desired the government to meet prior to their enlistment. These individuals often, however, refrained from enumerating specific legislative changes that could inspire them to volunteer. Instead, the North's African Americans spoke in general terms of equality, rights, and citizenship.

Nineteenth-century Americans recognized distinctions between natural, political, civil, and social rights that their modern-day counterparts do not, and prior to the Civil War no national category or definition of citizenship existed.[55] Given this reality, it is perhaps not surprising that black Northerners speaking of concepts like rights or citizenship did so without outlining their specific contours. More important than defining citizenship's essence for black Northerners was thinking strategically about how to use black service to achieve progress.

Black Northerners often invoked goals like equality and citizenship without specifying the changes that would realize them. Henry M. Cropper, who captained Philadelphia's Frank Johnson Guards, angrily disavowed rumors that his company had tried to volunteer; he and his comrades had "resolved never to offer or give service, except . . . on equality with all other men."[56] Cropper did not specify the changes that, in his opinion, would make this equality a reality. J. N. S. from Newton Falls, New Jersey, likewise believed that black men should serve only if ensured unspecified rewards for their service. African Americans should not fight, he wrote, unless they received "some *further* guarantee of benefits to be derived from it, as the just rewards of loyalty and patriotism." The United States' history of denying the fruits of victory to black soldiers dictated the course J. N. S. recommended: "If the Government *wants* us to *fight* and will reward us accordingly, I say, fight—not without, if we can help it."[57] Frederick Douglass also urged the government to make concessions to compel African Americans' service. He wanted black men to enlist whenever possible but stressed that black soldiers would fight best if "hereafter . . . recognized as persons bearing rights."[58]

Some black Northerners argued that they would reap the greatest advantage by waiting until entreated by the government to volunteer. "Argo," one of the *Christian Recorder*'s regular Washington correspondents, believed that the war presented a critical opportunity for African Americans that they should not squander by acting rashly. He denounced the actions of black Baltimoreans who had tried to volunteer as "folly, *neither more nor less*," and counseled black men to wait until *"called upon."*[59] In early May, William Lloyd Garrison's *Liberator* printed a letter from an unsigned black correspondent who encouraged black men to be "discreet." Their service ought to be "forthcoming" only "when most needed."[60]

Debate about enlistment became heated during the fall of 1861. In September, Alfred M. Green became involved in a lengthy exchange with a correspondent signing himself "R. H. V." in the pages of the *Anglo-African*.[61] According to R. H. V., black volunteers would only repeat the mistakes of earlier generations. He observed that African American veterans' descendants lacked "the rights of men and citizens." "Will the satisfaction," he then asked, "of again hearing a casual mention of our heroic deeds upon the fields of battle, by our own children, doomed for all we know to the same inveterate heart-crushing prejudice that we have come up under," be sufficient to inspire black men to serve? If black men "let [their] own heart[s] answer this question," R. H. V. stated, "no regiments of black troops will leave their bodies to rot upon the battle-field beneath a Southern sun."[62]

Green then lamented that black men were divided at this critical moment, and he criticized as "foolish" those who sought to "[nurse] past grievances to [African Americans'] own detriment." That earlier generations of black soldiers had been cheated of the fruits of victory mattered little to Green, because the present generation possessed "the manhood to defend the right and the sagacity to detest the wrong."[63] In reply R. H. V. predicted that black soldiers would never conquer white prejudice: "I am satisfied," he wrote, "that neither recruiting, drilling, or fighting will never break this innate prejudice, embedded in the hearts of the nation."[64] Green and R. H. V.'s dispute continued until November, and Green considered their exchanges of sufficient import—and the question of black enlistment still sufficiently unsettled—that he published both sides of the correspondence as a pamphlet the following year.[65]

This debate spilled out of the pages of black newspapers into community meetings, often called "war meetings," where black Northerners considered their best course of action. African Americans in the region possessed a long tradition of public debate, having discussed matters of community interest in their churches, debating societies, and mutual-aid organizations during the antebellum period. These bodies in turn selected delegates to attend black state and national conventions to debate matters of relevance to all black Northerners.[66] Drawing on this tradition, black Northerners congregated to discuss enlistment, often meeting in black churches. Leonard Grimes's Twelfth Street Baptist Church in Boston, Henry Highland Garnet's Shiloh Presbyterian Church in New York, Richard H. Cain's Bridge Street Wesleyan Church in Brooklyn, and Mother Bethel in Philadelphia, among many others, housed war meetings.[67] These were public spaces black Northerners had built and maintained themselves, spaces one might view as "safe houses" for the conduct of black politics. But black Northerners also met in public spaces whites frequented, including New Bedford's City Hall, Worcester's City Hall, and Buffalo's Old Court House.[68]

So far as is known, at no point during the war did white violence interrupt a black war meeting. Across the antebellum decades, white violence had flared in Northern cities, as it did in Philadelphia in 1838 when mobs burned multiple African American and abolitionist institutions.[69] The Civil War did not temper white Northerners' penchant for racist violence, as would become clear during the summer of 1863. That African Americans living in the North could debate in public the possibility of bearing arms highlights the comparative openness of Northern civil society, as such a meeting of free black Southerners would have been unthinkable. But it also reveals the extent to which many whites in the North ignored black politics altogether.

Black war meetings seem to have been fairly grassroots affairs announced through some local public medium and held shortly thereafter. Nationally circulated black newspapers carried notices for the regular gatherings of established black organizations, and for conferences planned for weeks or months, such as the Syracuse Convention black Northerners would hold in 1864. But war meetings were typically local gatherings convened on short notice. Black leaders wanted to know where their fellow community members stood and often hoped to convince them of the wisdom of a particular position. Meeting attendees could be assembled quickly, so advertising in a weekly, nationally circulated black newspaper like the *Anglo-African* would have made little sense. Instead, calls for war meetings seem to have been issued through (presumably white-run) local newspapers or by word of mouth. The *Liberator* correspondent who reported on a June 1862 meeting in Buffalo learned of it by a "call through the public journals of Buffalo, N.Y."; in spring 1863 black Philadelphians went to hear Frederick Douglass speak about the war and black enlistment because they had seen a "notice inserted in yesterday's papers"; and in December 1863, the *Liberator* reprinted a report of a war meeting held in "accordance with a published call."[70]

Some war meetings were ad hoc affairs. For example, in the spring of 1863, the "colored citizens of Pinebrook, N.J.," met in a private home belonging to a W. B. Nelson.[71] In August 1862 a black minister told of going to Washington's Israel Church to hear Amos Beman lecture, then listening as "a messenger arrived and spread the news like wild-fire, that at the Asbury M.E. Colored Church, there was a great war meeting of the colored people." The clergyman and several others left to attend. These proceedings' improvised nature did not harm turnout; when the minister and his companions reached Asbury, he estimated that 1,000 black Washingtonians had gathered there.[72] A February 1863 war meeting in New Bedford attracted 1,500 attendees.[73]

These meetings came together somewhat haphazardly, but once they began, attendees observed strict decorum. Black Northerners placed high importance on maintaining order at public gatherings as a way of countering white depictions of black incompetence.[74] African Americans who attended war meetings in the North had matters of vital interest and strategy to discuss; these gatherings were about more than simply demonstrating black capacity to master parliamentary procedure. Still, black Northerners typically ran their meetings as conventions and elected or appointed officers and committee members. Even the spring 1863 Pinebrook meeting held at W. B. Nelson's house began with a motion appointing the event's chairman and secretary.[75] Black Northerners used war gatherings not only to debate their stance on the conflict and enlistment, but also to prove that they possessed the capacity to conduct politics in a manner befitting the citizenship they claimed.

In May 1861, black New Yorkers held such an event in Wanarda Hall, and enlistment proved so controversial that several attendees declined the meeting's presidency because they had not made up their minds on the subject. After *Anglo-African* editor Robert Hamilton finally took the chair, James N. Gloucester gave the report of a committee appointed to consider the question of service. Gloucester, a well-known black Presbyterian minister and close associate of John Brown, recommended that black men offer themselves as firemen, form a Home Guard unit, or join the federal army.[76] Several speakers opposed this plan, including William J. Wilson, a black educator who had championed the black militia movement in the 1850s. While Wilson had supported volunteering, he said the government's rebuff of black service had cooled his military ardor: "Inasmuch as the offers of these patriotic black men had been refused he did not think that [they] should offer [themselves] to be kicked and insulted." Whites knew that black men would fight, and he did not think black men ought to court the humiliation of refusal "simply for the privilege of saying so."[77]

Evidently, Wilson or someone else insisted that these prospective servicemen should only enlist once the government had met their demands. When Gloucester spoke for enlistment, he declared that, with the nation at war, "this was not the time for argument in reference to . . . rights." The minister articulated an alternative take on the politics of service: rather than wait to enlist until granted terms, black men should join the military and trust that gains would come later. Gloucester's suggestion proved unpopular. He and his allies "exhausted the magazine of patriotism" in their arguments, but the meeting's attendees "by a very large majority" refused to volunteer.[78]

Black Philadelphians considered enlistment in various public forums. The city's Church Anti-Slavery Society discussed the topic in October and November 1861. In October, Alfred M. Green argued for enlistment and met strong opposition. One white man contended that African American men should not fight until the government abolished slavery and enacted black suffrage, and Isaiah C. Wears sounded the familiar note that the time for these men's service would come—but had not yet. Wears, a successful barber who had attained a position of leadership through his work on Philadelphia's Vigilance Committee and in the convention movement, feared that black soldiers would fall in battle like "sheep."[79] Debate over service occupied the entire session, as speakers "kept up a friendly and spirited meeting till a late hour of the evening."[80] A similar discussion transpired the following month. No record survives of the various positions staked out, but debate on the question "What action should be taken by the Colored People in the present contest?" inspired "very instructive" words from several prominent black Philadelphians.[81] At a meeting of the Banneker Institute, the educator Octavius Catto echoed Wears. In his "political essay" entitled "The Voice of 1861," Catto suggested that Northern war aims might change in ways that benefited black Americans. "The ultimatum of revolutions is not conceived at the outset," he said. "With time new motives arise." Nevertheless, he counseled black men to wait to enlist "until the government was compelled from circumstance to accept them."[82]

Black Philadelphians continued holding war meetings into the following year. In mid-August 1862, Alfred M. Green proposed to enroll all "able-bodied male citizen[s] of color" willing to enlist once they were granted "the rights of citizenship and equal privileges in common with other soldiers in the army and navy of the United States." Green now viewed service conditionally, having backed down from his 1861 endorsement of volunteering without qualifications. The meeting's principal controversy developed when David Bowser proposed to remove citizenship and rights as prerequisites for black service. Isaiah Wears concurred with Bowser's proposition, believing it "impossible to get [citizenship and rights] now, and therefore foolish and impolitic to ask for it, or make it a condition." Proponents and opponents debated the question at length, and the proposal passed. Evidently, by this point a majority of the attendees were ready to enlist without guarantees of rights or citizenship.[83]

At antebellum community gatherings, black Northerners had at times engaged in heated disagreements, and the war meetings of 1861 and 1862 inspired similar passions. In July 1862, an attempt to convene such a meeting in Washington's Asbury AME Church nearly turned violent. When black Washingtonians who favored enlistment attempted to hold a "great war meeting of the colored people," they met opposition from the church's trustees who, upon learning the event's purpose, shut the church doors. The parishioners who favored black service attempted to convene on the church steps, "but," reported

Henry McNeal Turner, "the Trustees here seemed to rout them again, and finally the crowd dispersed." Born free in South Carolina, Turner had worked in the employ of the white-run Methodist Episcopal Church until he learned of the AME discipline, at which point he switched his theological allegiance and began rising through the AME ranks. By 1860 he had become a deacon and received appointment as pastor to the federal district's largest black church, Union Bethel.[84] According to Turner, the violence between the antienlistment and proenlistment factions turned so serious that an Asbury trustee who attempted to block the church door confronted vicious resistance, escaping with his life only through the *"logic of fleetness."*[85]

Disagreements on the subject ran deep, but all black Northerners shared the same basic goal: they sought to use black service to change the nation fundamentally. The demand that African American service must bring fundamental change was intrinsic to the delayed-enlistment position. But immediate-enlistment advocates also wanted such reform, and, perhaps fearing that black men would see immediate enlistment as simply a repeat of past mistakes, they appended a clear description of their ultimate aim to their arguments. As early as the fall of 1861, immediate-enlistment advocates like Jermain Loguen and B. K. Sampson insisted that black men would fight not to preserve the antebellum Union, but to forge a new nation that would fulfill black aspirations. Loguen, the Tennessee-born son of an enslaved mother and her white master, had escaped slavery in the mid-1830s, relocated to Syracuse, and become a minister in the African Methodist Episcopal Zion discipline. A local leader of the Underground Railroad, he had helped recruit troops for John Brown's raid, and his militancy guided his thinking about service.[86] In September 1861, he urged the government to enlist African American troops. But Loguen said that black men should fight only because they had "[their] all at stake, hence something more than Union to fight for," and he predicted that those battling to destroy slavery "would do the cause of liberty more service than half a dozen regiments . . . merely fighting for the Constitution and the Union."[87]

Similarly, in October 1861 B. K. Sampson maintained before a war meeting in Cleveland that black men would fight "for more than country, more than a union of States," declaring, "We would defend more than human laws, we would defend those which are divine." These potential soldiers held their "country dear, but liberty [was] dearer." Sampson concluded, "That is a noble soul that would lay his life upon the altar of his country, but nobler far is he who dies to free his brother man."[88] Black leaders who urged enlistment without insisting on terms expected that black soldiers would fight to destroy

slavery rather than for the narrow principle of Union. This problematic expectation elided the fact that Union officials had not committed to abolishing slavery. Loguen and Sampson did not explain how they could ensure that
Union officials would *allow* African American combatants the chance to destroy slavery. Still, they made their ultimate aspirations for black service clear.
They would fight for the government but not for the principle of maintaining the government—rather, they would serve because they believed doing so
could advance their race's freedom.

Black Northerners' determination to use the war to do something more
than maintain the government contrasted with white soldiers' willingness to
fight for the Union. The idea of preserving the United States for its own sake
compelled white Northerners to enlist; many believed that the American experiment in democracy needed to be defended, that the government brought
forth by the founders needed to be maintained, and that they themselves
possessed a responsibility to defend the ideals of representative government.
White soldiers would fight and die to preserve the antebellum United States.[89]
To black Northerners, Union meant nothing; American democracy had too
long excluded African Americans for them to feel any desire to protect it for
its own sake. Black Northerners' reactions to the conflict and the prospect of
service differed, but they agreed that if they fought, they would do so not for
Union, but for black freedom and a new Union.

During early 1862, however, the debate over service slackened in response
to the widespread belief that the war would soon end. From January through
early June, Union armies won a nearly unbroken string of successes. Ulysses S.
Grant, the North's newest hero, took Forts Henry and Donelson on the Tennessee and Cumberland Rivers; Union forces captured New Orleans, Nashville,
the sea islands off South Carolina, and the critical rail junction of Corinth,
Mississippi; Grant again emerged victorious at the bloody Battle of Shiloh;
and by late May George McClellan had advanced his massive Army of the Potomac within six miles of Richmond. To many, the South seemed to be on its
last legs. Confederate authorities reacted to the crisis by enacting conscription
and martial law, while Union officials believed victory so assured that they
suspended recruiting.[90]

Black Northerners eagerly anticipated the Confederacy's collapse. The *Pacific Appeal*, a new black newspaper in San Francisco, declared the Confederacy all but dead in early April. Peter Anderson had founded the *Appeal*;
he was a black Philadelphian who, like William H. Newby, had gone to California after the discovery of gold. Anderson had become involved in efforts

to improve black education, participated in the state convention movement, and worked with Newby on the defunct *Mirror of the Times*. His new sheet gave voice to California's growing black community.[91] "The end is fast approaching," the journal declared. "Victory after victory perches on the banner of the Union."[92] The *Christian Recorder* welcomed the "culmination, decline and inevitable swift approaches of the final overthrow of the Rebellion," and thanked Providence for securing "[the nation] against a second year of [the war's] awful ravages, and [settling] . . . National existence on a stronger and better foundation than ever."[93]

Black Northerners saw that the soon-to-be-finished war would not end in slavery's destruction or racial equality, but they could not deny that it had created positive change, giving them hope for the future. With Southern legislators out of the picture, antislavery Republican congressmen had advanced their agenda. In March, Congress barred Union commanders from returning fugitive slaves. In July, it passed the Second Confiscation Act, creating several new mechanisms to free slaves of rebel masters. Congressional Republicans also struck at slavery wherever they had authority to do so, ending federal enforcement of the Fugitive Slave Act, approving a treaty with Great Britain for suppression of the international slave trade, prohibiting slavery in the territories, and abolishing slavery in Washington, D.C.[94] Black communities throughout the North held mass meetings celebrating D.C. emancipation, passing resolutions thanking the president and Congress, and pledging their devotion to the Union cause. On April 6, three days after the district emancipation bill passed the Senate, Frederick Douglass gushed to Massachusetts senator Charles Sumner: "I trust I am not dreaming but the events taking place seem like a dream."[95]

The spring of 1862 also saw Lincoln embrace antislavery and African American rights in new ways. On March 6, in a "Message to Congress," the president unveiled incentives to induce Border State slaveholders to cooperate with federally sponsored compensated emancipation, and he pressured Border State congressmen to adopt his plan through midsummer. Lincoln also reversed federal policies that had broadcast white Americans' low estimation of their black counterparts. In 1861 he had authorized the State Department to issue passports to black travelers, thereby allowing government officials to issue to African Americans a document that secretaries of state deemed a marker of its bearer's citizenship. In 1862 the president finally extended diplomatic recognition to the black republics of Haiti and Liberia.[96] As early as September 1861, when Henry Highland Garnet acquired a passport, the *Christian*

Recorder had crowed that the minister had departed New York "with a regular passport of citizenship," which, it added with glee, "must fill Judge Taney with horror."[97]

By the spring of 1862, signs that the nearly finished war was creating positive change were seemingly everywhere. Black Northerners rejoiced, for instance, that abolitionist speakers who had been assaulted the previous spring by angry mobs now spoke to enthusiastic, supportive crowds.[98] "The emancipation thunder of Dr. [George] Cheever, which has shaken the Smithsonian, and the walls of the Capitol—the interest which it called forth, the general approval it received," believed "Sacer," one of the *Christian Recorder*'s Washington correspondents, "is certainly a harbinger of the good times coming, when a man shall be considered a man, whether his face be black or white."[99] Sacer traveled with the New York minister James Gloucester to Alexandria, Virginia, where touring this former "monument of the barbarism of slavery" was "enough to make any colored man enthusiastic." Sacer and Gloucester saw former slave pens turned into army hospitals and watched black men and women enjoying, Sacer claimed, nearly all the same rights as whites. They departed "highly impressed with the wonderful change which was fast taking place on old 'Virginny shore.'"[100]

With the war ending, black Northerners saw little need to contemplate service and, although their debate about it did not cease, it slackened off noticeably from its 1861 level.[101] Black Northerners also abandoned some of the vitriol toward the Union cause they had expressed in 1861 and early 1862. U.S. officials had not proclaimed universal abolition, slavery lived, and so did discriminatory laws and practices. Nevertheless, the slaveholders' rebellion was doomed, and it had compelled legislative and executive actions that heightened black Americans' hopes for further positive change. The war had not brought African Americans' desired Union into being, but it had done enough to leave many black Northerners anticipating its end feeling sanguine.[102]

The rosy military picture that helped inspire this feeling did not last long. On June 1, following the Battle of Seven Pines, Robert E. Lee took command of the Army of Northern Virginia and seized the initiative, fighting several battles in late June known as the "Seven Days." The Virginia general lost all but one of these engagements, but his aggressive tactics and the heavy casualties McClellan's army suffered convinced the Union commander to retreat. In the late summer and fall the Confederacy pursued the offensive. Lee defeated Union forces at the Second Battle of Bull Run in late August and then marched into Maryland, and Confederate armies invaded Tennessee and Kentucky. None of these offensives gained Southerners much strategically, but it was clear that the crisis of Confederate existence had passed and the war would continue. In response, Lincoln issued a new call for troops in June.[103] Seeing that only heavy fighting would subdue the slaveholders' rebellion, black Northerners revived the debate over enlistment that had occupied so much of their attention the previous year.

As black Northerners considered enlistment anew, Congress legalized black service in the Second Confiscation and Militia Acts passed on July 17. Section 11 of the Confiscation Act authorized Lincoln to "employ . . . persons of African descent" and "organize and use them in such manner as he may judge best for the public welfare." The Militia Act repealed the 1792 ban on black militia service. Lincoln could employ African American men for "any military or naval service for which they may be found competent," but the act's framers seemed primarily to contemplate black men serving as noncombat laborers.[104] Some African Americans in the North rejoiced at the bills' passage. The *Pacific Appeal* betrayed no hint that its editors had been influenced by their deceased fellow Newby's attitude toward black service. Rather, the newly founded sheet gloried in the fact that "the Negro [was] at last acknowledged as a part of the effective force of the country," and it predicted that black combat troops would follow black laborers into the federal service.[105]

For other black Northerners, these laws changed little. After all, neither mandated any improvement in African Americans' rights in return for their service. Elisha Weaver's *Christian Recorder* pronounced the Confiscation Bill's black-service provision "good enough, and right," but still had one question:

> What provision has Congress made, or empowered the President, in relation to guarantying to the colored people of this country full protection from her laws, and the privilege of enjoying all the rights accorded to other human beings in the United States of America? IF provisions are made satisfactorily to our mind, we will frankly state that there is no class of people in this country who are or will be more loyal in every sense of the word than the colored people, or who will do as much service and honor to this—*the country of their* BIRTH![106]

The *Recorder* placed a capital "if" in the path of black service, putting the onus on federal officials to satisfy black demands. Henry McNeal Turner doubted that these new laws would inspire African American enlistment. He predicted of the government, "[It will] have a hard time raising negro regiments to place in front of the battle or anywhere else, unless freedom, eternal freedom, is guarantied to them, their children, and their brethren. To talk about freeing only those who fight and should happen to escape the ball, is all gammon. If our people have not got too much sense for that, they have too much instinct; at all events they will not do it."[107] Weaver and Turner both suggested that pragmatism would govern black Northerners' reactions to enlistment, and neither the Confiscation nor the Militia Act met the price they had determined to extract in return for their service.

Still, these laws gave the question of black service renewed vitality. Frederick Douglass still supported immediate enlistment, wondering why Lincoln waited to organize black regiments. "Where are the regulations which the President was to frame for the organization of the blacks in the service of the government?" he asked in August. "Nobody expects that these laws are to remain a dead letter; they were not passed to be neglected and suffered to become obsolete."[108] Other black Northerners followed Turner in demanding change in return for their service. Douglass's son Lewis, William H. Johnson, and white abolitionist Daniel Ricketson oversaw a First of August celebration in Myrick's Station, Massachusetts, where black Northerners qualified their support for enlistment. They coupled black service with improvements in black rights, calling for the removal of "all disqualifications from our statute books relative to the full recognition of the colored man's right to citizenship, and particularly for the end and purpose of enrolling him as a soldier upon equal forms with all other citizens." The *Christian Recorder* urged black men to embrace the politics of service, and in early August it paired black service with citizenship rights: "If the Union wants our aid, as citizens of the United States, and gives us the rights of men, there is not a colored man but what will readily shoulder his musket, and this Rebellion will soon cease—universal liberty proclaimed to all men, and the Union restored."[109] African American men would serve, said the *Recorder*, but only as rights-bearing Americans fighting for "universal liberty."

Despite the positive changes they had seen, some black Northerners remained unsure that the government had done enough to compel their enlistment in the late summer of 1862. Numerous aspects of the Union war effort and wartime North continued to trouble them. Both the Second Confiscation Act and the D.C. emancipation bills had contained funding for colonization. Racist violence flared in Toledo, Chicago, and Cincinnati, and black Kentuckians complained of harsh treatment from Union officials.[110] In August, Lincoln endorsed colonization, suggesting that black soldiers who fought for the United States might not have a place in the nation in the war's aftermath. On August 14, 1862, the president summoned five prominent black leaders to the White House: Edward M. Thomas, John F. Cook Jr., John T. Costin, Cornelius Clark, and Benjamin McCoy. "All," Kate Masur has written, "were members of Washington's well-educated and well-organized antebellum black elite"—ministers, teachers, cultural and intellectual leaders involved in various black civil-society institutions. The summons made black Washingtonians "frantic with excitement," some fearing that Lincoln intended to forcibly deport African Americans. Wild rumors circulated regarding Lincoln's intentions: "every imaginable idea, however absurd to common reason it might be, seemed to have gained a respectable idea of currency in the mind of some class of thinkers."[111]

Anyone who thought Lincoln might express support for abolition or black rights was sorely disappointed. Rather than blaming slavery for the war, Lincoln blamed the institution's victims, insisting, "But for [the black] race among us there could not be war." The president called slavery "the greatest wrong inflicted on any people." However, he insisted that white racism ran so strong that black Americans would remain "far removed from being placed on an equality with the white race" even after slavery ended. Thus total separation of the races would be best for everyone. Lincoln proposed colonizing black Americans in Central America, urging them to emulate the revolutionary generation by undergoing "hardships" and "[sacrificing] some ... present comfort" for the good of the race—to do otherwise would be "extremely selfish." He argued forcefully for the impossibility of a biracial America, but he did not suggest mandatory deportation, as had other Republicans. Nevertheless, the president's performance did not indicate that the Union black Americans wanted to emerge from the war was in the offing.[112]

The five black men who met with Lincoln did not seem particularly offended by his message, and their leader, Edward Thomas, told Lincoln his argument had been convincing.[113] Others were furious. Douglass branded the president an "itinerant colonization lecturer," asserting that his "illogical and unfair" statements were "quite in keeping with his whole course from the beginning of his administration up to this day." Douglass further explained his disappointment: " Mr. Lincoln is quite a genuine representative of American prejudice and negro hatred and far more concerned for the preservation of slavery, and the favor of the Border Slave States, than for any sentiment of magnanimity or principle of justice and humanity."[114] George B. Vashon also took Lincoln to task. Had African Americans' service in previous wars, he asked, not earned them a right to stay in the land of their birth? The president, Vashon asserted, knew the history of black service in American wars, and yet "the children of the patriotic blacks who periled their lives at Bunker Hill, at Red Bank, and on many another hardfought field ... [were] requested, not merely to take a lower seat, but to with draw entirely from the table."[115]

Black Northerners had considered emigration for several decades by 1862, and though some of their enthusiasm for this plan waned with the onset of war, others embraced the idea. "Hundreds ... likely thousands" of black Washingtonians volunteered to emigrate to Central America in the August 14 meeting's aftermath; black Northerners who opposed colonization could only see Lincoln's proposal as a real threat.[116] On the heels of this outrage came the Cincinnati incident of September 1862 in which city officials who had earlier refused African American volunteers violently impressed them into service. Evidently, the war had changed the government's attitude toward black citizenship to some degree, if black men could receive State Department passports. But passports did no good in the streets of Cincinnati. Here, black men could be driven like cattle in keeping with the long-standing American tradition that those ordinarily barred from military service could augment the army's strength in times of dire necessity.

Against this backdrop, many prominent black Northerners continued to oppose immediate enlistment. In mid-August, Weaver's *Christian Recorder* declared that it "did not favor at all" enlistment drives in Kansas and Rhode Island, counseling black men to "stay in their own State, and let the whites battle away at their pleasure."[117] Around the same time, the male members of Philadelphia's Mother Bethel Church opposed black volunteering. They "keenly [felt] the unfortunate troubles that [were] upon the country, yet ... [they had] too much self-respect to intrude themselves where they [were] not wanted." The churchgoers added, "Any person, or persons, representing otherwise, do not represent the colored people."[118]

Government policy and white racism caused some black Northerners to oppose black service totally; others continued to insist on terms, articulating a shrewd politics of service. Henry Highland Garnet insisted that prospective soldiers remained undeterred despite the discrimination they faced: "Throughout the North and South, tens of thousands ... [of black men] are ready and anxious to peril their lives in defence of the Government whenever they are called as free citizen soldiers."[119] J. M. W., writing to the *Pacific Appeal*, spoke in like terms. The government needed black help to put down the rebellion, which it would get if it overturned the *Dred Scott* decision and abolished slavery. Should the government fulfill these terms, he said, Lincoln would "stand at the head of the greatest and most valiant army the world ever saw."[120] In making these demands, J. M. W. became one of the first black Northerners to give the politics of service specific content by identifying the policy changes that could, in his estimation, inspire black enlistment.

The *Appeal's* next issue contained a similar item, in which a J. C. J. set forth the changes he believed necessary to inspire black enlistment. Black men would not fight, he asserted, "in the [present] degraded condition of things, looked upon as goods and chattels." They would fight if they could do so as "men, enjoying all the political rights and privileges of other men." For J. C. J., equality meant emancipation, the repeal of the Fugitive Slave Law, the nullification of *Dred Scott*, and, as he put it, an end to "all laws that destroy our position as men." These changes would "raise ... [African Americans] from the degraded position of goods and chattels to [the] true position of men, women and children."[121]

Black Northerners' late-summer debates over enlistment were eclipsed by Lincoln's preliminary Emancipation Proclamation, which he issued on September 22, five days after the Army of the Potomac halted Robert E. Lee's invasion of Maryland at Antietam. The proclamation contained several facets that troubled black leaders. It spoke of using federal subsidies to fund colonization and of compensating loyal slave owners whose slaves gained freedom. It framed emancipation as a war measure, employed lawyerly, colorless phrasing, and failed to describe emancipation as an act of justice. In fact, the document's text would later inspire Richard Hofstadter's famous quip that it contained "all the moral grandeur of a bill of lading."[122] Nevertheless, the preliminary Emancipation Proclamation sustained congressional enactments barring Union soldiers from returning fugitive slaves. More importantly, it proclaimed that on January 1, 1863, all slaves held in disloyal areas would be "forever free," and it committed Union forces to "recognize and maintain" any actions slaves took to win their freedom.[123]

The preliminary proclamation committed the Union to emancipation in an unmistakably public and official way. Unsurprisingly, many black Northerners enthusiastically supported the president's edict. "The proclamation of the President of the United States," wrote the *Christian Recorder*, "will be read with interest by all of our people, and all true lovers of freedom, irrespective of clime or caste, will give three hearty cheers for Abraham Lincoln."[124] In early October, Henry McNeal Turner issued a "Call to Action," asserting that the Proclamation "[had] opened up a new series of obligations, consequences, and results, never known to [African Americans'] honored sires." The document's aims satisfied him, for he stated, "The stern intention of the Presidential policy is, to wage the war in favour of freedom, till the last groan of the anguished heart slave shall be hushed in the ears of nature's God."[125] Yet not all black Northerners viewed the preliminary Emancipation Proclamation in such joyous terms. Some complained that it did not enact universal emancipation, and others objected to certain of its facets.[126] In fact, "a large

portion of our people," Turner reported, doubted that Lincoln "wrote his proclamation in good faith."[127] Most who doubted the proclamation's intentions or
efficacy, though—such as William Parham, who believed it would kill slavery
but fail to address the more intractable problems of white prejudice and racial
inequality—kept their doubts private.[128]

The preliminary proclamation did not intensify debate regarding black enlistment; if anything, debate slackened toward year's end. This likely stemmed
from the fact that the document said nothing about black enlistment, and the
fact that Lincoln's most recent public statements regarding the issue had denied any intention to enlist black soldiers.[129] When African Americans in the
North publicly discussed service in the interval between September 22 and
January 1, they were no more disposed to enlist immediately and trust that
subsequent gains would come than they had been prior to the proclamation's
release. The president's decree represented progress, but it failed to meet black
Northerners' demands.

African Americans in the North were glad to see the Union war effort
heading in an increasingly antislavery direction, but they wanted more than
the preliminary Emancipation Proclamation offered. Dr. Ezra R. Johnson,
who regularly published articles on the war for the *Pacific Appeal*, explained
this point in early October. Johnson, the son of a Revolutionary War veteran,
hailed from New Bedford and had been apprenticed to Philadelphia's James
Forten as a sailmaker before going into medicine. Like William H. Newby,
Johnson left for California in the wake of the Gold Rush, but he returned
home in 1851. Following Fort Sumter's fall, he chaired a New Bedford war
meeting that offered black men's services to the government. Rebuffed, Johnson returned to California to practice medicine.[130]

Since he had tried to volunteer in 1861, Johnson's thinking had shifted; he
now viewed service conditionally, and he was not satisfied with the proclamation. He believed that Lincoln would have to call on black help to win the
war, but he held that the government had still not "turn[ed] from the error
of [its] ways and done [African Americans] justice." Johnson did not identify
concrete measures that in his estimation would constitute "justice," but he
predicated black service on the United States meeting black demands. "Let
the Government do these things," he wrote, "and then we will feel a national
pride and glory for a Free Union, as it should be. Then we will have a home
and birthright in a free land for ourselves and children, and we will pledge
our highest vow to strive to make the Union what it ought to be, after the terrible ordeal through which it is called to pass." The preliminary Emancipation
Proclamation promised mass emancipations, but it did not meet the price the
doctor hoped to extract for black service.[131]

Johnson accounted the price of black service more specifically in November. The former immediate-enlistment advocate stated, "Before they enlist, the same rights, protection and remuneration which is enjoyed by the whites should be given to [black soldiers]."[132] Johnson did not specify the rights he sought, but he envisioned equal pay as a prerequisite for black service. In his demand for equal protection, Johnson seemed to have already heard that Southerners were threatening not to treat black soldiers as legitimate prisoners of war. Another correspondent of the *Appeal* labeled the proclamation "progress" but lamented that the government had refused to enlist black volunteers "while the Irish, Germans, French and Italians were all welcomed to the call." Black men "can wait," he resolved. "Our time has not come yet; but it will surely come, if we are faithful to ourselves." What changes precisely would inspire black men to serve, the writer did not say, but the preliminary proclamation had not been enough.[133]

While black Northerners continued in late 1862 to discuss what the government might do to secure their enlistment, some black troops were already fighting for the Union. Black sailors had served without controversy in the Union navy since the war's beginning, and a few courageous black men like H. Ford Douglas, who in 1862 joined the Ninety-Fifth Illinois, forced their way into white regiments.[134] Perhaps these men agreed with Douglas, who believed that emancipation would come and also stated, "This war will educate Mr. Lincoln out of his idea of the deportation of the Negro, quite as fast as it has some of his other proslavery ideas with respect to employing them as soldiers."[135] In 1862, white commanders also began to arm and equip black units. Sometimes working without sanction and sometimes with the War Department's blessing, white officers formed black units in Kansas, New Orleans, and South Carolina.[136] Lincoln neither endorsed nor opposed these efforts, but they suggested that the time when the Union might call on black men to enlist was approaching.

These first regiments do not seem to have inspired black Northerners to think differently about black service. Rather, at the conclusion of 1862 they placed more stock in their own evaluations of Union policy toward slavery and African Americans than they did in the fact that the massive U.S. Army now boasted three black regiments. Black Northerners waited anxiously to see if Lincoln would make good on his promise to emancipate the Confederacy's slaves on January 1, 1863. His proclamation unleashed a firestorm of protest in some quarters of the North, as many whites in the region believed it showed that abolishing slavery had replaced preserving the Union as the North's true cause. Backlash against the preliminary proclamation helped Democrats win significant gains in the 1862 midterm elections, and Democratic politicians pressured Lincoln to backtrack on emancipation.[137] Black Northerners, too, might have sensed the danger William Parham spoke of privately. He feared that the war might kill slavery but fail to eradicate the larger problem of white prejudice, and that the Union that emerged from the war would depressingly resemble the antebellum United States. In this context, many black Northerners continued to view enlistment cautiously.

Lincoln's preliminary Emancipation Proclamation capped Republicans' 1862 efforts to move the Union war effort in an antislavery direction, and as the year ended the United States had not embraced abolition, black rights, or black citizenship. Black Northerners could not be sure that a Union victory would result in the change they sought, and they remained divided over their race's service. African American leaders, though, were approaching a consensus that black men should only enlist once the government had met certain conditions. Since 1861, numerous prominent leaders and institutions had asserted that black enlistment must be predicated on the government meeting black demands: the *Weekly Anglo-African*, the *Christian Recorder*, William Wells Brown, Henry Highland Garnet, Alfred M. Green, Henry McNeal Turner, Dr. Ezra Johnson, and the members of Philadelphia's venerable Mother Bethel Church all at one time or another opposed or advocated delaying black enlistment. Perhaps because Congress had legalized black service and therefore the issue seemed more immediate, a few black men had begun to articulate *exactly* what types of changes they wanted to see in return for black service. In yoking these changes to the concept of citizenship, they pushed forward a conversation about the exact content of American citizenship that would result in a postwar constitutional revolution.

But that change lay in the future. By 1862's end, black Northerners had not achieved consensus on enlistment, and it would likely have been impossible for them to reach consensus on such a momentous, controversial question anyway. Many black Northerners had, though, declared their intent to extract a price in return for military service that included abolition, rights, and citizenship. The delayed-enlistment position gained strength over the course of 1862, winning increasingly widespread acceptance among leaders and institutions who would doubtlessly exercise a strong influence on black Northerners' decision-making. Considering it far from certain that Lincoln would issue his Emancipation Proclamation as promised on January 1, black Northerners waited to see what the new year would bring before making any definite determinations on the question of enlistment.

3

DECISION TIME

JANUARY–AUGUST 1863

O N JANUARY 1, 1863, following a lengthy New Year's reception at the White House, Abraham Lincoln retired to his office and signed his Emancipation Proclamation. It did not touch slavery in the Border States, Tennessee, or portions of Louisiana and Virginia. If the Proclamation fell short of black Northerners' fondest hopes, it markedly surpassed the document Lincoln had issued the previous September.[1] At Treasury Secretary Salmon Chase's urging, Lincoln went beyond citing military necessity in justifying the edict, affirming that he "sincerely believed" emancipation "to be an act of justice, warranted by the Constitution, upon military necessity." Lincoln also "invoke[d] the considerate judgment of mankind, and the gracious favor of Almighty God" in sanctioning his Emancipation Proclamation. Finally, he made no mention of colonizing emancipated slaves; instead, the president proposed to arm them. Freed slaves of "suitable condition," he stated, "will be received into the armed service of the United States to garrison forts, positions, stations, and other places, and to man vessels of all sorts in said service."[2]

Lincoln's black-service clause signaled a momentous shift in federal policy, and from early 1863 forward black Northerners debated enlistment with newfound urgency. Most black leaders, influenced by the proclamation, promises of equality, and a momentous legal opinion handed down late in 1862, counseled immediate enlistment. Many, including Frederick Douglass, became government-sanctioned recruiters. On April 27, 1863, Douglass spoke at Henry Highland Garnet's Shiloh Presbyterian Church in New York and mocked black men who hesitated to join the military. To Douglass's consternation, only one man volunteered. "This," reported a *Liberator* correspondent, "seem[ed] to put the meeting in a cowardly position." At this point, a man named Robert Johnson rose and, "by a few well-spoken words . . . convinced the meeting that it was not cowardice which made the young men hesitate to enlist, but a proper respect for their own manhood. If the Government wanted their services," said Johnson, "let it guarantee to them all the rights of citizens and soldiers, and, instead of one man, he would insure them 5000 men in twenty days." The audience awarded his "remarks . . . with tremendous and long-continued applause."[3]

Black Northerners had constructed their politics of service in hopeful anticipation of the moment when Union officials sought black help. Despite African American recruiters' best efforts, many joined Robert Johnson in opposing enlistment well into 1863. Prevailing conditions—slavery's continued existence, Northern discrimination, service inequalities—violated the emphases on equality, rights, and citizenship that had emerged as key tenets of this politics during 1861 and 1862. While historians have acknowledged that some black Northerners opposed enlistment into 1863, they have revealed neither the depth of this opposition nor the full range of factors that inspired it.

Looking back on early 1863, Francis Preston Stearns, whose father, George, became heavily involved in recruiting black troops, remembered that when a white abolitionist asked black Bostonians if they planned to volunteer, all but one answered in the negative. "We have no objection to white officers," they said, "but our self-respect demands that competent colored men be at least eligible to promotion."[4] Robert Purvis told white abolitionist Norwood P. Hallowell, "It augurs a sad misapprehension of character aspirations and self-respect of colored men to suppose that they would submit to the *degrading* limit which the government imposes in regard to the officering of said regiments." Purvis predicted that if the government did not change its policies, recruiters would have trouble securing "the right kind of men."[5] Securing the right kind of men would be imperative to black enlistment's success. Much depended on black leaders' ability to develop a call to service capable of inspiring their Northern brethren to enlist in spite of their objections.

Not all black Northerners needed to be convinced to enlist, of course. Some quickly joined P. B. Randolph of Utica in declaring, "We *have* rights, at last, which white men are bound to respect, and I regard the first of these as being the right to fight, and if God so wills it, nobly die for our country."[6] Nevertheless, black recruiters played a critical role in mobilizing black soldiers. Prominent black Northerners like Douglass, Brown, and Garnet had long careers as lecturers and public speakers under their belts. They could command large audiences and speak and write persuasively; they also possessed long-recognized community standing and had cultivated influential white allies. Their arguments, and the "war meetings" at which they aired them, played crucial roles in the individual decision-making processes of the tens of thousands of African Americans in the North who fought for the Union. Their tireless traveling and eloquent if controversial arguments filled the ranks of the first black Northern regiments, whose battlefield success was critical to U.S. officials' embrace of large-scale black enlistment. Understanding the way in which the African American recruitment network operated and the arguments that this group of recruiters developed illuminates how both black service and Union victory happened.

Eventually, most black Northerners of military age saw time in the Union army, but not all rushed to arms at the first chance. Their enlistment represented the culmination of a lengthy public discussion about what it meant to be black and fight for the United States. Many African Americans in the North were not convinced as 1863 began that the Union seeking their help was a Union they should go to war for. These potential combatants wanted confirmation that their service could fundamentally change the United States. In public meetings and print, black Northerners pushed back against the arguments made by black recruiters. Resistance to the immediate-enlistment position ran strong in some corners of the North through August 1863, then seemed to cease abruptly. By late 1863, most African American Northerners had become convinced that the war had been long and brutal enough that it could result in a radically changed nation, and they rejoiced that the war had progressed to the point where black soldiers could go into battle feeling that victory would usher in a Union equal to their aspirations.

AS THE NEW YEAR DAWNED, Congress debated the president's proposal to enlist black troops. In early January, staunch antislavery Republican Thaddeus Stevens introduced a bill to raise 150,000 black troops on terms of basic equality with white soldiers. His fellow representatives quickly rejected it.[7] Subsequent versions of Stevens's bill, amended to increase its chances for passage, included obnoxious provisions such as unequal pay and funding for colonization.[8] Congressmen from the Border States and lower North advanced outlandish racist arguments against the bill. Some predicted that black service would drive the Border States out of the Union and that black men's uncontrollable bloodlust would result in servile war.[9] Kentucky's John J. Crittenden maintained that black men "[were] not necessary for the putting down of this rebellion," further stating, "They are not worthy of being called to the aid of those who aspire to be considered free-born men." He inquired rhetorically, "Have not our citizens"—meaning white men—"the courage and strength to defend the country?" And why, Crittenden wondered, did Stevens's amended bill contemplate paying black soldiers less than white troops? Crittenden assumed that African American men could not be citizens and were not worthy or capable of fighting. "Do you not claim," he asked mockingly, "that they are as good citizens [as whites]?"[10]

Some proponents of Stevens's bill spoke in like tones. Ohio's Carey A. Trimble supported the proposal but clearly regretted its necessity. If Indian "savages" could fight for the government, he asked, why not African American men? Trimble predicted that most black soldiers would come from conquered Confederate territory because black Northerners saw they had nothing to gain by fighting. "The more intelligent among them," Trimble stated flatly, "say that they are not willing to risk their lives in a contest from which they are to derive no special advantage.... They cannot hope for an equality of political privileges, or any other equality, by the decision of this contest, and therefore they will decline to engage in it."[11] Even Stevens recommended the bill as a way to ensure that black men did their part alongside whites, denying that it mandated racial equality. The characteristically acerbic Stevens displayed his dissatisfaction with the bill's limitations, but he also grimly painted the opportunity enlistment offered to black men. "We propose to give them an equal chance to meet death, on the battle-field. But even then their great achievements, if equal to those of [Haitian general Jean-Jacques] Dessalines, would give them no hope of honor. The only place where they can find equality is in the grave."[12] Congress ultimately discarded Stevens's proposal, as the House Committee on Military Affairs found that the acts of July 17, 1862, had already authorized black enlistment.[13]

Though Stevens's bill was ultimately tossed aside, the debate surrounding it influenced black Northerners' thinking about enlistment. Black- and white-run newspapers reported on congressional debates, and black observers attended these sessions. Henry McNeal Turner visited Congress regularly during early 1863 and noted the vehemence of black enlistment's antagonists. Turner's newfound enthusiasm for black service persisted, but not all observers were so forgiving.[14] As 1863 began, Frederick Douglass, the most prominent advocate of African Americans serving in the military, had altered his stance and advised black men to volunteer only if they could do so on equal terms with whites. In the February issue of his *Douglass' Monthly*, he stated, "[Supporters of enlistment must] bear with our absence from the army until our own unbiased judgement and the action of the Government shall make it our duty and our privilege to become a soldier."[15] Douglass spoke in similar terms later that month at New York's Cooper Institute:

Do you ask me whether black men will freely enlist in the service of the country? I tell you that that depends upon the white men of the country. The Government must assure them of protection as soldiers, and give them a fair chance of winning distinction and glory in common with other soldiers.—[Cheers.] They must not be made the mere hewers of wood and drawers of water for the army.... Do your part, my white fellow-countrymen, and we will do ours.[16]

Douglass made this argument alongside affirmations that he saw the nation's willingness to enlist black men as a hopeful sign. The fact that he made this case at all after Lincoln's Emancipation Proclamation, however, demonstrated the pervasiveness of the belief that African American men should force the government to meet their terms.[17]

After learning of his sentiments, the *Weekly Anglo-African* criticized Douglass for putting an "'if' in the way" of black service, arguing, "[He did] himself and his brethren the wrong of misconceiving and mis-stating our duty at this hour." The next month, Douglass defended his words by setting them against the backdrop of the Congressional debates over black service. "When we made that speech at Cooper Institute, a bill was before the American Congress, to which all kinds of degrading amendments, were being offered and insisted upon, calculated, if carried out, to leave us after enduring all the hardships and perils of war, a degraded caste," he wrote. The debate had suggested to him that African Americans' service would fail to bring a new Union into being. Because the Union army enlisted black men under the auspices of 1862 legislation, historians have paid relatively little attention to Congress's 1863 debates about black enlistment. But black Northerners could not know that this congressional wrangling would come to naught, and they saw much in these debates to give them pause. Watching this debate caused Douglass— immediate enlistment's greatest champion—to momentarily change course; this dispute likely caused other black observers to doubt enlistment's advisability as well. Douglass pleaded that he did not then know what he had since learned of "the honorable terms" under which black soldiers could enlist.[18]

Douglass referred here to the promises of equality he was hearing from Massachusetts governor John Andrew, who had met with Lincoln and Edwin Stanton in January. Andrew left Washington believing that black troops would be allowed to join the military under the same basic terms of service as white troops—equal pay, clothing, and rations—but he failed to obtain permission to commission black officers. Thus, from the start, it was clear that African American troops would not enjoy *total* equality. By mid-January, however, Stanton had authorized Massachusetts and Rhode Island to recruit black units, and Andrew began corresponding with black leaders and making promises of equal opportunity.[19]

Andrew tapped George L. Stearns, a wealthy lead-pipe manufacturer and abolitionist who had funded John Brown, to head black recruitment efforts, and Stearns subsequently assembled an impressive roster of black recruiting agents. Working under Stearns's aegis, Douglass, Martin Delany, William Wells Brown, John Mercer Langston, Charles Langston and others crisscrossed the Northern states in 1863, urging black men to enlist. War-meeting activity intensified, and recruiters received help from local leaders in securing audiences. Their network was loose, and they were not always aware of one another's movements. In early May, a correspondent told the *Christian Recorder* that both Langston brothers and Charles Lenox Remond had recently arrived in Chicago, adding, "All landed here without a knowledge of each other's whereabouts." Enlisting the help of John Jones, a wealthy tailor and real estate speculator who had taken a prominent role in the prewar convention movement, "Mr. [John Mercer] Langston went to work, got up a public meeting among . . . which was quite numerously attended, and went off with considerable enthusiasm."[20]

Recruiters were representatives of the tiny black upper class, and they differed in terms of material wealth from most of the black Northerners to whom they counseled enlistment. This reality sometimes caused class-based tensions. African Americans in the North seem to have objected to the sense that they were being told what to do by well-off black professionals disconnected from the day-to-day realities of life for most black families in the region. When the Washington-based AME minister Thomas H. C. Hinton criticized those who jeered at his recruiting efforts and black draftees in August 1863, his description of black service's antagonists as "state prison birds, and work-house pimps" dripped with class invective."[21] Despite this obstacle, by utilizing their rhetorical talents and their contacts with the black militia units that had formed throughout the 1850s, black recruiters filled the ranks of the Fifty-Fourth Massachusetts, Fourteenth Rhode Island Heavy Artillery, and Twenty-Ninth Connecticut.[22]

Stearns oversaw this operation from Buffalo's luxurious Mansion House, where by April a small army of clerks contended with a "constant receipt of letters and telegrams" that kept them "all the time at work." Stearns wrote of the difficulty of his task: "Blacks are scattered in a population of Twenty Millions you can understand how much more difficult this is than recruiting the Whites." The businessman deployed his team of "Agents and Sub-Agents" across the Northern free states and Canada, and he required daily reports that resulted in a constant stream of "demand[s] for advice, direction, money and transportation." White prejudice circumscribed his agents' initial efforts, which "were secret and confined to the Blacks," but white leaders warmed to black enlistment. By late spring, Stearns's representatives could convene war meetings in public halls frequented by whites. In mid-May, John Mercer Langston reported that a gathering at a courthouse in Tiffan, Ohio, had been "so densely crowded . . . that it seemed every man, white and black, in the city was in attendance."[23] Stearns gloried in his operation's efficiency and predicted confidently that, with his help, "the Government [would] arm One Hundred Thousand [black men] with the approbation of the Entire North."[24]

Stearns asked men like Langston to join his recruiting network because their rhetorical abilities and reputations made them effective recruiters; not all black Northerners of Langston's stature accepted, however, that the time for black enlistment had come. In April, Henry Highland Garnet asked a war meeting at New York's Shiloh Church, "What have black men to fight for in this war?" The African American man who hesitated to enlist did so not out of cowardice, he insisted, but "because he has not justice done him." If the black soldier received an "equal chance with a white soldier," Garnet predicted, "he will show you how he can fight."[25] Robert Morris also opposed enlistment. The former militia captain told the New England Anti-Slavery Convention that when black men had been denied commissions in the Fifty-Fourth Massachusetts, he had "determined not to lift a finger for that Regiment, and he had never asked and never would ask any man to enlist it."[26] Months after the Union had begun recruiting African American regiments, a few high-profile black Northerners clung to the delayed-enlistment position.

Morris and Garnet's reactions did not typify prominent black Northerners' response to the call to enlist, however; almost overnight, many influential individuals and institutions that had once embraced delayed enlistment changed their minds. Several factors caused African American leaders to warm to immediate enlistment. The Emancipation Proclamation and its presidential endorsement of black service, the leaders' own analysis of the war's progress, the sincerity evinced by Andrew, and the promises of equality for black soldiers all likely played a role. Douglass made an abrupt about-face on the question of volunteering, and by late February he removed the "if" he had momentarily placed in front of black service. "Fred. Douglass enters heart & soul into this movement," Stearns informed Andrew on February 27.[27] Around the same time, John Rock explained why his thinking had changed. He said,

"[I have recently belonged to] the most intelligent portion of the colored men in [Massachusetts that did] not understand why we are to be proscribed in the Army, when we are willing to offer ourselves on the Altar of our Country." Rock remained troubled by the promotion issue but did not "believe that the door of promotion [was] to be permanently closed against" African American soldiers. He further declared, "[I have become] fully convinced that we shall not be doing right if we waive the opportunity to show that we will seize every thing that offers."[28] Rock challenged black men to show their willingness to fight rather than demanding change before joining the military.

The black press joined Douglass and Rock in endorsing immediate enlistment. The *Christian Recorder*—which, of the three major black newspapers, had taken strongest hold of the delayed-enlistment position—continued to advocate black service only conditionally. It urged black men to volunteer but cautioned them, before taking "hasty steps," to ensure that they would enjoy equality in the ranks.[29] The *Weekly Anglo-African* and *Pacific Appeal* embraced enlistment without qualification. "[African Americans] have been pronounced citizens by the highest legal authority, why should we not share in the perils of citizenship?" asked the *Anglo-African*. Black soldiers, the New York journal predicted, could "claim [black] rights" and "speedily overcome" racial prejudice.[30] The *Pacific Appeal* similarly told black men to forget past wrongs and enlist, observing, "[To be] considered good citizens we must possess ourselves with the necessary qualifications, and be prepared for military as well as civilian life."[31]

These newspapers' emphasis on citizenship suggests that a December 1862 opinion rendered by Attorney General Edward Bates convinced their editors that black enlistment's time had come. With the final Emancipation Proclamation looming, Treasury Secretary Salmon Chase had asked Bates to consider a case involving a black schooner captain whose ship had been detained due to his presumed noncitizenship. The attorney general used this opportunity to affirm blacks' status as Americans. The Constitution, he wrote, specified neither which rights and privileges citizenship entailed nor who qualified for it, but the document recognized the principle of birthright citizenship in referring to "natural-born citizens." Because the Constitution was "as silent about *race* as it is about *color*," free African Americans born in the United States, like the schooner captain, were citizens.[32]

A clear victory for activists who had argued throughout the antebellum period for black citizenship, Bates's opinion sharply limited citizenship's content.[33] Bates described citizenship as a reciprocal relationship between the individual and the nation; citizens owed allegiance to the nation, which in turn owed them protection. Citizenship did *not* imply possession of political rights like voting. Through discourses on U.S. and world history, Bates proved that noncitizens had sometimes exercised these rights and that persons recognized as citizens had not. His opinion was an important but limited victory that repudiated Taney's loathsome *Dred Scott* decision, showing how profoundly the exigencies of war had transformed America. But Bates's opinion did not require that the nation bestow political rights or legal equality on its citizens.[34]

The opinion quickly became a touchstone for supporters of immediate enlistment.[35] At an emancipation celebration in Boston's Tremont Temple on January 1, William C. Nell argued that Lincoln's proclamation and Bates's opinion inaugurated "a national era of fair play for the black man." At the same meeting, John Rock cited Bates's ruling and concluded that African American men should enlist and "enter upon [their] duties as citizens."[36] Black Northerners, who knew that citizenship had never existed as a well-defined, all-encompassing legal category, gloried in finally being recognized as Americans, however conceptually limited Bates's version of citizenship might be. In March, Richard H. Cain, an AME minister and future South Carolina congressman, presided over a public meeting at his Bridge Street Church in Brooklyn. There, attendees approvingly linked enlistment with Bates's description of citizenship and its "reciprocal obligations of protection and allegiance" between the government and "those under its control."[37] For some, the attorney general's opinion made it black men's duty to fight.

White leaders often stressed black men's duty as citizens to fight for their country, sometimes arguing that those who would *not* fight to gain rights did not deserve them. White abolitionist Wendell Phillips spoke in these terms when he addressed a recruitment rally for the Fifty-Fourth Massachusetts in February. Phillips conceded the injustice of Union promotion policy, but he argued that black men ought to respond by serving and earning advancement. "If you cannot have a whole loaf, will you not take a slice[?]!" he asked. "Make use of the offer Government has made you, for if you are not willing to fight your way up to office, you are not worthy of it."[38] Secretary of State William Seward gave this viewpoint official sanction. In late June, John Mercer Langston asked Seward what duty black men owed the United States in light of the fact that they were asked "to take an inferior position as Soldiers."[39] "The duty of the colored man to defend his country wherever, whenever, and in whatever form, is the same with that of the white man," Seward replied. "It does not," he continued, "depend on, nor is it affected by, what the country pays us, or what position she assigns us; but it depends on her need alone, and of that she, not we, are to judge. The true way to secure her rewards and win her confidence is not to stipulate for them, but to deserve them."[40]

Phillips and Seward asked much of black men but did not require white Americans to give justice to their black counterparts. At the least, their statements betrayed a lack of sensitivity to black concerns and an inability to empathize with well-founded long-standing grievances. African Americans could meet these white arguments for black enlistment with compelling objections: they could appeal to black service in previous American wars, or to simple justice, to argue that they already deserved equality. By pointing to the history of their efforts in the military, African Americans could also dismiss predictions by men like Phillips and Seward that change would come in the war's aftermath. In short, if arguments by men like Phillips and Seward had been the only proenlistment positions black Northerners heard in 1863, delayed enlistment might have won the day.

But black recruiters developed their own arguments, seemingly recognizing the problematic nature of white leaders' rhetoric. To be sure, some African Americans in the North believed that black men possessed a duty to fight for the United States as citizens, but recruiters did not generally argue in these terms. They contended that, practically speaking, fighting despite inequalities would be more effective than making a principled refusal to serve. Black recruiters urged black men to forget past injustices. As these future combatants possessed a unique chance that, if rejected, might never come again, they should bear temporary injustices to serve the greater goal of bringing the Union they sought into being. Frederick Douglass's famous appeal for the Fifty-Fourth Massachusetts, "Men of Color, to Arms!," published in March 1863, spoke in exactly these terms. "There is no time for delay," he wrote, further stating, "NOW OR NEVER." Black troops could win equality through service. "When the war is over," Douglass predicted, "the country is saved, peace is established, and the black man's rights are secured, as they will be, history with an impartial hand, will dispose of that and sundry other questions." He believed talk did no good: "Action! action! not criticism, is the plain duty of this hour. Words are now useful only as they stimulate to blows."[41] Douglass implored African American men to shelve their objections and enlist, for change would only come if they fought.

Black recruiters linked the ideas that the war presented a fleeting opportunity and that black men should bear present-day inequalities for the sake of long-term gains. At a February 1863 war meeting in New Bedford, William

Wells Brown urged African American Northerners not to hold back because they had not received *all* they sought. "If [black men] had refused to avail themselves of the public conveyances and public schools when first allowed those privileges," he argued, "because the right to bear arms was not also granted, they would be in a ridiculous position." If these individuals let the "opportunity" to enlist pass, "they would forever be left out in the cold."[42] "Inactivity now on our part will be certain death to us," wrote California's Dr. Ezra R. Johnson, having abandoned his resolve to delay enlistment. If black men "held back," the nation would not grant them new rights. But if they took "an active part," Johnson said, "we may have all our rights as citizens given to us when peace is again restored."[43]

African American recruiters knew they needed to assuage the anxiety that underlay the politics of service, the nagging fear that history would repeat itself. In this vein, "Hope," the *Anglo-African*'s correspondent in Troy, New York, offered these suggestions to his fellow black men: "First aid in putting down this rebellion . . . then *claim* our rights as men and citizens; we will have earned it *then*, and who will dare dispute them[?]"[44] Thomas H. C. Hinton insisted that service would win black rights in the postwar period. Speaking of efforts to form a Washington-area Home Guard regiment, Hinton urged black Washingtonians, "[Leave] no stone unturned . . . in showing the Americans that we have attempted to do our duty." He made the suggestion in the hopes that, after the war, "legislators" would confer on African Americans "every immunity, every right, and every blessing the most favored of its subjects deserves."[45]

In encouraging black men to fight for rights that would come later, these black Northerners voided the delayed-enlistment position, which was designed to ensure that history did not repeat itself. But black recruiters did not, for the most part, depict black men as having a *duty* to fight for the United States. Too familiar with the oppression black Northerners had suffered, these recruiters realized that African Americans might balk at the language of "duty." Moreover, the argument that black men owed the nation service as citizens was logically problematic. If this was the case, then white Americans might argue that black men had simply done their duty and deserved no further compensation. African Americans in the North thrilled at Edward Bates's recognition of black citizenship, and his opinion convinced many to volunteer for the military. It is striking that black recruiters tended not to frame black men's duty to fight as their responsibility to the nation as citizens.[46]

Instead, black men owed it to themselves and their enslaved brethren to fight. In a speech to an Ithaca war meeting, Jermain Loguen repeatedly reminded his listeners, "Who would be free, themselves must strike the blow";

Douglass's March 1863 appeal invoked the same phrase.[47] Here, black recruiters drew on a strain of American political thought dating back to the American Revolution: that peoples unwilling to fight for their own liberty did not deserve it.[48] They also seized on an effective rhetorical strategy through which they could express the vital necessity of enlistment without asserting that African American men were obligated to fight for the nation that had so long mistreated them. In making the phrase "Who would be free, themselves must strike the blow" key to the rhetoric of black enlistment, they assured black Northerners that they would go to war not for the antebellum Union, but for themselves.

While black recruiters urged prospective Northern servicemen to submit to temporary inequalities, they somewhat contradictorily insisted that, in day-to-day matters, black troops *would* serve as equals with white troops. Andrew and other Northern officials had promised equal pay, clothing, and rations, and African American recruiters frequently repeated these pledges.[49] In March 1863, Douglass told African Americans would might serve, "[I have been] authorized to assure you that you will receive the same wages, the same rations, the same equipments, the same protection, the same treatment and the same bounty secured to white soldiers."[50] He repeated this vow in May, telling a New York City war meeting that black servicemen would be "treated in all respects as white soldiers [were] treated."[51] At the end of this event, George T. Downing read a letter from Andrew in which the governor promised black troops equality.[52] When black recruiters like Downing and Douglass promised black men equality in their day-to-day treatment, they expressed their sincere belief in the promises they had received; only later in the year would it become clear that African American combatants would be paid less than their white counterparts.[53] In a sense, though, with these promises of fairness black recruiters deliberately tried to distract from the obvious fact that black soldiers would not enjoy parity in *all* aspects of their service.

When they authorized black enlistment in January 1863, Lincoln and Stanton refused to commission black officers, barring black soldiers from rising above the rank of sergeant major. Some black commissioned officers had served in the Kansas and Louisiana regiments formed in 1862. However, Lincoln and Stanton believed that commissioning black officers for the new regiments would run afoul of public opinion, which was only just accommodating itself to black enlistment.[54]

Many African American Northerners objected to Union promotion policy, and black recruiters effectively explained why these detractors should bear this insult and enlist. William Wells Brown contended that denying commissions to black men at first made sense given white racism and black men's general inexperience as soldiers. White prejudice, he explained, would only dissipate gradually, and black troops would conquer this bias faster under white officers than black ones. White observers would not believe an African American officer's praise for his troops as readily as they would praise from a white officer.[55] White soldiers had been fighting for nearly two years by the spring of 1863, and had gained combat experience that black men lacked. Martin Delany cited this consideration, arguing that no African American men were "eligible or capable" of serving as officers.[56] Moreover, added the *Weekly Anglo-African*, "The general rule of promoting men from the ranks for courage or conduct will quickly instal these sub-officers into commands earned by their bravery!"[57] That most soldiers did not enter the army as commissioned officers, instead ascending to this position as a result of meritorious service, allowed recruiters to answer opposition to Union promotion policy comparatively easily.

Black recruiters could not answer black Northerners' concerns regarding their prisoner-of-war status so easily; no argument could justify Confederates' refusal to recognize captured black soldiers as POWs. As early as December 1862, Jefferson Davis remanded captured black soldiers to the various Confederate states, all of which treated black insurrection as a capital offense, for punishment. The following May, the Confederate Congress confirmed this policy. Northern efforts to arm slaves enraged Confederates, and slaves turned soldiers were their chief targets; Southern officials had not by 1863 decided how to treat captured free African American soldiers. Still, black Northerners knew that they might be executed or enslaved if captured, or perhaps murdered on the field by Confederate soldiers seeking to implement government policy more speedily. As early as the summer of 1863, reports came from several battlefields that Confederate troops had murdered captured black soldiers.[58]

Confederate POW policy acted as a powerful brake on black Northerners' willingness to enlist. It is striking, then, how infrequently black recruiters directly addressed the POW issue, especially in comparison to their frequent discussions of Union promotion policy. Black recruiters discussed Confederate POW policy occasionally. Frederick Douglass rather blithely asserted that, "although the colored men were not to be considered prisoners of war when taken by the Confederates . . . he was sure the colored men were as ready to give their services to the country now as they were at the commencement of the war."[59] From time to time, recruiting agents acknowledged Confederate POW policy as a legitimate argument against enlistment, and in late May the

Weekly Anglo-African praised black men who had volunteered though they could "rightfully dodge [enlistment], as some do, behind the fact that the government [would] afford them no protection if captured."[60] No rhetorical strategy could rationalize Confederate practice, and so black leaders seem to have declined to try to make it seem less objectionable than it was. Black men would have to accept that the price of their capture might be enslavement or death.

The POW issue and other indignities inspired some black Northerners to resist joining the armed forces, and black recruiters found they could not easily brush aside delayed enlistment. Rather, recruiters conceded the validity of black Northerners' objections while maintaining that the benefits service could win outweighed any temporary inequalities.[61] Black recruiters had to walk a fine rhetorical line, John Mercer Langston recalled.[62] To contend with African American Northerners' general "feeling against taking any part as soldiers in the war," these figures relied on "cautious, truthful statements, made with such candor and appeal as to create after meeting their prejudices, favorable and effective impressions." At the beginning of his time as a recruiter, Langston's work was "largely . . . of such character."[63]

John Rock followed Langston's blueprint at the New England Anti-Slavery Society's convention in late May. Rock said that some Northerners wondered why black men hesitated to enlist. "But," he continued, "if you will consider . . . how nearly every post of honor and profit is denied us . . . and when you add to all this the fact, that many colored man [*sic*] in the service of the government have been taken prisoners and sold into slavery, without even a protest from the Federal Government, you ought not to be surprised why we have hesitated, and not rushed pell-mell into the service." African American men had fought before and gotten nothing: "Many of our grandfathers," said Rock, "fought in the revolution, and the battles of the revolution we are obliged to fight over again to-day." Nevertheless, he supported enlistment, arguing that temporary concessions to racism would bring long-term gains: "If the government will not come to us, we will go to it. We will leave no excuse for these who would deprive us of our rights."[64] Black Northerners, Rock argued, were more likely to bring the Union they sought into being by fighting than by maintaining a principled refusal to fight.

In the summer of 1863, the obstacles black recruiters faced increased. The Union government implemented a new and especially galling policy in June, announcing that it would pay black servicemen less than white troops. African American soldiers would receive ten dollars a month, with three dollars deducted for clothing costs; white privates received thirteen dollars a month with a pay increase if promoted. All black soldiers would receive seven dollars a month, and none would receive the one-hundred-dollar federal bounty paid to white volunteers since 1861. These pay discrepancies contradicted the promises of day-to-day equality John Andrew and black recruiters had been making since early 1863.[65]

Ironically, this decision came because government officials pleased with black enlistment's initial results were ready to undertake it on a large scale. As spring turned to summer, Stearns's recruiting operation continued to hum, and African American troops proved their mettle on multiple battlefields, fighting well at Port Hudson, Louisiana, on May 27; Milliken's Bend, Mississippi, on June 7; Honey Springs in Indian Territory on July 17; and especially at Fort Wagner in Charleston Harbor on July 18. These servicemen's efforts received praise from white officers and the white press. Recognizing black enlistment's success and importance, Edwin Stanton established a federal Bureau of Colored Troops in late May that imposed centralized authority over the recruiting process. The units that formed from the summer of 1863 onward were designated as part of the United States Colored Troops (USCT).[66] After creating this new bureau, Stanton asked War Department solicitor William Whiting what monthly rate of pay black troops should receive. Whiting cited the 1862 Militia Act, which had prescribed unequal pay for African American soldiers. The War Department announced this policy on June 4, by which point black troops had seen combat.[67]

Black Northerners' anger over the pay issue and other inequalities kept delayed enlistment alive during the momentous summer of 1863. The story of black recruiters and their appeals is only one-half of the story of how black military service happened—the other half involves individual black men's decisions that fighting for the Union made sense. African Americans in the North saw that joining the armed forces remained a gamble. Why, many surely wondered, did recruiters think it axiomatic that gains would result after the war when the crisis of the war itself, a massive internal rebellion threatening the nation's existence, did not force the government to concede equality to all who risked their lives in its defense? Did black citizenship truly exist when African Americans suffered discrimination in and out of the army? Black recruiters tailored their arguments to validate and overcome these counterarguments, but many Northern blacks remained unconvinced.

White Northerners like George Stearns saw recruiters like Frederick Douglass as "intermediaries" between white and black Northerners; their wealth and status set them apart, and rank-and-file black Northerners listened when they spoke. Listening, though, had never implied automatic deference. In 1817, black Philadelphians had pushed back against Richard Allen and other "black elites," repudiating colonization.[68] Lincoln's August 1862 meeting with black leaders from D.C., Kate Masur has written, precipitated "a crisis . . . of leadership in black Washington," as many objected to the idea that such a small group could represent African Americans' interests. The five men who met with the president were "racial representatives" to whom whites often turned as "intermediaries."[69] This description applies to Stearns's network equally well. Black Northerners were no more willing to be represented by a committee of five than they were inclined to automatically act on recommendations made by black recruiters. As with colonization, African Americans in the North would make their own decisions.

Evidence from across the region shows that hesitation to enlist or opposition to enlistment remained widespread in Northern black communities past the time African American men began to fight and die for the Union. Many who recorded such resistance attributed it to concerns over service inequalities or the state of black rights and citizenship. This opposition has long gone underappreciated. No organized network of speakers argued for delayed enlistment, and as a result, its advocates did not carve out as prominent a place in the historical record as did black recruiters.

To be sure, black Northerners sometimes wrote to black or abolitionist newspapers to argue against immediate enlistment. Junius, the *Christian Recorder*'s regular Brooklyn correspondent, believed that service inequalities would inhibit black enlistment.[70] "[Black] [m]en in the North will not leave their homes and families, their avocations, at wages of $25 and $30 per month, to be sent to South Carolina, or Georgia, to fight rebel white men, with the prospect of dog's death by the minions of Jeff. Davis, should they be captured, all for $10 per month, without bounty at that." Junius further said of black men eligible for service, "[They are willing to] wait [to volunteer] till they raise the soldier's wages, and secure us from Jeff's halters, or from his merciless whips and tortures."[71] "Box," a Washington, D.C., correspondent for the *Anglo-African*, asked black recruits, "For what do you expose your lives?" In his opinion, African American men had no interest in restoring the antebellum Union, and they should only fight when assured that their service could "guarantee . . . fighting for a country and a home."[72]

These statements might only confirm scattered resistance to immediate enlistment that was representative of the unpopular or idiosyncratic opinions of an isolated few. Evidence that in early 1863 defiance remained strong in black Northern communities comes from a different set of sources. Namely, it comes from records of community meetings in which recruiters labored to neutralize the points made by advocates of delayed enlistment, and from the often

disgusted reports of community correspondents who told of apathy, hesitation, or outright opposition to service during the spring and summer of 1863.
For instance, resistance to immediate enlistment flared in Delaware, where
slavery survived. In late July, Frisby J. Cooper, a schoolteacher who would
become a leading AME clergyman, reported that black Wilmingtonians possessed "little war spirit" and would rather take their chances with the draft
than volunteer.[73] Black Delawareans did not consider their citizenship fully
recognized while they lacked the rights and privileges their white counterparts enjoyed, whatever Edward Bates said on the matter. Cooper explained
that Black Wilmingtonians were "perfectly willing to go and fight the battles
of the country, in its hour of trial and danger, if they [were] to have and enjoy
all of the rights and immunities of a *bonafide* citizen of these United States,
in common with other citizens, irrespective of color, cast, or condition."[74] He
wrote that he ultimately expected great things from the war, but as late as
August 1863 racist injustice cooled the military ardor of Wilmington's black
community.

Resistance also manifested itself in the nation's capital. In late July,
Thomas H. C. Hinton participated in a debate at the Israel Lyceum, a black
debating society, on the question of black enlistment and failed to bring the
meeting to consensus.[75] The next month, Hinton's anger at black Washingtonians' reluctance to serve boiled over in a letter to the *Christian Recorder*. He
admonished black draftees to "have some other plea than 'what am I going
to fight for[?]'" He decried the District of Columbia's "colored copperheads,"
which he called the "the slush hounds of our kindred," who jeered at Hinton and black draftees.[76] Hinton's harsh rhetoric did not harmonize D.C.'s
black men to enlistment; in late August, Henry McNeal Turner noted general
"mourning" over the draft. A short while later, Hinton reported that the only
activity taking place among black Washingtonians was sporadic substitute
hunting. Those who sought to avail themselves of the March 1863 conscription
law's substitution clause were buying their way out of service.[77]

If evidence of opposition to enlistment had been limited to areas of the
North in close proximity to slavery's continued existence within the Union, it
might be seen as a regional quirk. It makes good sense that black men who interacted frequently with the hated institution might have felt little pull to join
the military. But opposition also manifested itself in Northern states where
slavery had died out decades earlier. Black Pennsylvanians were divided on the
question of service when they considered it at a "Grand Emancipation Demonstration" in Harrisburg in mid-January. One of their resolutions pledged black
men to "give [their] faithful service in any manner when legitimately called

upon by the proper authorities, that will not involve [their] self-respect." After reading their resolutions aloud, those in attendance debated enlistment's merits. Thomas Early, a veteran of the Underground Railroad, "was not in favor of going to war unless he received as much money as white soldiers." Another speaker, a Mr. Cann, joined Early. Several others took the opposite position, including the Reverend David Stevens, who said he would fight if he did not receive a cent. Remarking, "They whipped my mother down South; [and] they whipped my sister down South," Stevens then said "he was ready to go whip them." Evidently, the audience was as divided as the speakers, as it rewarded all who spoke with loud applause.[78]

In March, as recruiting agents for the Fifty-Fourth Massachusetts fanned out across the North, the *Weekly Anglo-African* commented that enlistment proceeded slowly: "There is so much about the brigade which our men cannot understand, that they approach it as carefully, and as suspiciously as a man-trap." Cowardice did not explain black Northerners' hesitation to enlist, insisted the New York sheet; they hesitated to enlist because of their continued mistreatment.[79]

The same month, William Wells Brown and J. W. C. Pennington, a Presbyterian minister who, like Brown, had risen from slavery to prominence, solicited black recruits at a Brooklyn war meeting.[80] Brown and Pennington's "best reasoning powers . . . were taxed to overwhelm" the "opposition, among the colored people, to the enlistment of [their] brethren because of the many indignities heaped upon [them], both at home and in the camp." Brown and Pennington apparently argued persuasively, as the meeting concluded with resolutions approving enlistment, but resistance proved hardier elsewhere. In April, "Hope" from Troy, New York, complained that many black men who would otherwise volunteer hesitated because they felt "as if there [was] no sufficient inducement. Not," he clarified, "in regard to pay, but in a social and political view."[81] Later that month, Pennington, visiting Poughkeepsie, conceded, "In certain quarters among us there is some shy fighting in regard to the war question." He also admonished black men who hesitated to enlist and cautioned his readers to "beware of black Copperheadism."[82]

Black Northerners in the states carved out of the Northwest Territory, where slavery had never been legal, also opposed immediate enlistment. In late January, attendees of a black convention in Michigan expressed willingness to fight but determined to hold out until state legislators eliminated color-based distinctions from the state's constitution.[83] Black Ohioans gave enlistment an especially cold reception. The *Weekly Anglo-African's* Ohio correspondent "L'Occident" reported in late April that several recruitment meetings for the

Fifty-Fourth Massachusetts had been "thinly attended," also arguing that black Ohioans who objected to leaving their native state to fight did so to conceal their desire not to go to war at all.[84] William Parham met with a recruiting agent from Massachusetts but wrote in March that he thought few black men would volunteer, as they had observed the war's brutal progress and did not want to risk their lives any more than white Northerners.[85] Parham attributed black Ohioans' slowness to enlist to "the very discouraging facts regarding differences of pay and bounty."[86] L'Occident shared this judgment. In November he explained why assembling Ohio's Fifth USCT—which had mustered into the army as the 127th Ohio Volunteer Regiment—was an "arduous task," stating, "The decision concerning the pay and bounty of colored troops is so manifestly unjust that a man needs a large stock of patriotism to enlist on such terms."[87]

In assessing the strength of delayed enlistment during the early months of 1863, it is important to note that not all of the authors quoted above specifically mentioned objections related to the politics of service. Personal and idiosyncratic concerns surely motivated at least some of the opposition mentioned in these reports. And while many of the above-quoted accounts *did* specifically mention service inequalities, they usually did so secondhand; rather than quote black Northerners who opposed enlistment directly, the correspondents rendered this opposition in their own words, depriving historians access to the actual phrasing enlistment's opponents used. It is impossible to know the exact contours of the language black Northerners used in 1863 to argue for delaying military service, but it is reasonable to conclude that much of their 1863 opposition to enlistment grew out of the politics of service they had developed during the war's first two years.

In correspondence with government officials, black Northerners sometimes removed any doubt on this point. In late March, Mitchell S. Haynes of Newport, Rhode Island, asked John Andrew whether black soldiers could become commissioned officers, whether black POWs would be protected, and whether Edward Bates's opinion on citizenship had overturned *Dred Scott*. Haynes's questions came on the heels of a Newport war meeting called "to consider the question [of] enlisting." No one had answered these questions, and so Newport's black men remained undecided regarding service, having "adjourned to meet on fryday April 3/63 in order to receive the answer."[88] Black Northerners posed similar queries through late summer, when C. J. Grimes of Boston, wife of the Twelfth Street Baptist Church's Leonard A. Grimes, asked Andrew about black soldiers' pay.[89] "The question," she insisted, "is of vital importance to the Coled people of this State." Grimes's husband was away in Washington, and since his departure, she said, "a Number [of men] have been to me to make the enquiry whether there is a difference or not."[90]

In the summer of 1863, service inequalities actually caused Frederick Douglass himself to momentarily stop recruiting. Dedicated though he was to black enlistment, the horrors of Confederate POW policy weighed on Douglass, and by August 1 he had seen enough. Unaware that on July 30 Lincoln had issued a retaliatory proclamation promising to execute or put to hard labor one rebel soldier for every black Union soldier so treated, Douglass penned a public letter to George Stearns resigning his post as recruiting agent.[91] "I owe it to my long abused people, and especially those of them already in the army," he said, "to expose their wrongs and plead their cause. I cannot do that in connection with recruiting. When I plead for recruits, I want to do it with all my heart, without qualification. I cannot do that now." Douglass acknowledged that he and other black recruiters had counseled enduring temporary inequalities in the service of winning long-term gains, but he could no longer stomach this proposition:

> I know what you will say to this [letter]; you will say; "wait a little longer, and after all, the best way to have justice done to your people is to get them into the army as fast as possible." You may be right in this; my argument has been the same, but have we not already waited, and have we not already shown the highest qualities of soldiers and on this account deserve the protection of the Government for which we are fighting? Can any case stronger than [the Fifty-Fourth Massachusetts's assault on Fort Wagner] ever arise? ... How many 54ths must be cut to pieces, its mutilated prisoners killed and its living sold into Slavery, to be tortured to death by inches before Mr. Lincoln shall say "Hold, enough?"[92]

Douglass likewise assailed William Seward's injunction that black men forget service inequalities and do their duty as citizens by fighting for their country. While black troops were rendering the nation allegiance, they were not receiving the protection the government was obligated to provide in return. "Mr. Seward's lecture to colored men," he fumed, "would be considered everywhere as twaddle if applied to white men. . . . Colored men have a right not only to ask for equal pay for equal work, but that merit, not color, should be the criterion observed by Government in the distribution of places."[93] Black Northerners had enlisted as Douglass had instructed, but the weight of service inequalities, combined with the audacity of white officials who brushed these inequalities aside, caused him to stop recruiting.

Shortly after firing off these missives, Douglass learned of Lincoln's retaliatory proclamation; a few days later, he met with Lincoln and Stanton in Washington. These meetings did not result in immediate alterations to Union pay or promotion policy, but Douglass came away satisfied enough to resume recruiting.[94] When he published these pieces in his newspaper's August issue, he appended an editorial note acknowledging the president's retaliation order.[95] That Douglass published his withdrawal from recruiting and rebuke of Seward at all was significant: by doing so, he signaled his recognition that the terms under which black men fought could become so degrading that they might actually undermine the policy of using service to create a new Union.

Anger over service inequalities, discrimination, and slavery loomed large in the enlistment debate, but they were not the only reasons black Northerners hesitated to volunteer. By 1863, the length and brutality of the war had surpassed the expectations of nearly all Americans. The casualty lists that had become a regular feature of U.S. newspapers told an unprecedented tale of pain and suffering—for the killed and maimed, and for the families and friends left to deal with the pain of lost loved ones, or of loved ones returned but forever changed by the horrors they had witnessed. The same aversion to participating in this carnage that slowed white enlistments in 1863 acted as a brake on black men's willingness to serve. Joining an army during wartime is always a wrenching decision involving the pain of separation and the fear of never seeing family and friends again; like all would-be soldiers pondering enlistment, black men had to grapple with the harsh realities involved in serving one's country.

The poverty in which many black families lived, and the extent to which their survival depended on husbands' and fathers' wages, also hindered black enlistment. The prospect of widowed wives and orphaned children struggling to survive following their husbands' and fathers' deaths in the federal service gave black men pause. The notoriously slow pace at which the Union paymaster worked meant that even those who survived could not ensure that their wages would reach their families in time to meet the needs of household finances, and black men sometimes did not feel able to volunteer unless they could ensure prompt payment. George Stearns informed John Andrew in March 1863, "There are many Colored men who hesitate to enlist for fear that their families may suffer before the Regt is mustered in, and the bounty paid." Timely payment of the Fifty-Fourth, Stearns predicted, "would do more to promote enlistments than the influence of all the white Officers in the West."[96]

Transportation also proved an obstacle to enlistment. Black men joining the first Northern regiments often had to travel long distances to reach New England, and recruiters could not always fund their passage. In March 1863,

Albany's Stephen Myers, a former slave turned newspaper editor and Underground Railroad operative, told Andrew he had secured a substantial number of volunteers but lacked the money to pay for their trip. In December, Boston's Lewis Hayden reported similar difficulties in Harrisburg.[97] Even black Northerners who decided quickly to volunteer could be forced to delay their enlistment by such logistical considerations.

In the volatile Border States, would-be black volunteers faced violent opposition to their attempts to enlist. In Maryland, when abolitionist Colonel William Birney began enrolling enslaved and free black men, they became the target of reprisals from local whites. In August, Birney complained to the Bureau of Colored Troops that Maryland officials had arrested one of his recruiters, which had "intimidated the people of color, giving them the impression that the United States was powerless to protect them." The incident had cost him some 200 recruits. In addition, "the enemies of the enlistment of U.S. Colored Troops" had driven livestock away from fields belonging to families of black volunteers and even turned some out of their homes. Birney told of the arrest of John Singer, a free black man who, while leaving for Baltimore to enlist, was arrested on a writ "not known to the law of Maryland"; the officials who arrested Singer had also "avow[ed] their intention to prevent enlistments by issuing the writ in all similar cases."[98] White Marylanders kept up resistance to black military service until January 1864, and in Kentucky and Missouri African American recruits had to face the possibility of violent reprisals throughout the war.[99]

Would-be recruits might also have been put off by the words and attitudes of white supporters of black enlistment. The Union turned to black volunteers in 1863 partially because white enlistment had fallen off dramatically. With conscription looming, many whites saw African American military service as a way to keep their own sons safe from rebel guns. When he took up "the *'negro'* subject" with Union general-in-chief Henry Halleck in August 1862, Iowa governor Samuel Kirkwood explained, "When this war is over . . . I shall not have any regrets if it is found that a part of the dead are *niggers* and that *all* are not white men."[100] White soldiers began to see the logic in the proposition that black soldiers could stop rebel bullets as well as they could. One bluntly recommended, "If [black combatants] can kill rebels I say arm them and set them to shooting. I would use mules for the same purpose if possible."[101] Black enlistment was popular with many Northerners, George Stearns recognized, "because they want to get rid of [African Americans]." Stearns further stated, "If the President would conscript them . . . men women and children and take them south he would be so popular that it would insure his election for the coming term."[102]

Even ostensibly well-meaning whites sometimes echoed this attitude. A public circular issued by the Pennsylvania Committee on Colored Enlistment in late June 1863 contained two appeals: one urging black men to enlist, and one urging white Pennsylvanians to support black enlistment. Speaking to African American Pennsylvanians, the committee both acknowledged that the United States had cheated black veterans of earlier wars and nodded toward service inequalities' injustice. The committee's appeal to white Pennsylvanians began by stating that black troops would be counted against the state's draft quota. As if to appease white prejudice, the organization added that black troops would receive "about one-half the pay of the white troops, and . . . no bounty." In addition, the circular posited that the state contained only 6,000–7,000 black men capable of fighting and lamented that, of these, 400 had already enlisted in Massachusetts. While the flyer acknowledged black troops' patriotism and bravery, it concluded by appealing to white self-interest: "Since . . . recourse to conscription becomes necessary, unreasoning prejudice only can be blind to the fact that every colored recruit acts as an unpurchased substitute for a white man."[103] Black soldiers were bodies, replacements for white men. This document carried the signatures of many prominent white Pennsylvanians, including well-known abolitionist J. Miller McKim and antislavery congressman William D. Kelley.

If they read this circular, with its appeals to racially distinct audiences, black Northerners would surely have wondered whether their service could bring the changes black recruiters claimed. Here were avowed friends of the African American community depicting their fellow men as substitutes. Speaking to white Northerners, whose approval would be necessary for black men to parlay service into postwar gains, the Pennsylvania Committee on Colored Enlistment did not present any legal changes as concomitants to black service. It might be argued that this "white appeal" for black service did not reflect the true feelings of its signatories, that this approach was simply necessary to conquer white prejudice and facilitate large-scale black enlistment. Still, African American men surely wondered whether, if such a cynical argument was necessary to convince white Northerners to drop their opposition to black enlistment as Confederate troops drove into Pennsylvania, it was reasonable to expect that when danger passed, white opinion would countenance black equality.

Racist violence on the home front likely encouraged some black Northerners to delay enlistment, causing them to feel that they needed to remain home to protect their families and property. In 1863, mobs raged in Detroit and Harrisburg, and in July predominantly Irish American hordes terrorized New York City for four days, lynching dozens of black men and destroying African Americans' property. An estimated 5,000 black New Yorkers fled the city to escape the mob's murderous wrath.[104] The riots shocked the nation and might have caused some black Northerners to doubt the advisability of going to war.[105]

In the riots' aftermath African Americans feared similar disturbances in other Northern cities and concentrated on home defense. Days after the violence in New York stopped, John Rock worried a revolt would erupt in Boston, warning John Andrew that a friend of his had discovered a "bushel and a half of minie balls" hidden in a city dump meant for use in "an outbreak."[106] In late July, the *Christian Recorder* reported, "[Philadelphia's] citizens are expecting every day that a mob will break out here." The paper offered the city's black residents some advice: "Have plenty of powder and ball in your houses, and use it with effect, if necessary, in the protection of your wives and children."[107]

As they had in the aftermath of the 1850 Fugitive Slave Law, African American Northerners talked of forming organizations for self-defense. "Junius Albus" wrote to the *Christian Recorder* about appointing black policemen and starting black self-defense leagues. For his part, Brooklyn's Junius reported that individual efforts to protect homes and property had evolved into a larger communal discussion about founding a self-defense organization.[108] "Many," he wrote, "are thinking about powder, lead, and military companies, self-defence, and death to the man or men that dare invade their homes."[109] "Sea Side," an occasional *Recorder* correspondent, predicted more violence and recommended forming "in every city protective associations . . . to resist violence and massacre." Those who weren't fighting "owe[d] it to the brave colored men that [had] left [behind] their homes, families, and little ones . . . and [were] perilling their lives on the battle-field."[110] These calls for black men to take up arms on the home front came in the aftermath of appalling violence, and no one knew when similar atrocities might occur next. The Draft Riots receded from view as time passed, and black Northerners' talk of organizing for self-defense slowed. But fear and uncertainty gripped African Americans in the riots' aftermath, and these emotions inspired some to think that their duty was to remain home in readiness to meet the next onslaught of white rage. The insurrections shifted black Northerners' attention away from the battlefield and toward their own communities, likely helping to explain why some men hesitated to enlist in the late summer and early fall of 1863.

Despite the opposition to immediate enlistment that some black Northerners manifested through mid-1863, the fact remains that a remarkably high
percentage of these men eventually wore Union blue. How does one explain
this result? First, volunteering always enjoyed substantial support. This study
highlights those oft-ignored voices who dissented, but it is likely that by 1863
opponents of immediate military service were in the minority among black
Northerners, although they remained a substantial, vocal minority. It is impossible to know with certainty what percentage of African Americans in
the North at one point or another opposed immediate enlistment. But a close
analysis of black newspapers from these months suggests that at any given
moment more black Northerners would have supported enlistment than opposed it.

Nevertheless, resistance to immediate enlistment was widespread, and
the high percentage of Northern blacks who eventually served in the Union
army suggests that, at one point or another, many of them resisted immediate
enlistment and changed their minds. To explain their service, we must first
acknowledge that black recruiters performed their task well. They held regular, well-attended meetings throughout the North, and at many they secured
volunteers on the spot.[111] Their task was difficult; recruiting work confronted
them with the familiar antebellum dilemma between principle and pragmatism. Recruiters ultimately had to encourage African American men to put
their bodies on the line as part of a practical campaign to win long-term gains.
Indeed, when Frederick Douglass downplayed service inequalities and highlighted the gains service could win, he became, according to David W. Blight,
a government "war propagandist." When in July 1863 Douglass resigned in
protest, he temporarily abandoned this new wartime duty and became once
again an advocate for his community. Only after receiving assurances from
Lincoln and Stanton that they would protect black soldiers did Douglass resume recruiting. In other words, once Douglass the black activist was satisfied, he could become a recruiter again.[112]

Blight's observation about Douglass applies generally to the recruiters in
George Stearns's network, men like John Rock and William Wells Brown who
had built public careers protesting slavery and racism. They were used to advocating for their communities and protesting the government's treatment of
black Americans. Recruiting put them in the novel position of continuing to
oppose government policy and yet encouraging black Northerners to fight for
the government. Enlistment agents had to adjust to the conflicting demands
of their position by acknowledging the validity of objections to service while
nevertheless urging black men to join the military. They also needed to remain

willing to sever ties with the government if its treatment of black servicemen became too objectionable to bear. In the aftermath of the Fifty-Fourth Massachusetts's bloody repulse at Fort Wagner, African American soldiers' predicament became too much for Douglass to endure, and he momentarily stopped recruiting. By printing his letter to Stearns, Douglass signaled to black Northerners that he would end his connection with the government if circumstances eroded his belief that black service could win a new Union.

In the face of powerful obstacles and conflicting pressures, black recruiters developed a compelling call to service. By October 1863, they had convinced substantial numbers of black men to enlist: 9,050 had joined regiments formed in Massachusetts, Pennsylvania, Rhode Island, Michigan, Iowa, Ohio, and the federal district.[113] Not all of these enlistees hailed from the states in which these units were raised. Some traveled from their home states to enlist, others came from Canada or other foreign destinations, and at least a few, especially in the federal district, were surely runaway slaves for whom service offered an avenue of escape from bondage. But the majority of these enlistees would have been free African American men residing in states in which slavery had been abolished, and this number represented more than a quarter of the total number of black enlistees credited to these states by war's end. By the time Confederate armies surrendered in 1865, more than 70 percent of free black males of military age living in states in which slavery had ended before the Civil War had served in the Union army. Surely, many were influenced by Douglass and his fellow recruiters.[114] Their efforts filled the first African American regiments while the success of black enlistment hung in the balance. Given historians' claims regarding black service's importance to Union victory, we must rate highly the contributions to Union triumph made by this network of black recruiters.

African American soldiers began to enlist just as white recruitment flagged, and they served as combat and garrison troops as Union armies subdued the Confederacy. Historian Joseph T. Glathaar has explained, "Blacks alone did not win the war, but timely and extensive support from them contributed significantly and may have made the difference between Union defeat and stalemate."[115] Andrew Lang has argued convincingly that African American troops' disproportionate assignment to garrison duties—which was specifically envisioned by Lincoln in his Emancipation Proclamation—labeled them as second-class citizens in the eyes of many white Americans who viewed such duty as incompatible with republican ideals. However, William W. Freehling has shown that black soldiers' garrison service contributed to the "decisive" numerical superiority Union armies enjoyed in 1864 and 1865.[116] Lang has also shown that black troops on occupation assignments transcended the limitations implied in their responsibilities by participating in the "unbalancing [of] traditional southern power dynamics." African Americans unsettled these dynamics through the very fact of their presence as armed black men on Southern soil, their participation in raids and counterinsurgency missions that extended their power across the Southern countryside, and their liberation of friends and family members in the surrounding areas.[117]

Both Freehling and Stephanie McCurry have emphasized the Confederacy's failure to arm its black population as key to its defeat.[118] McCurry has pointed to male slaves' military potential as a great resource that the Confederacy failed to tap, not because white Southerners refused to contemplate arming slaves altogether, but because they could not devise a system that would accord slaves enough rights to induce them to fight while also maintaining the racial and class hierarchies that defined their slave society.[119] The Confederacy's failure to enlist black men stood in stark contrast to the massive black presence in the Union army from 1863 forward.[120] African American recruiters deserve much credit for the Union's ability to avail itself of black military power, as their arguments influenced black Northerners' decisions regarding enlistment during one of the war's most critical junctures.

Black recruiters' efforts aside, some African Americans in the North surely warmed to enlistment because of their analysis of the war's progress. As Union armies conquered Southern territory in 1863, increasing numbers of slaves found freedom under Lincoln's Emancipation Proclamation. Lincoln also dropped his support for colonization; after signing the proclamation, he never publicly mentioned it again.[121] The president's July 1863 retaliatory decree also helped harmonize black Northerners to the prospect of service, despite the fact that Lincoln never followed through on the threats it contained. African American troops' performance on the battlefield also likely played a role. The first black regiments' battlefield successes might have chipped away at intransigent black Northerners' resolve. The praise these servicemen garnered from white officers and reporters likely convinced some that though service inequalities persisted, black service could erode the white racism that inspired them. These units' service might have encouraged black Northerners to feel that they needed to take part in the struggle. Finally, while some Northern blacks feared the draft, it likely motivated others to enlist; volunteers perhaps reasoned that their course was better than having the details of their service dictated to them. African American Northerners longing for rights and citizenship might have seen self-determination in this realm as consistent with their goals.

The black press highlighted incidents that suggested that the war and black service were eroding white racism. In November, Ohio's A. M. Taylor attended a ceremony at Camp Delaware where the state's former governor William Dennison spoke. Dennison had refused black recruits in 1861, but he now, as Taylor told the *Christian Recorder,* stood "on the same platform with colored orators . . . and addresse[d] a colored regiment as citizens." His remarks, said Taylor, "show[ed] how public opinion has changed in [African Americans'] favor."[122] In September, Thomas Smith, the president of the Bank of North America, stood up for a black serviceman harassed on a Philadelphia street-car. When a white patron objected to the soldier entering the car, the bank executive knocked the man flat and gave the soldier his seat. In the words of *Weekly Anglo-African* correspondent Parker T. Smith, the banker forced "ruffians [to] remember that colored men have rights which white men are bound to respect."[123]

The most famous incident of this type happened in Baltimore and in-volved Alexander T. Augusta, the U.S. Army's first black physician. When local whites attacked the uniformed Augusta, white troops assisted him in arresting his assailants. Augusta expressed his pride in this incident: "Even in *rowdy Baltimore,*" he wrote, "colored men have rights that white men are bound to respect."[124] Incidents such as these suggested that white opinion was changing, and they likely contributed to the slackening of opposition to enlist-ment. In any case, after September 1863, evidence of resistance to immediate volunteering was few and far between, suggesting that the topic ceased to be a divisive one for black Northerners.

Black Northerners stopped debating enlistment because they had become convinced, by a combination of the above factors, that the hope they had ar-ticulated since 1861 had been realized. The war had proved long and costly enough to provoke white Northerners to accept radical change; it might now result in a transformed United States. By the middle of 1863, African Ameri-cans in the North had not seen *all* the change they desired, but they had seen much of it. And in keeping with their long-standing tendency to favor prag-matic action over purity of principle, they took the chance to win a new Union. In 1863, delayed enlistment became a casualty of black Northerners' growing conviction that the Civil War could change the United States' basic character.

In 1863 black Northerners expressed their belief that the war had become a crucible through which a new nation might be formed. California's Wil-liam H. Hall referenced the Revolution in urging black men to enlist. Born free in Washington, D.C., Hall had studied for the ministry at Oberlin College, fought black disenfranchisement in New York, and joined the Gold Rush in

1849. Having improved his material station considerably, Hall took up permanent residence in Oroville, California, and worked alongside William H. Newby and others in the black convention movement.[125] In 1863 he answered his late colleague's mid-1850s injunctions that African Americans be *absolutely sure* they would be getting something in return before again fighting for the United States. "It matters not now," he wrote, "in the hour of emergency, to inquire into the policy that has been pursued toward us for over eighty years. Its results have been benevolently and sublimely borne, and it should be remembered that the circumstances which once proscribed our limits and denied a recognition of merit, has been entirely changed, and we find the generation of '63 separating from compromises and compacts to return to that sublime doctrine of '76, which so freely disseminated the germs of liberty to all mankind."[126] Hall believed that by 1863 the war presented Americans the opportunity to enact their great first principle.

The *Pacific Appeal* linked the Civil War to the Revolution, because by 1863 the former offered black men the chance to fight for more than Union. In its Fourth of July issue, the *Appeal* stated that no July Fourth since 1776 "[had] been fraught with so much significance to human freedom." The publication elaborated on the connection between present-day events and those of the previous war:

> [Eighty-seven years before, black men fought] side by side with white men, for the maintenance of the sentiments of freedom enunciated in that sublime document—the Declaration of American Independence. In 1863, black men have emerged, through 87 years of Babylonian-like captivity, and are placed in a position by the National Government in which they may obtain their reward. In this age of freedom, with our citizenship restored, our soldiers accepted to fight the country's battle in behalf of human rights, we join in hailing this "auspicious day."[127]

Black soldiers went to war because, as Peter Johnson Jr. put it in an August letter to the *Appeal*, by 1863 "the covenant with death [was] broken, the agreement with hell [was] annulled. No more Union as it was and Constitution as it is." Johnson added, "But give me the Union with slavery annihilated forever, and the Constitution to read as the Declaration of Independence, proclaiming that all men are created free and equal."[128]

By mid-1863, black Northerners believed the war presented them a chance to "refound" the United States. At a first anniversary celebration for Washington's Association for the Relief of Contrabands, John F. Cook Jr. presented a flag to members of Washington's First USCT. "If the doctrine of the equality of man was announced by the American people in 1776, its adoption has been left for 1863," he thundered. "For the present give to the winds the wrongs, the unrequited services of 1776. Dwell not upon the faithlessness of 1812, but build your hopes, your faith upon the nature of the present strife. . . . The conflict is not between the North and South, it is of nobler aspect, of transcendently higher nature. It is of freedom, the equality, and of slavery, the oppression of man." Cook did not take the Constitution as his reference point, but rather the equality of the Declaration of Independence. Black men could erase the wrongs done to their forebears by participating in a struggle in whose balance hung interests that transcended party, region, race, and skin color. By fighting, African American soldiers could ensure that "1776 and 1863 in glory, in moral significance, in practical effects upon Christianity, civilization and human-ity must ever grace the pages of history, ever illume and adorn the annals of America, and stand forth prominent among the world's most favored years."[129]

Perhaps a letter written to the *Weekly Anglo-African* in late April 1863 best expressed black Northerners' identification of the Civil War as an opportunity to refound the nation. In the missive, an S. T. Johnson of Susquehanna Depot, Pennsylvania, advised African American men to enlist at once, stating, "For-bearance ceases to be a virtue." He also stated that black men should become "brothers in arms, associates in the foundation of a new republic whose watch-word shall be Liberty."[130] Here, clearly and eloquently, was the language of refounding: the war offered African Americans the chance to become mem-bers of a second founding generation. In addition to the factors earlier cited, black men's belief that the Union war effort was sufficiently antislavery to allow their service to result in a national refounding helps explain why black Northerners stopped arguing over enlistment in late 1863.

At the beginning of the Civil War, most white men fought to save the Union, although an abolitionist minority wanted to achieve this end by destroying slavery. As the war ground on, many Union soldiers saw slavery up close for the first time and determined to kill the institution. Others recognized that slavery strengthened the Confederacy and came to see its destruction as nec-essary to winning the war; and still others, witnessing the unimaginable car-nage all around them, came to believe that perhaps God had ordained that the fighting would not end while slavery lived.[131] White soldiers came around to the idea that winning the war would entail fundamental change to the United States. In 1863 black Northerners who had always sought this end joined them in the Union army.

Abraham Lincoln had always hated slavery, but constitutional law, North-ern public opinion, and the need to prevent Border State secessions had constrained him from taking decisive steps against it at the war's outset. By November 1863 he had committed the Union to a massive program of military emancipation, and he began to see the war as a chance for a national rebirth. When the president spoke at Gettysburg on November 19, 1863, he employed the language of "refounding." As John F. Cook Jr. and William H. Hall had earlier, Lincoln reached past the Constitution to the Declaration of Independence and emphasized its equality as fundamental American law, depicting the United States as "conceived in Liberty, and dedicated to the proposition that all men are created equal." The war, he said, had come as a test of "whether that nation, or any nation so conceived and so dedicated, can long endure."[132]

At Gettysburg, Garry Wills has argued, in depicting the war as a test of the viability of American equality, and in venerating the Declaration's equality as the fundamental American founding principle, Lincoln "remade" America. The president intended his speech to point toward the country he hoped would emerge from the war, in which the Declaration's equality would move into a "newly favored position."[133] The "new birth of freedom" Lincoln movingly invoked was all about equality. In the project of bringing forth a new nation dedicated to egalitarianism, Lincoln had by November 1863 accepted the help of new and willing partners who likewise used the language of refounding to describe their participation in that nation.

If by 1863 Lincoln saw the war as a chance to remake the nation in the image of equality, he yet retained faith in Union. At Gettysburg, Lincoln depicted preserving the Union as an effort to ensure "that government of the people, by the people, for the people shall not perish from the earth." The president here evoked an ideal of democracy that the United States had failed to live up to. Black Northerners had felt this failure keenly, and to them Union was meaningless. American democracy had not included African Americans, having served as a vehicle for black oppression and enslavement; black Northerners fought not to preserve "government of the people, by the people, for the people," but to create it. Black men fought because by 1863 they believed the war over slavery had turned into a war capable of killing that institution and resulting in black rights and citizenship. By 1863, African American soldiers could go to war confident that if victorious, they would enjoy what former slave William Wells Brown called "a new Union."[134]

4

CONTRACTS OF WAR

O N MARCH 5, 1864, some eight months after white mobs terrorized black New Yorkers, the city's Twentieth USCT marched proudly down Broadway as thousands of enthusiastic spectators, white and black, watched. New York's Union League Club hosted a flag presentation ceremony addressed by the president of Columbia University, and the regiment boarded a steamer bound for New Orleans afterward. Contrasting this day of celebration with the previous summer's violence, Thomas H. C. Hinton declared, "A new era has been ushered in, colored soldiers gloriously welcomed in the streets of New York City, and protected by the whole force of police . . . and as they passed along . . . the white and colored ladies wave[d] their handkerchiefs. . . . The national ensign hung out at every window; on they go, cheer after cheer. Ain't that a victory?"[1] White New Yorkers' reactions to the procession confirmed Hinton's belief that African American service was changing the United States.

Not all black regiments headed South under such cheery circumstances. In January, as Loudon S. Langley traveled south with other Vermont recruits bound for the Fifty-Fourth Massachusetts, he recorded their anguished reaction to the news that they would receive lower pay than white troops: they "received [the truth] with . . . much cursing and swearing, accompanied with the declaration that they never would have enlisted had they been truly informed." The incident, Langley wrote, left his fellow soldiers "somewhat down-hearted."[2] Later that spring, Rev. William W. Grimes reported that as the Twenty-Ninth Connecticut left New Haven, "there appeared to be a cloud hanging over them, notwithstanding [which] they wanted to go." This "cloud," Grimes continued, was the "same cloud that [had] disheartened all the colored troops now in the field. Namely, money." The anger the men of the Twenty-Ninth felt over Union pay policy inspired them to make a striking symbolic gesture. When local leaders presented them a regimental flag, they refused it. "From the treatment they received," Grimes explained, "they declared they would not receive the colors; and when they were presented, not one grant, not one word, not one cheer was given by the regiment; the whole thing was coolly done." The soldiers' wrath did not affect their sense of purpose; they embarked on their troopship as "stern men of war," but they did so under protest of the government's failure to deliver on its promises.[3]

In 1864, black troops' anger over Union pay policy flared, and they flooded black newspapers with calls for equal wages. From his post with the First USCT at City Point, Virginia, Henry McNeal Turner wrote, *"Unless the colored troops get their full pay very soon, I tremble with fear for the issue of things."*[4] African American soldiers protested Union salary rules because of the resulting economic hardship, but also because they understood that, given their own vulnerable claim to citizenship, the terms of their service mattered as much as their service itself. If black combatants acquiesced in discriminatory treatment while they fought, they might undermine their citizenship. Edward Bates had affirmed blacks' status as American citizens in December 1862, but his decision's practical effect was narrow. As James Oakes has observed, Bates's opinion lacked "the force of statute . . . or the weight of judicial precedent."[5] It might be overruled in court or canceled by a subsequent attorney general. African American troops sensed the tenuous nature of this recognition of their citizenship and believed that the citizenship they possessed meant little in practical terms when it did not preclude them from being treated unfairly. Moreover, they sought a more robust type of citizenship than Bates had described, one grounded in the cherished founding principle of equality.

In recent decades, historians have chronicled the campaign for equal pay black soldiers waged from late 1863 through the war's end; none, however, has linked this protest to the conversations that took place in Northern black communities earlier in the war.[6] When black Northerners began enlisting in 1863, they discarded delayed enlistment, and their politics of service might have died at this juncture. But the politics of service had always been principally concerned with African Americans and their relationship to the United States, and this topic remained relevant as black soldiers went South with the Union army. Thus, black Northerners' discourse about the war, citizenship, and military service did not end once African American men began serving; it continued, its focus shifted. African Americans in the North knew they needed to press for change while they wore Union blue, seeing no incompatibility in fighting for the Union while opposing U.S. policy.

When black Northerners ceased debating enlistment itself in late summer

1863, they adapted their politics of service to new circumstances. African American soldiers protesting Union pay policy claimed that their enlistment had created a new contractual relationship of reciprocal obligation between themselves and the United States. Blacks who joined the first Northern regiments led the way in protesting Union compensation practices, arguing that refusal to pay them equal wages constituted breach of contract. Congress began to equalize their salaries in June, and this victory occasioned celebration. But Congress did not equalize all black troops' pay with its June 1864 bill, and Union paymasters' notorious slowness kept some regiments from receiving equal wages for months, so black soldiers continued to protest Union pay policy into the spring of 1865.

Black civilians in the North conducted parallel campaigns on the home front. They knew they owed it to black soldiers to serve as their proxies at home, and to advance racial equality they wrote and spoke publicly, held conventions and mass meetings, and lobbied state legislatures. These civilians supported black soldiers' campaign for equal pay, but they also targeted everyday forms of discrimination whose eradication would be vital to achieving a meaningful black citizenship. African American Northerners remained sensitive to the treatment their husbands, fathers, and sons received in the Union army. As service inequalities persisted into the summer of 1864 and began to chip away at black Northerners' patience, some temporarily resurrected public debate over whether African American soldiers should fight at all.

In their protest, black soldiers and civilians showed that, despite its practical limitations, they put great stock in Edward Bates's formulation of citizenship. They knew this decision had the potential to fundamentally remake the relationship between black men and women and the United States, and they sought to make the nation fulfill its terms. Bates defined citizenship as a relationship of mutual allegiance and protection between the citizen and the state. By serving the federal cause, African American men did their part. However, while the federal government could disregard promises it made to African American soldiers, and while these troops could not earn wages sufficient to support their families, the government failed to meet its obligation of protection. Black Northerners understood that, despite Bates's ruling, black citizenship did not mean much if it did not compel the government to protect black soldiers and treat them justly.[7] At the same time, they sought to broaden the citizenship Bates described and claim rights, like the vote, without which enjoying citizenship meant little.

With concerns about the state of black citizenship uppermost in their minds, black troops and civilians conducted a vigorous campaign of dissent while they helped win the war. Rather than waiting to seek postwar redress, they fought a two-pronged crusade for victory on the battlefield and the home front similar to black troops' "Double V" campaign during the Second World War. Edward Bates's opinion, the Brooklyn correspondent Junius wrote in November 1863, did not change the historical fact that African Americans had not been treated as citizens. The possibility that, in the future, they might enjoy statutory citizenship and yet lack key rights and privileges loomed large in his mind. Black protest during the war's final year and a half was fueled by African Americans' recognition that it remained an open question whether they would *assume that position as a part and parcel of the bona fide citizens of the Republic.* "Without some great effort on the part of the colored people themselves," Junius predicted, "their status will be that of serfs in all coming time."[8]

AS BLACK ENLISTMENT CONTINUED and expanded in 1864, black re-cruits in the Northern states moved through the various camps established for their enlistment and training: Readville in Massachusetts, New Haven in Connecticut, Riker's and Hart's Islands in New York, Camp William Penn in Pennsylvania, Camp Stanton in Maryland, Camp Delaware in Ohio, and Benton Barracks in Missouri. Union officials in the South continued to enlist former slaves, and a new dynamic developed as often-unscrupulous North-ern recruiters descended on Southern states looking for ex-slaves to fill black Northern regiments. Federal officers understood how important black troops were to the Union cause. Lincoln wrote in August 1864 that if the United States abandoned all the posts African American soldiers occupied, it "would be compelled to abandon the war in 3 weeks." Black enlistment remained unpopular in certain circles, but Lincoln showed no public signs of retreating from it, or from the promise that slaves turned soldiers would remain free. The president saw that black men fought for motives beyond Union and would only be inspired to risk their lives for the United States if they were guaranteed they were fighting for liberty. "Why should [African American soldiers] give their lives for us, with full notice of our purpose to betray them?" he asked. "If they stake their lives for us they must be prompted by the strongest motive—even the promise of freedom. And the promise being made, must be kept."[9]

All African Americans wanted to see slavery's end, but those in the North wanted more than abolition and emancipation, and some still remained un-convinced that black men ought to serve. For instance, speaking at a first anniversary celebration of the Emancipation Proclamation in Boston, Edwin Garrison Walker—son of the black pamphleteer David Walker, as well as one of the first black men admitted to the Massachusetts bar, and one of the two first black representatives elected to the state legislature—argued that the Lincoln administration "ha[d] not done enough." He "wanted a better state of things before he could consent to enter the ranks and fight the enemy."[10]

Black correspondents in Indiana and Connecticut attributed local drop-offs in recruiting to service inequalities, and enlistment proceeded so slowly in Baltimore that a white recruiter convened a meeting of black Baltimoreans on February 29 to "ascertain the cause of the tardiness, on the part of intelligent and respectable colored men in the State of Maryland, in joining the army." The next month, AME minister Jabez P. Campbell, the *Christian Recorder*'s former editor and a future bishop, declared that black Marylanders wanted "free soil, free speech, free men, and no slaves, with equal pay, equal bounty, equal pensions, equal rights, equal privileges, and equal suffrage, under the Government of the United States, with no distinction on account of color. The want, or demand, of equal remuneration in the Union army," he said, "has been a cause of hindrance to the enlistment of colored men in this State."[11] The question of enlistment no longer preoccupied black Northerners as it had in 1863, but some of them continued to object to enlistment into 1864.

These holdouts represented a minority of black Northern opinion; by this point, most African Americans accepted the proposition that their male brethren ought to enlist when possible. In the North, focus now shifted to the service inequalities under which black troops labored, particularly Union pay policy. During 1863's final months, black newspapers ran letters from African American soldiers that blasted Union compensation practices and other indignities. These missives acquainted black civilians with the anger and deprivation black soldiers felt. In September, John R. Tunion of the First USCT told the *Christian Recorder*'s readers about his unit's reaction to Union pay policy. "The men are very angry about it," Tunion reported. "I think it will cause insubordination among them. Fifty-two of the non-commissioned officers are going to hold a meeting upon the subject; we don't feel like serving the United States under such an imposition."[12] From South Carolina, George Stephens of the Fifty-Fourth Massachusetts wrote the *Weekly Anglo-African* several times to protest Union wages, declaring in September, "There may be some reason for making distinction between armed and unarmed men in the service of the government, but when the nationality of a man takes away his title to pay it becomes another thing."[13] Letters from soldiers like Tunion and Stephens dramatized the government's betrayal of its promise of equal pay.[14]

The early Massachusetts and South Carolina regiments protested the wage discrepancy especially loudly, and many soldiers in these units refused to accept unequal pay. The Fifty-Fourth and Fifty-Fifth Massachusetts regiments even declined an offer from their state legislature to use state funds to rectify the disparity. Principle, not desire for financial gain, inspired their refusal to accept lesser pay, Stephens explained. "We did not enlist for money," he wrote, "but we felt that the men who enlisted us and those who accepted our service never intended that we should be treated different from other Massachusetts men."[15] The Massachusetts regiments' protest angered some white officers but stayed within acceptable bounds. But in November 1863, tragedy ensued when ex-slaves in the Third South Carolina led by Sergeant William Walker stacked arms in protest of their pay. Walker told a court-martial hearing that he and his comrades had been poorly treated by their officers, and he noted that they had all enlisted under a "promise solemnly made . . . that [they] should receive the same pay and allowances as were given to all soldiers in the U.S. Army."[16] His commander, Colonel Augustus Bennett, sympathized with his cause but charged him with mutiny anyway. For demanding the pay he had been promised, William Walker died before a firing squad in February 1864 while his entire brigade looked on.[17]

By the end of 1863, black soldiers' agitation inspired black newspapers and civilian leaders to protest Union pay practices. In late December, the *Christian Recorder* issued a public protest on the compensation issue. The *Recorder* speculated that the pay discrepancy could not possibly reflect government policy and was rather a locally perpetrated fraud, concluding, "It would be manifest injustice in the Government to offer the colored soldier seven, while the white receives thirteen dollars, besides the large bounties given."[18] On the home front, community action started to reflect black Northerners' wage concerns as well, as war meetings turned into occasions for protesting Union pay policy. In October, black Bostonians gathered in Leonard Grimes's Twelfth Baptist Church to protest the U.S. approach to compensation. After hearing a letter from a member of the Fifty-Fourth read aloud, they resolved the injustice of the policy and created a community fund to aid soldiers' families.[19] The correspondence that black soldiers sent to black newspapers in 1863, as well as the protest these servicemen began to inspire on the home front, prefigured the agitation for equal pay that suffused the black press in 1864.

A few black soldiers criticized their comrades' disapproval of Union pay policy. But most African Americans, soldiers and civilians alike, saw these practices as inconsistent with the citizenship they hoped black service would win and therefore supported protests against them.[20] Black soldiers had enlisted knowing that they would not serve on terms of *complete* equality, but they remained determined to use their service to bring change and refused to bear discrimination silently. No one had to be a constitutional scholar to see that paying black troops less than white troops was unfair, and sometimes African American soldiers' protests appealed simply to the principle of fair treatment. Much resistance to Union wage scales likely emanated from this consideration. But close analysis of the language black soldiers employed to protest Union pay policy suggests that they also understood that this policy jeopardized black citizenship. It undermined the relationship of protection and allegiance Edward Bates had defined as citizenship's core.

African Americans who had enlisted in Northern states often asserted that the government had violated the contract it had made with them. In early 1863, black recruiters and white officials had promised black Northerners equal pay, and black soldiers argued that these promises constituted an agreement that was binding from the moment of enlistment. The government violated this contract by its decision to pay African American servicemen under the terms of the 1862 Militia Act. Daniel Walker of the Fifty-Fourth Massachusetts issued this complaint in mid-January: "[While the men of my unit have] fulfilled all our agreements to the Government, and have done our duty wherever we have been . . . thus far the Government fails to fulfil their part of the contract, by not paying us."[21]

That same month, "Barquet," also of the Fifty-Fourth, maintained that while he and his comrades would not take less than the thirteen dollars per month they had been promised, they would "perform [their] part of the contract" until mustered out of service.[22] In July, J. H. Hall of the Fifty-Fourth warned, "The educated negro does not enter into contracts without knowing what recompense he is to receive or is promised for his services," and he also suggested that black men would "prosecute the [pay] matter" when they returned from the field. Hall answered one of the greatest fears that underlay black protests against Union pay policy—that the refusal to pay black soldiers equal wages might serve as prelude to the U.S. government's continued denial of black equality in the war's aftermath—by asserting that he and his comrades would not "tamely submit to the infliction of wrongs most foul, as did [their] forefathers."[23]

African American newspapers understood black soldiers' enlistment in contractual terms as well. Commenting on the pay controversy in February, the *Christian Recorder* asked, "Has the compact, now sealed in the blood of Africa's sons, been kept?"[24] Once Congress began to equalize black pay, the *Weekly Anglo-African* reflected on the wage issue and pronounced, "There was but one side to it, the side of justice and of good faith in the obligation of contracts."[25]

Sometimes black soldiers spoke explicitly in the language of contractual obligation, but more often they employed language that, while not *explicitly* contractual, implied that their enlistment had created a relationship of reciprocal obligation between themselves and the government that the government had violated. In April 1864, Edward W. Washington of the Fifty-Fourth Massachusetts asserted, "[Black soldiers] must be slaves, for we put our lives in peril for the defence of a government, that refuses us what it *solemnly promised* us."[26] That same month, "Bay State" of the Fifty-Fifth Massachusetts reacted to the government's failure to offer equal compensation: "Promises have no weight with us now, until the past and present is fulfilled—future ones we will not heed."[27] In late May, a sergeant of the Fifty-Fifth Massachusetts explained bitterly what John Andrew could do if he not fulfill his "promise" of equal treatment: "[He can] replace us where he got us from."[28]

Black soldiers often enumerated the specific terms under which they had enlisted to highlight the government's breach of contract. E. D. W. of the Fifty-Fourth Massachusetts remembered that, "In time of enlisting. . . . [the soldiers of the Fifty-Fourth] were promised the same pay, and the same rations as other soldiers."[29] In June, J. H. B. P. wrote, "Governor Andrews, of Massachusetts enlisted me as follows: three years, or sooner discharged, with the same pay, rations and medical and hospital attendance as other soldiers, forty-two dollars per annum for clothing, fifty dollars bounty from the commonwealth of Massachusetts when mustered in the service, one hundred dollars bounty from the General Government, when mustered out of the service, a land warrant of one hundred and sixty acres of land, and a pension from the General Government, and the same treatment, in every respect, as the white volunteers receive." J. H. B. P. saw Union pay policy as "a great insult and an unequivocal breach of contract."[30] These servicemen's insistence on keeping the terms of their enlistment at the forefront of the discussion over pay suggested the great stock black soldiers placed in the moment of enlistment, when their entrance into the Union army created a new relationship between themselves and the U.S. government.[31]

Black soldiers wrote directly to Northern officials, especially John Andrew, to complain that their treatment violated the terms of their enlistment. Just days after their bloody assault on Fort Wagner, the "Members of the Mass 54 Regiment That Still Lives" asked Andrew to bring them home in response to the Confederacy's barbarous POW policies. "We Wer told that We Would Be Treated as White Soldiers that had Went into the field," they said. While they acknowledged that they had been treated fairly in many respects, the Confederacy's refusal to exchange black POWs "s[truck] [them] to the heart."

In conclusion, the soldiers asked Andrew, "For The Sake of the Old comonwelth . . . call us Back to our old Home once more."[32] Frederic Johnson, a sergeant in the Fifty-Fourth, told Andrew that many of his comrades "seem[ed] to feel . . . duped." Their "general feeling" was that they would rather be called home for state defense duty or honorably discharged than submit to Union compensation rules.[33]

Black soldiers let Andrew know that he had not made good on his promise of equal pay. An anonymous member of the Fifty-Fourth told him indignantly, "I think the labor[er] is worthy of his hire, for if I agree to give A man $13 A month. . . . my conscious force me duty bound to do so." Some newly freed slaves who had enlisted balked at black Northern soldiers' protests over compensation, believing they reflected poorly on these servicemen's reputation as fighters. But others joined black Northern soldiers in viewing service contractually. Ex-slave Joseph Holloway told Andrew that the government had "come short of their promish" to give black soldiers the "same pay, rations, bounty & lands . . . as all other soldiers," then added, "[The government] ought to come short of keeping us hear."[34]

First Sergeant Stephen A. Swails of the Fifty-Fourth Massachusetts took his grievances to the adjutant general's office, writing Colonel E. D. Townsend to "respectfully demand to be mustered out of the service of the United States." Swails argued his case for discharge in explicitly contractual terms, painstakingly describing his entrance into an agreement with the government and the statute that governed that agreement's terms. "I am a Sergeant of Co 'F,' 54th Regiment Massachusetts Volunteers," he began.

> I enlisted at Readville Mass, April 8th 1863, as a "volunteer from Massachusetts, in the force, authorized by an Act of congress of the United States, approved on the 22nd day of July, A.D. 1861, entitled, 'An Act to authorize the employment of Volunteers to aid in enforcing the laws, and protecting public property.' This act distinctly states in Section 5, That the officers, non commissioned officers, and privates, organized as above set forth, shall, in all respects, be placed on the footing, as to pay, and allowances, of similar corps of the Regular Army." I was accepted by the United States, and mustered in with the company to which I belong, April 23, 1863, by Lieut. Robert P. McKibbon, mustering officer; since that time I have performed the duty of a soldier, and have fulfilled my part of the contract with the Government. But the Government having failed to fulfill its part of the agreement, in as much as it refuses me the pay, and allowances of a Sergeant of the regular Army.[35]

The well-educated Swails could demonstrate the legality of his claims to equal pay in eloquent prose.[36] But his understanding of his service mirrored that of his less-learned comrades, underlining the extent to which a contractual view of service pervaded the ranks of black regiments.

In viewing their enlistments as contracts with federal or state governments, black troops displayed an understanding of military service consistent with earlier American soldiers' thinking. Fred Anderson has demonstrated that New England servicemen during the French and Indian War balked at performing duties not covered under the terms of their enlistment. They also protested military authorities' failure to fulfill the terms of their enlistment contracts by failing to provide them with proper rations or extending their terms of service beyond their agreed-on dates of discharge. Typically, these militiamen protested by deserting, striking, or staging "peaceful mutinies" that aired their grievances without violently altering their units' command structures.[37] Like black Civil War soldiers, New England militiamen kept track of the terms under which they were employed, often recording their promised rate of pay and length of service in their journals.[38]

Militiamen who fought in the Revolutionary War and Red Stick War saw service similarly. Revolutionary militiamen, Charles Royster has observed, "repeatedly refused to serve beyond the time for which they had been called up," sometimes insisting on departing early to ensure that they would be home when their enlistments expired. They would fight only "under conditions to their liking, for an agreed upon number of months."[39] Adam Rothman has documented similar behavior by the Western Tennessee militiamen and volunteers who served under Andrew Jackson during the Red Stick War of 1813–14. In the winter of 1813, Jackson's troops began to abandon him because they had "enrolled for specific terms of service and were unwilling to fight any longer than legally required." The bulk of his soldiers, poor farmers with few or no slaves, could not endure a long campaign that would keep them from their livelihoods, and so "Jackson's army crumbled."[40] These who in early American wars clung to contractual notions of service were militiamen, not members of regular armed forces, as were black Civil War soldiers. Nevertheless, militia units fought beside regular troops in both wars. Militiamen's conceptions of service likely influenced regular soldiers' thinking, and they surely influenced Americans' thinking about military service more generally.

Black men fought in all of these wars, and they likely shared this contractual view of military service to some degree. African American veterans might have transmitted this view to their friends and families once they returned home, and thus it is possible that antebellum black Northerners came to see military service in explicitly contractual terms whose violation justified protest and resistance. It is possible that African Americans in the North enlisted in the Civil War with such notions already engrained in their consciousness, and that these long-held ideas explain their furious response to Union pay policy.

Like soldiers in French and Indian War–era New England militia units, black troops protested by engaging in resistance that, while subversive of military discipline, usually stopped short of outright violent mutiny. Black combatants from Massachusetts, Michigan, and Rhode Island refused to accept the wages offered them—an action that constituted mutiny—despite entreaties and warnings from white officers to take their pay.[41] African American soldiers organized work stoppages, refused certain kinds of duties, and petitioned for their rights. In June, E. W. D. of the Fifty-Fourth Massachusetts reported, "[The Fifty-Fourth Massachusetts is] still in the field without pay, and the Government shows no disposition to pay us." The correspondent and his comrades had "declined doing active field service, except in cases of the greatest emergency, and [were], therefore . . . doing garrison duty."[42] In mid-July, following two attempted strikes, Company D of the Fifty-Fifth Massachusetts petitioned Abraham Lincoln "demand[ing]" proper pay from their date of enlistment, and asking for their "immediate discharge, having been enlisted under false pretence." The men of Company D took their protest further than most; they threatened the president with the specter of armed mutiny by vowing to "resort to more stringent measures" if the government failed to meet their demands.[43] Black soldiers never resorted to massive violent revolt in protest of Union compensation policy, but they refused to dignify the terms of a contract altered without their consent.[44]

Black soldiers also approximated earlier Americans' contractual understandings of service in demanding that the government either fulfill the terms of their enlistment contracts or discharge them. Servicemen who demanded discharges sometimes used pseudonyms, perhaps to shield themselves from potential discipline. Such was the case with "A Soldier" of the Twenty-Ninth Connecticut, who informed the *Weekly Anglo-African* of service inequalities effect on the members of his unit: "If it continues they will lay down their arms and go to prison, as they would much rather be there than to be treated worse than slaves are in the South." If the Union continued to treat black soldiers unfairly, this anonymous soldier had one request of the government: "Call us home, and let the white soldier fight it out."[45] Likewise, a soldier from the Sixth USCT signing himself "Unknown" told the Senate, "[Either] pay us full wages and bounty, or else send us home."[46] J. H. B. P. elaborated the consequences of Union pay policy starkly when he argued in June 1864 that if black troops did not "receive the same pay and treatment as other soldiers, [they owed] no allegiance to the Government."[47] Demanding discharges or making inflammatory statements to black newspapers were less direct forms of resistance than some of the actions discussed previously. Still, these bold statements revealed the depth of black troops' anger over Union pay policy while indicating that that anger emanated from a contractual view of service.

Black soldiers protested Union compensation rules and other service inequalities in evocative, passionate rhetoric but generally kept their dissent within acceptable bounds.[48] They petitioned, struck, engaged in peaceful mutiny, and vented their anger in print; all were powerful forms of resistance that yet fell short of the type of outright violent resistance that would require severe retributive justice.[49] This commonality, in addition to the language of contract and reciprocal obligation that black men used to describe their enlistment, suggests that the pay issue emerged as a flashpoint for black troops partially because unequal pay violated their contractual understanding of military service, an understanding common to American soldiers.

But black soldiers also objected to Union pay policy because of concerns related to citizenship. A relationship of mutual obligation between the citizen and the nation formed the heart of Edward Bates's depiction of national citizenship. The attorney general did not use the word "contract" to describe the relationship between the country and the individual, but his description clearly lent itself to contractual interpretation. Union pay policy *directly violated* the terms under which black Northerners had enlisted in the spring of 1863, unlike Union promotion and Confederate POW policies, both of which these men had understood when they entered the military. This fact presented troubling implications for African American citizenship in two ways. First, if citizenship was based on a contractual association between the United States and individuals, what did it say about black citizenship that the nation did not feel bound to honor the agreements it had made with its black citizens? Second, did the government not fail to live up to its obligation of protection when it failed to pay African American soldiers wages sufficient to allow their wives and children to survive?

Black soldiers saw that Union pay policy could undermine black citizenship, and this concern helped inspire their resistance to it. "A Soldier" of the Fifty-Fifth Massachusetts argued, "It is the color and quality and citizenship of the United States that is the reason they want us to take" unequal wages.[50] Another member of the Fifty-Fifth claimed that accepting unequal pay would mark African American troops as "second class soldiers." That status, he said, "does not at all accord with our ideas and wishes."[51] J. H. Hall of the Fifty-Fourth Massachusetts spoke of Union compensation practices and other inequalities when he held that, like Andrew Jackson before them, Northern officials had "promised the negroes every thing pertaining to a citizenship, in order to get them into the field," but failed to honor those promises.[52]

Black civilians shared the view that Union pay policy could undermine African American citizenship. Reciting a list of black soldiers' grievances, the *Weekly Anglo-African* opined in April 1864 that if these men accepted the "[base] offer" of unequal pay, it would "strip them of all the attributes of soldiers and free American citizens."[53] And on July 6, a meeting of black Bostonians addressed by Robert Morris, John Rock, and others resolved, "That notwithstanding the Attorney-General of the United States has more than once declared our citizenship, it is more than evident that his decision has been neither confirmed by the President, Cabinet, Congress, or United States Supreme Court, and is therefore liable to be reversed at any time." The United States, they declared, "[remains determined to] withhold from [African Americans] every right of citizenship and to perpetuate our degradation so far and so long as it can do so without too greatly endangering its own rights and liberties."[54] Bates's opinion might be canceled if other government agencies failed to honor its findings.

While some black soldiers and civilians proclaimed that the promise of citizenship remained unfulfilled while Union pay policy discriminated against black soldiers, others argued that the nation failed to live up to its obligation of protection while it refused to pay black servicemen wages sufficient to support their families. African American troops who learned they would be paid less than promised when they had enlisted knew that their unexpectedly meager salary would only increase the already considerable hardships under which black families labored to survive. When relatives on the home front wrote to their soldier husbands, fathers, and sons to tell of their ordeal, these letters made a heavy emotional impact. It was surely gut-wrenching for African American troops performing the nation's service hundreds of miles from home to read of their loved ones' trials and know they could not do something to immediately rectify the situation.

Black women wrote to black newspapers to report on their charitable work or give their thoughts on the war and black service, but wives of black soldiers did not typically protest Union pay policy or detail their own sufferings in the black press.[55] Instead, they addressed their complaints to Union officials. Buffalo's Hannah Johnson, whose son fought in the Fifty-Fourth Massachusetts, told Abraham Lincoln himself that he needed to treat rebel prisoners harshly as retaliation for Confederate POW policy: "You ought to do this, and do it at once. . . . Meet it quickly and manfully, and stop this, mean cowardly cruelty." Rosanna Henson, whose husband had joined the Twenty-Second USCT, likewise castigated the president for the hardship Union compensation rules were causing her family. Writing in July 1864, she informed Lincoln that her husband had not been paid since May. "I have four children to support and I find this a great strugle. A hard life this!" As a black woman, she told him, she did not receive any assistance from the state, "yet [her] husband [was] fighting for the country." She had been told that the president would "see to" securing black troops their proper pay, and she demanded that he fulfill his duty. "I speak for my self and my Mother and i know of a great many others as well as ourselve are suffering for the want of money to live on," wrote Rachel Ann Wicker of Piqua, Ohio. "For my part i Cannot see why they have not th same rite to their 16 dollars per month as Whites." As black soldiers' families experienced the economic consequences of Union pay policy, black women took their grievances to the highest offices in the land.[56]

Black women also wrote to their husbands in the army, and their descriptions of their sufferings made their way into public discourse through their husbands' letters.[57] African American troops took their anger and pain to the black press, asking how the United States could betray the wives, parents, and children who remained behind when black troops left to fight the nation's battles. "Bay State" of the Fifty-Fifth Massachusetts asked in April 1864, "[Does the government intend] parents, wives, children, and sisters to suffer, while we, their natural protectors, are fighting the battles of the nation?" Bay State wrote about seeing "a letter from a wife in Illinois to her husband, stating that she had been sick for six months, and begging him to send her the sum of *fifty* cents. Was it any wonder," he asked, "that the tears rolled in floods from that stout-hearted man's eyes[?]"[58]

"Mon," also of the Fifty-Fifth, asked whether the government cared "for the heart-rending appeals of the wives, children, and other relations, to the soldiers, for aid in their suffering—yes, in some cases, starving condition?" He continued, "Is it not delightful to hear your wife and darling babies crying to you for the necessaries of life, while you are so confined that you cannot help them?" Only with difficulty could black soldiers keep their minds on their duty when "every mail [brought] news from home . . . of destitution."[59] More often, African American servicemen detailed their families' hardships briefly, mentioning loved ones' plight in their larger arguments against Union pay policy. Typical of this approach was a letter written by Edward J. Wheeler of the Fourth USCT. Wheeler lamented, "Whilst the argumentation [over pay] is going on, our families are suffering for the want of sustenance."[60]

In linking their families' suffering to Union compensation practices, black men vented their frustrations at the heavy financial burden military service placed on their families; they also displayed a gendered discomfort with the fact that their salaries prevented them from fulfilling their masculine duties as husbands and fathers. Historians have long recognized that African American soldiers hoped their service would validate black manhood. When they invoked considerations of manhood, though, black men did not always speak in the language of masculinity, suggesting that they simply wanted black military service to cause whites to see African Americans, male and female, as fully human.[61]

While in the Civil War African American men sought to use military service to win citizenship, Chandra Manning has shown that black women and children—alongside those men who did not enlist—likewise provided services to the Union army. These efforts earned them citizenship in the form of a "new, direct relationship with the U.S. government" that often included a contract for wages.[62] The Civil War was a moment in which African American women and children worked alongside African American men to achieve citizenship, but focused as they were on their own enlistment contracts and service, black soldiers did not always give those serving the Union army in nonmilitary capacities the credit they deserved for their work to make black citizenship a reality.[63] And when black servicemen linked Union pay policy to home-front privation, they often spoke in explicitly gendered language. Union wages prevented black men from fulfilling their roles as protectors of and providers for their families. "Bay State" conveyed this meaning when he referred to African American males as their relatives' "natural protectors."

A. Kristen Foster has argued that Frederick Douglass's linkage of black men's service with black citizenship caused him to develop a gendered conception of citizenship that rested on men's ability to fight and die for their country. It may be that in these letters linking Union pay policy and black families' suffering, containing as they did the implicit assumption that enlistment should not prevent black men from fulfilling their accustomed gender roles, black Northerners were articulating a similar understanding of a connection between black service and a specifically male version of citizenship.[64] But African American soldiers also invoked the suffering their inadequate wages caused their families because they felt that suffering deeply, and because they understood that the powerful image of servicemen's wives and children starving and freezing could shame Union officials into equalizing their pay. In deploying this image, African American soldiers buttressed their arguments about the federal government's violation of the enlistment contracts it had made with them.

Black civilians' understanding of the relationship black service created between the federal government and their race mirrored the contractual relationship black soldiers insisted had taken shape upon their enlistment. They did not talk in explicitly contractual terms as often as their soldier counterparts, but African American civilians linked their demands for change to their fellow men's military service. This linkage demonstrated their belief that black service had created a new relationship not just between black soldiers and the federal government, but between *all* African Americans and the government. Determined that African Americans' service would not be brushed aside, that their patriotism would not go unrewarded in the conflict's aftermath, black civilians did not wait for the war's end to use black service to demand change. Rather, they contrasted this service with the shabby treatment black civilians endured on the home front to highlight the need for immediate reform.

Black soldiers and civilians kept each other informed of the progress of events in their various locales through newspapers and private letters, developing a mutual appreciation for the fact that they were working in complementary ways toward a common goal. In April 1864, R. H. C. urged African American Northerners, "Look after the interests of the soldiers; see that no injustice be done them by subordinates of the government, for it is from this class they suffer more than from any other." Black civilians' duties did not end at protesting service inequalities. In R. H. C.'s opinion, they must agitate for fundamental change: "Now that there is a great progressive movement on hand, let not any man among us stop, in his efforts to elevate and honor his race."[65] A female black author challenged African Americans in the North to agitate by asking pointedly, "Do not those noble and brave men who face the cannon and shake hands with death, demand of those who sit quietly around their comfortable fires, reading the 'war news,' to get for their children that for which they fight and die?"[66] African American soldiers recognized that service and home-front agitation served a common end. From his regiment's encampment at Jacksonville, Florida, R. H. B. of the Third USCT celebrated black Pennsylvanians' campaign against railcar discrimination, predicting that if "every section of the country, town or hamlet . . . agitate[d] the question of equality before the law, and demand[ed] by the law the rights that citizens enjoy," the combined efforts of "[black] leading men at home, with the co-operation of their brethren in the field" would bring speedy change.[67]

When black delegates from across the United States met in national convention in Syracuse in October 1864, they admitted that black men had gambled by enlisting without extracting terms in the hope that service would win long-term gains. But they insisted that black Northerners' abandonment of delayed enlistment did not mean that African Americans would wait quietly until the war's end to agitate for change. Delegates to the Syracuse Convention were intimately familiar with the politics of service and the debate it had inspired: Frederick Douglass, William Wells Brown, Peter Clark, John Rock, George T. Downing, Robert Hamilton, Jermain Loguen, Henry Highland Garnet, Elisha Weaver, Alfred M. Green, Octavius Catto, Jacob C. White, George B. Vashon, and John Mercer Langston all attended.

In the convention's published address, the delegates acknowledged that "colored people [had] enlisted in the service of the country without any promise or stipulation that they would be rewarded with political equality at the end of the war." They also recognized that some might use this fact to argue against postwar change. Turning this logic around, the convention's representatives insisted that black men's decisions not to make their service contingent on the government's accession to their demands proved their patriotism: "The fact, that, when called into the service of the country, we went forward without exacting terms or conditions, to the mind of the generous man enhances our claims."[68] Now that widespread enlistment was a reality, African Americans on either side of the soldier-civilian divide recognized the need to use black service rhetorically to push for change. Only by a sustained multipronged effort would they win the gains they sought.

From the time large-scale black service began, black civilians linked it to their demands for immediate change. Black Philadelphians used this tactic in their campaign against railcar companies' practice of refusing black patrons service or forcing them to ride on their cars' outdoor platforms.[69] In July 1864, after he and his dying child were denied entry to a car on the Lombard and South Street line, the black Episcopal minister William Johnson Alston penned a public letter of protest that ran in white and black newspapers. He inquired pointedly, "[Is it] humane to exclude respectable colored citizens from your street cars when so many of our brave and vigorous young men have been and are enlisting to take part in this heavenly ordained slavery extermination, many of whom have performed commendable service in our army and navy—in the former of which your humble subscriber has two brawny-armed and battle-tried brothers?"[70]

A mass meeting held in Philadelphia's Sansom Street Hall asserted that black men were "responding earnestly to the call of the general Government for soldiers" and exhibiting "loyalty . . . beyond question." Those at the gathering also lamented the "anxiety, the apathy and indifference of . . . white citizens" to their campaign to change the policies of the city's railway companies.[71] In March 1865, Britton Lanier exploded in anger at a report that a railcar conductor had forced two black soldiers off a car's front platform. He said that "the bare recital" of this outrage on two wearing the "uniform of that Government which promises protection to the fullest extent to all who wear its uniform" was enough "to cause the blood of every colored man in the land to boil, as it were, in his veins."[72]

In their campaign for equal railcar rights, black Philadelphians adopted the same tactic black soldiers used in their protests over pay by highlighting the particularly appalling fact that wives and female relations of African American servicemen were denied entry to these conveyances. In April, J. O., a Philadelphia correspondent of the *Weekly Anglo-African* alleged that, "while husbands, brothers, and fathers [were] going forward, daily giving their lives to save the country from dismemberment and ruin, their wives, sisters, and old, white-haired, tottering mothers" were confined to the front platforms of the city's railcars. "How atrocious!" he exclaimed.[73] At the same Sansom Street Hall meeting referenced above, presiding officer John C. Bowers, who had played a leading political role in the Philadelphia black community for decades, proclaimed it little wonder that Northern arms struggled when "even old women, whose sons [were] at Camp Wm. Penn, [were] obliged to ride on the front platform" of the city's railcars. Later in the meeting, those assembled resolved, "In the sight of the present national struggle, no more shameful sight can be presented to an intelligent, sensitive mind, than that of respectable females standing upon the platform of empty cars, with sons, husbands, and brothers beside them in United States uniform."[74] That black civilians appropriated the trope of the wronged, vulnerable woman that black soldiers also employed says much about gender ideologies of the day, which involved a belief in female helplessness and the need for male protection. The reliance on this idea says that, like black soldiers, black men who did not enlist felt the insult to their wives, daughters, sisters, and mothers keenly. And it suggests that African American civilians were paying close attention to African American soldiers' rhetorical strategies, highlighting the extent to which soldiers and civilians were engaged in a single campaign for change.

Black noncombatants supported black soldiers and were determined to use their service to agitate for change. However, civilians knew that the inequalities black soldiers faced could undermine black service's potential to win the rights and citizenship for the race as a whole. Remembering Frederick

Douglass's example from the previous year, African Americans were willing, even as increasing numbers of black soldiers fought and died, to withdraw their support from the war effort and enlistment when Union policy toward black servicemen was too offensive to bear. During the summer of 1864, African American Northerners' anger over service inequalities flared, individually and collectively. In August, black Philadelphians passed a series of resolutions criticizing black soldiers' treatment, particularly the Union army's refusal to commission these men as officers. Alfred M. Green, now a sergeant major in the 127th USCT and a recruiter, read these resolutions aloud. They asserted that African Americans' loyal service "call[ed] for better treatment . . . from the Federal government," as well as, in the delegates' words, "just treatment at the hands of our fellow-citizens, whose proper places [in the army] are filled by our self-sacrificing brothers, fathers, husbands, and kindred."[75] The meeting's attendees did not withdraw their support for black service or the war effort, but their words represented a sharp rebuke, as well as a frank acknowledgment of the fact that white Northerners' desire to avoid service had greatly influenced the Union's adoption of black enlistment.

While Green and his fellows registered their dissent in measured terms, Philadelphia's William Forten raged in a private missive to Charles Sumner. Forten, son of the sailmaker and abolitionist James Forten, belonged to one of Philadelphia's most prominent black families and had long been active in various antislavery societies. He had helped resurrect the city's Vigilance Committee after the passage of the Fugitive Slave Law, fought for black suffrage, and supported black enlistment.[76]

Forten also mourned the recent death of his brother Robert. Robert Forten had been so disillusioned with the prospects for black equality that before the war he and his family had emigrated to England. The Emancipation Proclamation had convinced him to return, and he had joined the Forty-First USCT. He then contracted typhoid fever and died in April 1864. Writing to Sumner in June, William Forten lamented that his brother had died serving a government that refused to treat him as a citizen. "My God! Where, oh where is the justice?" he exclaimed. "Who Sir," he continued,

will give the true history of this war? The black-man, disowned—dishonored—disgraced and dehumanized, trampled in the dust for a long century now lifts his head and proudly walks into the front ranks of certain death unprotected, unregarded, in order that the country may have a Constitution, and his oppressors *liberty & law*, who in return for this exhibition of disinterested patriotism and bravery hurl him out from its benefits, and brand him a felon. Sir, very keen are my feelings on this subject at present as but a short time has elapsed since my hand was laid on the cold brow of my brother who came from the enjoyment of liberty equality & citizenship in England to do battle for their recognition in this his own native land.[77]

The Union's refusal to grant equality to African American troops left William Forten furious and disillusioned, his faith shaken. Moreover, the tragic irony of his brother's decision to forsake citizenship in England to fight for a government that continued to discriminate against black citizens weighed heavily on his mind and perhaps his conscience. But Forten had not given up on the idea of black enlistment, as he also asked Sumner for advice on securing a commission for a friend of his.

By mid-August, some black Bostonians *had* given up on black service. At a public meeting in Leonard Grimes's Twelfth Street Church, erstwhile recruiters William Wells Brown and John Rock withdrew their support for the Union war effort. Anger over the inequalities servicemen faced had been brewing in Boston for some time, as shown by the resolutions black residents passed the month before affirming that such disparities undermined black citizenship. After the meeting's first speaker, the Reverend H. H. White, defended his role in encouraging black enlistment, Brown emphatically repudiated his previous recruiting efforts. "At first I desired that colored men should go to the war," he admitted, but the "imbecile" Lincoln administration's policies and black soldiers' treatment had changed his mind. "Our people have been so cheated, robbed, deceived, and outraged everywhere, that I cannot urge them to go," he concluded.

Rock concurred: "I think we have just cause of complaint for our treatment at the hands of the government." He rehearsed African American soldiers' complaints over Union pay and promotion policies, and he lambasted abolitionists who thanked Lincoln for enlisting these troops:

If [black] enrollment meant equal chances and a fair fight, I should gladly accept it, but when it means to be drafted and forced to fight to defend and perpetuate a government which has always persecuted us, which promises nothing better now, and which still refuses to pay, to defend, to protect or retaliate for the outrages committed upon us while in its service! This requires a greater amount of patriotism than any one except a negro is expected to have. Is not the government carrying out the Dred Scott policy in refusing to retaliate and to pay us? If we are not to be treated as men now when in this hour of peril we have come forward and forgiven two centuries of outrage and oppression what reason have we to expect anything, or even if we should receive anything, how do we know that it may not be wr ested from us?

In his invocation of *Dred Scott*, Rock showed his concern that the inequality black troops faced reflected the fact that, Edward Bates notwithstanding, African Americans remained noncitizens.

After Rock concluded, Carteaux Bannister, a well-known hairdresser and female abolitionist, spoke. Two of her brothers were serving in the Union army, she said, but she hoped no more black men would enlist. Indeed, Bannister declared she would "rather beg from door to door than that her husband should go to the war." Robert Morris spoke last. The former militia captain had never warmed to volunteering, continuing to insist that black soldiers only serve under terms of absolute equality even as other prominent black Northerners abandoned this stance. Morris's observation of African American service had only confirmed his position. He would not prevent any black man from enlisting—"if any one chooses to make a fool of himself, he can do so"—but he would act otherwise. Morris also believed that the government's denial of equality to black soldiers suggested that the war would bring little change. "[Black people] have rights as well as the white people," he said, "and it looks to me as though they intend to use us and do not mean to do anything for us. If we are not careful, they will give us what they gave our fathers in the Revolution."[78]

This outburst of anger was likely inspired by more than simply service inequalities. The summer of 1864 saw a precipitous drop in Northern morale generally. Northerners witnessed unprecedented killing as Ulysses S. Grant and George Meade drove the Army of the Potomac against Robert E. Lee's troops in Virginia. As the spring offensives undertaken by the army in the East and William Tecumseh Sherman's force in the West stalled during the summer months, many began to wonder whether the Confederacy could be conquered at an acceptable cost.[79] Additionally, black Bostonians' anger seems to have been generated in part by white Northerners' tendency to blame African American troops for the disaster of the Battle of the Crater on July 30, as well as by Lincoln's seeming receptivity to Confederate offers for a negotiated peace, and his repeated insistence that his actions against slavery had been prompted only by necessity.[80]

Nevertheless, black Bostonians' anger, Alfred M. Green's disappointment, and William Forten's anguish demonstrated the effect service inequalities and home-front discrimination were having on black Northerners. African

Americans in the North knew that black men had enlisted without forcing the federal government to accede to terms. They had sacrificed short-term leverage for long-term gains, and they understood that they might get nothing. Rock's references to *Dred Scott* and colonization hinted at the torment and doubt that beset those whose relatives, friends, and neighbors were fighting the country's battles while being treated as second-class citizens. The anger black Northerners and their leaders manifested during the summer of 1864 mirrored Frederick Douglass's reaction to Lincoln's slowness to retaliate against Confederate POW policies the previous summer. This rage also reflected the desire to bring a new Union out of the war. In service of this goal, African Americans in the North remained willing to withdraw their support from the war effort if the terms under which black soldiers fought became inconsistent with their hope for a new America. Had black civilians continued to make the kind of statements Brown and Rock made at that Boston meeting, a rift might have developed between them and their military brethren. Many black soldiers would have looked unkindly on black leaders who withdrew their support from the war effort and enlistment, no matter their motivations.

Such a rift did not happen because by the time black Bostonians met in August, soldiers' and civilians' protests had begun to bear fruit. On June 14 Congress passed the Appropriations Act, equalizing the pay of all black soldiers, whether or not they had been promised equal pay upon their enlistment, retroactive to January 1, 1864. In deference to black Northern soldiers' claims that they had volunteered under the promise of equal wages, the law—when combined with Edward Bates's finding that black soldiers' pay should never have been determined by the 1862 Militia Act anyway—also allowed for black troops who could swear they had been free on April 19, 1861, to receive equal pay retroactive to the date of their enlistment. This act caused great celebration in the Massachusetts regiments that had spearheaded the protests against Union compensation policy, but it struck many as a half measure. In March 1865, Congress acted one final time, allowing the South Carolina regiments that had begun forming in August 1862 to receive full pay. Legislators also allowed Stanton to make case-by-case decisions on the wages due to black troops whose pay had not been equalized retroactive to their date of enlistment, such as those in the Kansas regiments. Most, though not all, black troops eventually received the equal wages for which they had clamored so loudly.[81]

In equalizing black soldiers' pay, Congress was influenced by abstract considerations of justice and by the principle advanced by these servicemen in their letters of protest: that the government's compensation rules violated their enlistment contracts. Whether or not Northern officials who had promised African American soldiers equal pay at their enlistment had been legally authorized to do so, argued Representative John F. Farnsworth of Illinois in May 1864, "if the promise was given, and [black men] enlisted and were mustered into the service with the expectation of the fulfillment of that promise, the Government [was] bound to fulfill the contract between the contract officers and these black men."[82] In February 1864, Massachusetts's Henry Wilson referred to the Massachusetts regiments' refusal to accept unequal wages, read a letter of protest from one of their white officers into the *Congressional Record*, and claimed to know "from different sources" that Northern black leaders who had supported black enlistment would withdraw their support if Union pay policy was not changed.[83]

As Herman Belz has observed, using contractual principles to justify equalizing black soldiers' pay did not imply that these men deserved additional wages because they were equal to their white counterparts. Nevertheless, that Congress accepted black soldiers' argument—even if they encountered it not from the servicemen themselves, but through white officers and black civilian leaders serving as intermediaries—counted as a signal victory for the cause of African American citizenship.[84] When the federal government fulfilled black troops' enlistment contracts by equalizing their pay, it began also to fulfill the larger contract integral to Edward Bates's conception of citizenship by providing protection from economic hardship to the soldiers who showed it allegiance.

Nor was this victory regarding the pay issue anomalous. During the war's final months, black Northerners rejoiced at a series of new laws and policy changes that suggested that the new Union they sought might be on the horizon. Black men began to gain entry to places previously reserved for whites only. In February 1865, John Rock became the first black lawyer to receive accreditation from the United States Supreme Court, and in the House of Representatives—which, along with the Senate, had only begun allowing black spectators in its gallery since the war's start—Henry Highland Garnet preached an impassioned sermon imploring the government to do justice to black soldiers.[85] That same month, Martin Delany received a commission. His appointment, when added to the handful of Kansas and Massachusetts soldiers who had already been commissioned lieutenants, took some of the sting out of Union promotion policy. Congress also legalized African Americans' testimony in federal courts, permitted African Americans to carry the federal mails, and desegregated streetcars in the nation's capital.[86]

Changes at the state level also bred optimism. Since the days of William H.

Newby, black Californians had sought to end their state's ban on black testimony, and in 1863 they succeeded. Black Illinoisans won a similar struggle to repeal their state's black laws in February 1865, and the campaigns for railcar desegregation in Philadelphia and other Northern cities began to attract support from Republican politicians and newspapers.[87] Moreover, slavery continued to crumble. Federal armies overran previously untouched portions of the South and liberated the slaves who came within their lines; Maryland, Missouri, Arkansas, Louisiana, and Tennessee abolished slavery; and in January 1865, Congress passed a new constitutional amendment abolishing slavery.[88] Despite the obstacles to legal equality that remained and their own recognition that military necessity had driven many positive wartime changes, African Americans could not help but see these developments as hopeful signs, perhaps preludes to more fundamental change.

Still, as Confederate resistance collapsed in early 1865, African Americans recognized that peace brought peril—a nation at peace might regress. It was imperative that they confirm black citizenship while the memory of black military service remained fresh. This impulse to strike quickly helped inspire the call for the Syracuse Convention in October 1864. This impulse also inspired that convention's delegates to form the National Equal Rights League (NERL) to give the fight for black rights an institutional basis.[89] In a public appeal for support, John Mercer Langston, the NERL's first president, detailed the organization's mission and the need for immediate action. "We know too well," he said, "by our bitter experience of wrong and degradation, how [black soldiers] were treated after [earlier American] wars. Wisdom, then, dictates that we should profit by this lesson." Langston further described black civilians' responsibility to black soldiers: "[We must] make every effort in our power to secure for ourselves and our Children all those rights, natural and political, which Belong to us as men and as native-born citizens of America . . . while the devotion, the gallantry, and the heroism displayed by our sons, brothers, and fathers at Port Hudson, Fort Wagner, Petersburg, and New Market Heights are fresh in the minds of the American people."[90] As George Vashon told an audience of black Pittsburghers in January 1865, "While the public sentiment is so favorable to us, delays are dangerous, and the present propitious moment should not be suffered to slip away unused."[91]

The recognition that a return to peace might endanger black citizenship was nothing novel. African Americans had enlisted without securing guarantees of change. Slavery appeared doomed and positive developments had occurred, but the possibility loomed that wider systemic changes might prove elusive. William Wells Brown delivered a stern warning regarding the dangers of peace to the New England Anti-Slavery Society in May 1864. "The colored man has everything yet to fear," he told his audience. "Even when Grant's army shall be successful, we, the colored people, will be yet in danger." Military necessity had played a large role in creating positive change. "The advantages that we have so far received," Brown recognized, "have come as much through Jeff. Davis as through President Lincoln."[92]

Frederick Douglass likewise grasped this danger. In a letter to a British abolitionist in September 1864 he worried that, after securing peace, the government would "hand the negro back to the political power of his master, without a single element of strength to shield himself from the vindictive spirit sure to be roused against the whole colored race."[93] When Douglass gathered with other black delegates in Syracuse the next month, the address they issued displayed anxiety about white Republican leaders' postwar commitment to black rights. In "surveying [African Americans'] possible future," they knew that their "cause [might] suffer even more from the injudicious concessions and weakness of our friends, than from the machinations and power of our enemies."[94]

Because African Americans knew that peace's return endangered their cause, news of Robert E. Lee's surrender on April 9 inspired both celebration and trepidation. "If we feel less disposed to join in the shouts of victory which fill the skies," wrote the *Weekly Anglo-African* just days afterward, "it is because with the cessation of war our anxieties begin." Would the government continue to support black citizenship? Would it grant black men suffrage? Would it ensure that slavery's death would result in meaningful freedom for ex-slaves? Only time would tell but, the *Anglo-African* warned, "Our fear is that the government will not be equal to its duty."[95]

The end of hostilities between North and South betokened an uncertain future for African Americans. The transformation the war had wrought inspired hope for further change. But black Northerners knew that the alterations they had already seen had been spurred only by Confederate rebellion. Once that rebellion ended, change might cease. While the war raged, black soldiers were indispensable to the Union, and federal and state officials' recognition of their contribution to the national survival helped propel reform. But policies that undermined African American citizenship had persisted. Although many black soldiers still had substantial time left to serve in their enlistments, the war's cessation changed the relationship between black soldiers and the nation. African American troops continued to serve, but they might no longer be seen as allies whose cooperation was vital to the United States' survival.

As Confederate armies laid down their arms in the spring of 1865, slavery lived. The hated institution only died with the Thirteenth Amendment's ratification that December. Discriminatory laws and practices lived too, still pervasive in the North and South. Moreover, the Constitution did not include a definition of citizenship that counted black men and women as Americans. And Abraham Lincoln lay slain at the hand of an assassin, the actor John Wilkes Booth. Booth had long planned to murder the president, but he had been inspired to follow through by Lincoln's speech of April 11, 1865. As he stood outside the White House among an otherwise jubilant crowd, Booth listened as Lincoln endorsed black suffrage, at least for the "very intelligent" and soldiers. "That means nigger citizenship," the assassin growled. "That is the last speech he will ever make."[96] Booth's murderous rage at the president's moderate call for limited black suffrage prefigured many whites' reactions to African Americans' postwar campaign for rights, equality, and citizenship.

Despite their determination to make black service in the Civil War count in a way that black service in earlier wars had not, black Northerners knew that black soldiers might again suffer betrayal. It remained to be seen what black citizenship meant practically, and if it entailed any new rights, privileges, or immunities. Watching the war's end in Charleston, the AME minister James Lynch recognized rightly that black Americans' "status [was] not yet fixed." Only time would tell whether "that citizenship given us to make us liable to the draft, will ripen into that which will give us the ballot box and make us liable to the legislative seat or Gubernatorial chair."[97]

5

MAKING BLACK SERVICE MATTER

1865–1883

I N THE SUMMER OF 1865 Henry McNeal Turner lamented the nation's slowness to reward black military service. "Theoretical . . . freedom has been secured," he conceded, but "practical [freedom]" still eluded African Americans. The nation owed black soldiers a great debt, and he demanded change in their name. "The dying groans and crimson gore of ten thousand colored heroes," he wrote, "ask in tones of thunder for their children's rights, at the hands of the same nation, and better that she drink hemlock and bitter gall than prove treacherous to their demands."[1] Black men had fought and died to bring forth a nation that would live up to American founding ideals. For Turner, it was better for the nation to perish than to fall short of fulfilling this aspiration.

Despite Turner's fear that the United States would forsake its black soldiers, less than five years later, the minister could declare that African Americans' demands had been met and that the struggle over slavery and black rights that had divided the nation for so long was finished. Much had changed since the summer of 1865: by 1870 slavery was abolished and Congress had confirmed black citizenship, passed equal-rights legislation, imposed military rule on the unrepentant South, and forced Southern states to enfranchise black men. The March 1870 ratification of the Fifteenth Amendment, which forbade states from using race or color as suffrage qualifications, inspired Turner to proclaim that the "drama of national purity and excellence [was] fast reaching its zenith and culminating in the climax of fadeless glories." He believed the nation had been changed fundamentally, calling the amendment's ratification the "finish of our national fabric . . . the crowning event of the nineteenth century; the brightest glare of glory that ever hung on land or sea."[2]

Turner believed the long fight against slavery and discrimination was over, but during the 1870s and 1880s Reconstruction's achievements unraveled. A key blow to Republicans' Reconstruction program came when the Supreme

Court invalidated congressional civil rights legislation in the 1883 *Civil Rights Cases*. The Court ruled that the citizenship encoded in the Fourteenth Amendment did not authorize Congress to prevent private owners of public accommodations from discriminating on the basis of color.

In 1863, Turner had been instrumental in convincing black Washingtonians to enlist in the U.S. Army; the organization of the First USCT had begun in his own church.[3] Now, in an irate missive to the *Memphis Appeal*, Turner insisted that the court's decision "absolve[d] the allegiance of the negro to the United States." The black man who would enlist and fight for the United States, he said, "ought to be hung by the neck." "As long as that decision is the law of the land," he declared defiantly, "I am a rebel to this nation."[4] The Supreme Court's ruling, combined with other legislative and judicial setbacks, Southern violence, and the personal frustrations Turner experienced in Reconstruction-era Georgia, had by the 1880s convinced him that some African Americans ought to emigrate to Africa, where they could escape violence and discrimination and Christianize the continent.[5] As the clergyman embraced emigration, a doctrine many black leaders had abandoned during the Civil War, he came to see the United States as a "failure" with "no disposition to protect the rights of a man who is not white." The Supreme Court had "decitizened the Negro" in 1883, and all African Americans could expect was "perpetual degradation or ultimate re-enslavement."[6]

Turner's evolving views did not necessarily typify African Americans' reactions to Reconstruction and its failures in its conclusion. The minister's thinking, though, was emblematic of the hopes and fears blacks shared as they entered the postwar world, the elation they felt as it seemed their goals had been achieved, and the anguish they experienced as they saw Reconstruction undone.[7] Despite the differences in birth, status, and class that divided them, African Americans emerged from the war united in purpose and determined to remake the nation. In service of this goal, from the summer of 1865 forward they once again adapted the politics of service to fit new circumstances. African Americans appealed to their military service as justification for government recognition of black rights and citizenship to ensure that, this time, white Americans did right by the nation's black warriors. Black Northerners, joined by black Southerners afforded the chance to discuss political issues publicly by slavery's death, continued to insist that the United States harmonize its laws with its founding principles.

In the war's aftermath, African Americans pushed for a meaningful citizenship that conferred on them the same rights and privileges white citizens enjoyed. Edward Bates's opinion had been an important victory for black citizenship, but African Americans knew they would need new laws that confirmed their status and expanded civil liberties and freedoms. Black men had willingly enlisted and fought to save the nation despite the discrimination African Americans continued to face while they did so, and this fact was key to the arguments black leaders made as they pushed for change.

No consideration of the postwar struggle for black rights is complete without an exploration of the connection between wartime service and postwar agitation. As they considered what achieving a full degree of citizenship meant, African Americans overwhelmingly identified it with black male suffrage and legal equality; without these things, they contended, citizenship counted for little. To realize their goals, they organized on the local, state, and national levels, held conventions, signed petitions, wrote letters, and lobbied public figures. Black veterans figured prominently in this activity, participating in state- and national-level political campaigns and occasionally organizing veterans' conventions to agitate collectively on the basis of their service. Using black military service as a key rhetorical touchstone, black activists, veterans and nonveterans alike, played a key role in forcing federal officials and white politicians to devise a constitutional definition of American citizenship and specifically define black men and women as Americans.

African Americans entered the postwar period with lofty aspirations for themselves and their nation, and they embarked on a determined campaign to win a meaningful citizenship that would allow black and white Americans to live together as equals. "The reconstruction of this Union is a broader, deeper work, than the restoration of the Rebel States," wrote Henry Carpenter Hoyle, a veteran of the Forty-Third USCT, in 1867. "It is the lifting up of the entire nation into the practical realization of our republican idea."[8] In this project, African Americans were successful in legal terms. Congressional Republicans passed legislation codifying many of the changes they demanded as the price of black service. As African Americans embarked on this ambitious crusade, they did so not as constitutional scholars familiar with modern understandings of citizenship, but as would-be citizens in a nation in which citizenship had existed as a vexed, unstable concept equated with membership in the military.[9] They trusted in the founding principles they had always proclaimed as their own, the example of their meritorious service, and their powers of persuasive rhetoric to wrest black citizenship from unwilling whites. In spite of Reconstruction's failures, their postwar successes laid the legal groundwork for future generations to claim the rights, privileges, and immunities that nineteenth-century African Americans identified with meaningful citizenship.

AS CONFEDERATE ARMIES surrendered in the spring of 1865, the question of the United States' postwar shape took on new urgency. African Americans knew that the Confederacy's defeat and slavery's death were momentous events by themselves, but when, in the words of AME minister Thomas Strother, they celebrated the nation's birthday "in a becoming manner, for the first time in eighty-nine years," they looked forward to further changes.[10] "A.," a correspondent of the *Christian Recorder*, attended a Fourth of July celebration in Washington, D.C., at which John F. Cook Jr.—to whom Lincoln had recommended black colonization in August 1862—read the Declaration of Independence and various speakers advocated universal suffrage. "A." left the gathering enthused yet unsatisfied, remarking, "[I hope the day is] not far distant when every man will stand equal before the law, and every right given him which is due to a free and enlightened American citizen."[11]

That African Americans gathered to mark the national birthday, abandoning their common antebellum tactic of holding counter–July Fourth gatherings, showed how much the war had changed. But African Americans were not satisfied with the change they had already seen. James H. Payne, quartermaster sergeant of the Twenty-Seventh USCT, reported that his regiment spent the Fourth in prayer. Payne's comrades wanted more than abolition, entreating the Almighty, "Grant us and all of our race a 4th of July in this country when we would be able to dwell under the bright and genial rays of universal liberty, enjoying the right of suffrage, and the rights and immunities accorded to others."[12] While they knew that peace might bring danger, many African Americans approached the postwar period confident that black service would receive its proper reward.

African Americans remained determined to wrest more than freedom from the federal government. Michael Vorenberg has noted that black activists took relatively little interest in the Thirteenth Amendment's passage through Congress. African Americans supported and celebrated the amendment, but they sought "forms of empowerment more immediate and tangible" than abolition: land ownership, legal equality, and suffrage.[13] By the spring of 1865, abolition's progress, combined with tangible evidence of slavery's destruction in many parts of the South, convinced numerous black Northerners that slavery was all but dead. At the Pennsylvania State Equal Rights League's February 1865 convention, Alfred M. Green announced that he would no longer ask black men to enlist to free the slaves, but would "[invite] [them] to the field" to secure suffrage and "equal rights and privileges" for their race. The convention's published address affirmed this stance, stating flatly, "Colored men are no longer fighting for the freedom of the slaves in the South." Black men *were*, however, asking, "What is our reward for [fighting?]." They were also demanding suffrage and government recognition of black rights and interests.[14]

African Americans knew they needed to strike while the crisis of the war remained fresh in the public mind. The slaveholders' rebellion had represented the greatest threat to the nation's existence since its birth, and as Frederick Douglass told the Massachusetts Anti-Slavery Society, the war's "chastisement" had almost brought the nation up to the point of enacting black suffrage. He warned that if black Americans failed to press their cause home, "centuries" might pass before they saw again "the same disposition that [existed] at this moment."[15] Black leaders had told black Northerners during the war that it was "now or never," imploring them to enlist immediately or lose forever their chance to win black rights and citizenship. The same dynamic applied as African Americans sought in the postwar period to translate their military service into legal change.[16]

Some white abolitionists, including William Lloyd Garrison, thought black rights were a question to be worked out gradually, but African Americans insisted on citizenship and rights immediately.[17] Black commentators, veterans and nonveterans both, joined Corporal William Gibson of the Twenty-Eighth USCT in asking whether the nation would prove willing "to pay the laborer for his hire." "It is to be seen in all past history," Gibson wrote in May 1865, "that when men fought for their country, and returned home, they always enjoyed all the rights and privileges due to other citizens. We ask to be made equal before the law; grant us this, and we ask no more."[18] In asserting that citizenship *always* followed service, Gibson was incorrect, as the history of black service in earlier American wars proved; Gibson elided the nation's history of failing to reward black veterans, hoping that this time would be different, and that confident assertions of the nation's duty to black veterans would achieve the desired result.

African Americans' postwar demands for citizenship proved that they were not satisfied by Edward Bates's opinion; it lacked the force of legislative or judicial decree and had conferred no rights. African Americans had changed citizenship already, but they sought more. They knew, as F. H. Sawyer told the black-run *New Orleans Tribune* in November 1865, that the attorney general's version of American citizenship "[would] mean nothing" since, within its terms, "each and every State in the Union [could] deprive such of every right that makes citizenship valuable."[19] Black soldiers had fought Union pay policy to establish their inclusion within Bates's relationship of protection and allegiance; with the fighting over, African Americans demanded a more meaningful citizenship than Bates had described, a citizenship under which they were guaranteed the same rights and privileges as whites. They did not, however, demand an end to a version of citizenship that doled out rights, privileges, and immunities to different groups of citizens based on factors like ascriptive identity and community standing. In effect, African Americans argued that their ascriptive identity as black Americans should no longer deprive them of citizenship, that by donning the nation's uniform black men had proved themselves solid community members deserving of *all* the rights, privileges, and immunities associated with being an American.

In pushing for this more meaningful version of citizenship, African Americans did not develop a single concrete definition of the status they sought, but they overwhelmingly identified suffrage and legal equality as its key components. African Americans insisted that they would be citizens when they were no longer subject to discriminatory legislation and when black men could vote—if not universally, then at least under a set of qualifications applied equally to black and white males.[20] In July 1865, the *Christian Recorder* expressed this view, stating that black men needed to push for the "right of suffrage and equality before the law" while "the great revolution of public opinion . . . [was] still in motion." When the United States gave African Americans the vote and legal equality, they would then enjoy "the rights and privileges of full citizens of the country for which [they] fought, bled and died."[21] When the NERL convened in Cleveland in October 1865, delegates connected citizenship with suffrage and legal equality, and William Forten proclaimed these goals the organization's "much desired end." To make clear their interpretation of the phrase "equality before the law," the delegates proposed an equal-rights amendment to the Constitution that would have barred legislation "against any civilized portion of the inhabitants . . . on account of race or color" and voided any such existing laws as "anti-republican in character."[22]

Undoubtedly African Americans *associated* suffrage and equality before the law with citizenship, but in describing the exact relationship of suffrage and legal equality to citizenship their rhetoric was a bit fuzzy. Sometimes they depicted these rights as inherent to citizenship, and sometimes they described them as rights that some citizens might possess and others might not. Some black commentators saw certain rights as inherent to citizenship and held that, as long as individuals lacked these rights, they lacked citizenship. In May 1865, a black political meeting in New Orleans declared the right of suffrage "inherent to citizenship, in a true republican Government," and later that year San Francisco's *Elevator* included the rights to vote, testify in court, and hold office among a list of the "privileges annexed" to citizenship.[23] Denver's W. P. Allen insisted that black citizenship did not truly exist while black men remained disenfranchised. Allen bitterly complained that although African American males had loyally served the United States, the government had not yet enacted black suffrage and thus continued to deny these servicemen the "right of citizenship."[24] Statements like Allen's envisioned citizenship as a universal status implying certain inherent rights for all its holders—a strikingly modern vision.

In other instances, African Americans spoke of suffrage and legal equality as rights enjoyed by "full citizens," a term that carried different and potentially problematic implications. In February 1865, Frances Ellen Watkins Harper demanded that the government "clothe" African Americans "with all the rights . . . necessary to a complete citizenship."[25] When newly enfranchised black Washingtonians voted in a local election in the summer of 1867, a triumphant James A. Handy described their "elat[ion]" at "exercising for the first time the right belonging to full and complete citizenship."[26] Implicitly, in talking of the rights necessary to "complete" or "full" citizenship, Harper and Handy suggested that other levels of citizenship existed under which persons might enjoy only *some* of the rights available to full citizens and yet remain citizens. It seems likely that few at the time sensed a meaningful distinction between this position and the more modern understanding of citizenship described above. Speakers who depicted the rights they desired as inherent in citizenship and those who sought "full" citizenship were, in practical terms, trying to secure the same legal gains. With hindsight, though, the tension between these positions is evident. Black Americans knew they wanted citizenship, and they agreed about which legal rights they wanted to achieve, but their rhetoric was a bit inconsistent when they described these rights' relationship to citizenship.

Following the Confederacy's defeat, citizenship remained a concept in flux with no concrete constitutional definition, and African Americans' thinking about that status reflected its uncertainty. Edward Bates had confirmed the principle of birthright citizenship but had not identified any political or civic rights and privileges as inherent to it. He had also explicitly stated that persons might lack key rights, like the vote, and remain citizens. In this atmosphere, it likely seemed unclear which entitlements inhered in citizenship and which did not, and African Americans likely found questions involving the inherent and noninherent rights of citizens beside the point. It was enough to know that they would not enjoy meaningful citizenship until they could influence state and federal policymaking through their votes and enjoy legal equality. Crafting arguments capable of inspiring white lawmakers to enact black suffrage and equality was more important than devising a comprehensive conceptual understanding of citizenship. African Americans were not, as an 1869 *New Orleans Tribune* headline declared, "theorists" familiar with modern scholarly debates about citizenship; they argued for citizenship as members of a community long denied rights they had watched others enjoy, and they cared far more about making compelling arguments than about developing an exact consensus regarding what it meant to be an American citizen.[27] African Americans' widespread agreement that winning suffrage and legal equality would bring them closer to meaningful citizenship formed a sufficient basis for agitation.

To win that meaningful citizenship, African Americans North and South threw themselves into political action, seeking to exert as much influence as a largely disenfranchised group could on state and national legislators. Many worked under the auspices of the NERL and its network of local and state auxiliaries. Black delegates met in statewide and national conventions, drawing on the network of civil-society organizations that had long supported African American protest. As most black men and all black women lacked the vote, much of their political activity was rhetorical in nature, but African Americans also petitioned Congress and other government bodies, met and corresponded with high-level public officials, and held parades and other public celebrations in support of black rights.[28] In the South, recent ex-slaves convened to demand rights and citizenship, channeling their political activity through the kinship, church, and community networks they had developed while enslaved. As black Southerners gained the franchise and participated in formal political processes, they agitated for further change through local Union Leagues and the Republican Party.[29]

In public statements and private communications, black leaders North and South cited black service as a central justification for the changes they demanded, adapting the politics of service to the demands of the postwar period. Appealing to black soldiers' service was central to black leaders' strategy of, in Charles Lenox Remond's words, "sham[ing] ... the ruling power ... into doing them justice."[30] Within days of Lee's surrender, black North Carolinians asked Charles Sumner for the vote on the basis of their service. "Many of us have done service for the U.S. Government, at Ft. Fisher, elsewhere, & we shrink with horror at the thought that we may be left to the tender mercies of our former rebel masters," they wrote, further noting that "the *franchise* alone [could] give [them] security for the future."[31] Looking to turn the galling inequalities under which black troops had served to their advantage, African

Americans cited the pay discrepancy and other indignities to enhance these troops' claims to justice; black men had enlisted under especially disadvantageous circumstances and were especially worthy of reward. The Pennsylvania State Equal Rights League reminded the nation that African American soldiers had fought "without the incentive of large bounties, full pay, or promotion" and had under these trying circumstances "contributed [their] full share towards saving the flag and the Union."[32] At Boston's March 5, 1865, Crispus Attucks Day celebration, John Mercer Langston tied his argument for suffrage and legal equality to the fact that black troops "volunteered under circumstances highly creditable to them, and went to the ranks, where 90 per cent of men would have returned to peaceful homes under the circumstances."[33] Humiliating service inequalities had taxed black military families to the breaking point, but black leaders realized that citing these injustices might shame whites into acceding to black demands.

Black veterans played prominent roles in black political campaigns, attending postwar conventions across the United States and occasionally organizing conventions to urge the government to repay them for their sacrifices. As early as November 1865, a convention of African American soldiers from Iowa proclaimed it the state's duty to enact black suffrage, arguing, "He who is worthy to be trusted with the musket can and ought to be trusted with the ballot."[34] The following year, to give "organizational force to [their] moral authority," black veterans inaugurated a national convention movement. Their call to convene invited all to attend who believed "that they ha[d] not received from the Government a due recognition of their services, rendered her in the hour of need, and that in sustaining the Union with the musket, they have won their right to the ballot."[35]

At the Colored Soldiers' and Sailors' Convention that resulted, held in Philadelphia in January 1867, black veterans echoed their wartime demands. They called for "equality of rights with the white soldiers who [had] also fought against the armed traitors to the American flag." Delegates from across the country listened approvingly as speakers demanded suffrage and legal equality or, as Sergeant A. Ward Handy termed them, "all the rights of American-born citizens." Numerous black leaders who had not served in the armed forces participated, including Henry Highland Garnet, William H. Day, Jermain Loguen, George B. Vashon, William Forten, Elisha Weaver, and Octavius Catto. These figures' attendance signified their recognition that the politics of service remained salient, and that black veteranhood, the ability of hundreds of thousands of black men to portray themselves as saviors of the Union, rated as one of the most valuable political weapons in their arsenal.[36]

African Americans' service had increased their political leverage, but it had not changed their agitation's ultimate goal. In the postwar years, African Americans still sought to bring the nation into conformity with its founding principles, linking rewards for black military contributions with the Declaration of Independence's equality clause.[37] In October 1865, black Indianans declared that black soldiers had "fought, bled and died" to secure the rights the Declaration of Independence identified as "inalienable."[38] The next month, African Americans gathering outside the capitol building in Harrisburg, Pennsylvania, to honor returning black veterans affirmed that these men had fought for "the truths enunciated in the Declaration of Independence." Those in the crowd also decried all "distinctions based on race or color."[39] For decades, African Americans had seen the founding American text as the blueprint for the change they wanted to create, and they had envisioned their participation in the Union war effort as part of the struggle to bring American reality into line with American principles. After the war they continued to anchor their political agitation on the Declaration of Independence.

Black activists did make some arguments not directly related to military service. Some pointed out that African American men had voted and enjoyed numerous rights under colonial and state governments in earlier periods of American history; in recognizing black citizenship the nation would merely be restoring to its black citizens the rights it had unjustly taken from them. The New Orleans Tribune observed that "colored citizens" had voted under the Articles of Confederation, and that no provision of the Constitution barred black voting. In demanding suffrage, the sheet claimed, African Americans only asked the United States to return to its earlier practices and honor its founding principles.[40]

Some black commentators argued pragmatically that, no matter how uncomfortable black suffrage made white Northerners, only African American votes could counter the electoral might of disloyal rebels returning home and regaining the franchise. "The condition of the South, and of the country," argued Frederick Douglass in early 1865, required black voting, as "the rank undergrowth of treason" would survive Confederate defeat, and only black voters could "counterbalance this spirit."[41] As a committee of Norfolk black leaders pointed out, slavery's death voided the Three-Fifths Compromise, meaning increased congressional representation for voters of doubtful loyalty if African American men remained disenfranchised. Under these circumstances, John Mercer Langston predicted in October 1865, "As military necessity brought us emancipation and arms, political necessity may yet bring us enfranchisement and the ballot."[42]

Despite Langston's confidence and the exertions of black leaders North and South, whites did little to expand black rights and citizenship. In the North and West, between 1865 and 1869, only Wisconsin, Iowa, and Minnesota legalized black voting. Voters in Connecticut, Ohio, Kansas, Michigan, and New York defeated black suffrage, and white Republicans in other states kept the issue from coming to a vote.[43] Matters stood even worse in the former Confederacy. As Elizabeth Varon has shown, many white Southerners saw in the terms offered by Ulysses S. Grant at Appomattox a sign that they would be allowed to control their states' restoration to the Union. Even in slavery's death, they would reclaim as much as possible of the antebellum Southern social order, "an imagined era of racial order and deference" in which whites monopolized political power and "recognized the incapacity of blacks for citizenship." Although the myth of Lee's surrender as a moment of healing has proved persistent, in reality, even in the hour of defeat many white Southerners remained unrepentant, bristling at the idea of federal interference in Southern society despite the war's verdict of federal supremacy.[44]

Moreover, as 1865 progressed, white Southerners found an ally in newly elevated president Andrew Johnson, whose harsh rhetoric quickly turned to conciliation. By the fall of 1865 Johnson was pardoning former Confederate leaders "wholesale"; his lenience encouraged white Southerners to defy federal authority, pass Black Codes that limited black economic freedom and mobility, and oppose black suffrage.[45] South Carolina governor Benjamin Franklin Perry issued a reminder to Northern Republicans advocating black suffrage: "This is a white man's government, and intended for white men only, and . . . the Supreme Court of the United States has decided that the negro is not an American citizen under the Federal Constitution."[46] Perry's reference to *Dred Scott* as binding precedent shows why, in the summer of 1865, black suffrage and legal equality seemed to many African Americans as far away as ever.

As early as that summer some feared that history had repeated itself and the government had forsaken black soldiers. On July 4, 1865, William Wells Brown told an antislavery gathering in Framingham, Massachusetts, that he "feared the rebellion ha[d] closed too soon," that African Americans were "to be cheated out of what [they had] been promised, what the brave men [had] been fighting for." White Southerners were enacting a new form of slavery, black suffrage was impossible, and the nation "ha[d] broken faith with the black man."[47] Writing to the *Anglo-African Magazine* in September 1865—the weekly New York newspaper had changed its name and format that spring— an A. Atwood recounted how black soldiers had "cheerfully obeyed" when called as citizens to fight during earlier American wars, then had watched their citizenship "[ooze] out, when the storm subsided." Atwood saw the same dynamic at work in the Civil War's aftermath, and he predicted that peace would not come until the nation did justice to its African American population.[48] Black anger burst forth at the NERL's 1865 Cleveland convention as well. "We have been deserted by those we faithfully supported," thundered William Forten, "and insolently informed that this is a white man's country, though it required the strong arms of over 200,000 black men to save it, *and that the elective franchise is not now a practical question.*"[49]

In blasting the betrayal they saw occurring before their eyes, black agitators drew on the contractual arguments soldiers had made during the war. Just as African American servicemen had insisted that the government honor their enlistment contracts, African American leaders spoke in contractual terms when they implored the government to recognize black citizenship. At the Cleveland convention, Forten and the other delegates—including former black recruiters like Alfred M. Green and John Mercer Langston—affirmed their determination to "agitate, entreat, and demand in the name of *justice, humanity*, and *truth*, the fulfillment of the nation's pledges made to [African Americans] in her darkest hours of trial, when bankruptcy, ruin, and dissolution were rushing madly upon her."[50] The same month, a convention of black Arkansans demanded "*bona fide* citizen[ship]," which they associated with "equality before the law and the right of suffrage." The federal government, Arkansas's William H. Gray reminded his listeners, had "pledged" itself to secure these rights, writing "the contract in blood, when [the nation's] own children stood ready to destroy her."[51] African Americans' continued use of contractual principles displayed both their faith in the sanctity of contract as a bedrock principle of a free-labor economy and their recognition that the political positions black soldiers took during the war remained relevant in its aftermath.

African Americans might of course have accepted that the changes they sought would take time; their refusal to countenance even temporary denial of rights underlined their determination to make black service count. White abolitionists, recruiters, and officers had frequently insisted that African Americans' enlistment would bring new rights, but black Northerners had extracted no positive pledge for passage of specific legislation from either President Lincoln or Congress in return for black military service. Although Andrew Johnson in 1865 recognized Southern state governments that continued African American disenfranchisement, he also publicly acknowledged the possibility that states might enfranchise black voters as they saw fit. Johnson knew it was unlikely that any state would do so voluntarily; but had African Americans been at all disposed to accept gradual change, statements like

Johnson's might have soothed their postwar anger.[52] Black Americans might have been appeased by vague promises of progress and accepted that change would come eventually. They might have decided that, given how fundamentally emancipation changed American life, they ought to hold off on pushing for additional *immediate* changes and trust in their ability to gradually win new rights.

But African Americans would not be sated by emancipation and vague suggestions of further change; heeding the lessons of the past, they demanded instant, sweeping reform. The immediacy of their demands flowed from the reality that, as Stephen Kantrowitz has noted, black Northerners' struggle against slavery had never aimed solely to end chattel bondage. These African Americans had always wanted to abolish the hated institution as part of a larger project of winning rights and citizenship. With slavery dead, Northern blacks who had cut their activist teeth during the late antebellum period remained true to that project.[53]

Most African Americans only countenanced political agitation, but a few insisted that they would have their rights even if they had to resort to arms to get them. Speaking for an 1865 convention of black Virginians, Henry Highland Garnet, Joseph T. Wilson, and others hinted at violence when they informed white Virginians of a threat to their "perfect security"—"the existence of a colored population of four millions and a half, placed, by your enactments, outside the pale of the Constitution, discontented by oppression, with an army of 200,000 colored soldiers, whom you have drilled, disciplined, and armed, but whose attachment to the State you have failed to secure by refusing them citizenship."[54]

Seeing that the Black Codes were an attempt to revive slavery under a new guise, African American leaders insisted that black men would fight before they would submit. In October 1865, the *Anglo-African Magazine* invoked the horrors of the Haitian Revolution and the emotionally charged issue of Civil War prison camps to describe the black response to an attempt to reinstitute slavery: "If you want to see a bloody time, if you wish to witness horrors compared with which even Andersonville was a Quaker meeting—then try to reduce back to slavery the four millions of our brethren!"[55] Even Alfred M. Green—on the eve of the Colored Soldiers' and Sailors' Convention in January 1867, no less—suggested publicly and apparently seriously that African American men might not accept the government's denial of their rights peacefully. Of the upcoming convention, Green said that he and his fellow black veterans desired "if possible, to peaceably secure [their] right to be treated as men." At the same time, he declared, "[We stand ready to] avail ourselves of such other means as will secure the end or prove us worthy of it, though we fail in its attainment."[56]

Black men who threatened violence believed that their wartime service had given them the moral capital to make inflammatory public statements. Only four years earlier, white Northerners were so offended by the idea of arming African American men that they had refused their assistance in putting down a massive internal rebellion; events would subsequently prove that armed displays of force by black men could in the war's aftermath provoke furious white responses. In this atmosphere, threats of black violence were particularly bold, even if they appeared in black newspapers unlikely to fall into the hands of the white Southerners who would be most horrified by them. That black men risked making these kinds of statements likely stemmed from their belief that their contribution to Union victory had afforded them new rhetorical latitude. The government's failure to quickly reward black service infuriated and discouraged African Americans, and these remarks represented some of the most extreme manifestations of black anger in the early postwar period.

Discouraged though they were, African Americans had developed astute political instincts through their decades of agitation, and they displayed a sophisticated sense of Reconstruction's political dynamics. They saw that they could reap long-term benefits from Johnson's lenience and white Southerners' intransigence. Just as, early in the Civil War, the United States' limited efforts to subdue the Confederacy had prepared white Northerners to accept emancipation, African Americans saw that the reactionary course the president and Southern political leaders steered might provoke Northerners to adopt a more robust approach to Reconstruction. As early as August 1865, the Pennsylvania State Equal Rights League had concluded, "The insane rage that blinds the Southern people, and prompts them to persecute and maltreat the freedmen ... will work its own cure." The state league's annual meeting expressed the following hope for the Southern states: "[They will go] from bad to worse in their mad career, till the United States Government is compelled with its strong arm, to place the franchise in the hands of her loyal black sons, who will with the ballot save the South, as they have with the musket saved the Union."[57]

In May 1866, the *Christian Recorder* speculated on the effect Johnson's "unexpected policy" could have on African Americans: "[It might] be just as necessary to the great work of our enfranchisement in this country as were the defeats sustained by McClellan to the employment of colored soldiers and the recognition of our citizenship."[58] By October, the *New Orleans Tribune* confidently predicted that the "folly of the Southern oligarchy" would again provoke more radical change than most white Northerners would initially accept. The paper urged its readers, "Let the rebels do our work."[59] African Americans used their wartime experience to evaluate the evolving American political landscape. To help them navigate the postwar period, they drew on the confidence they gained through military service, and on the ability to interpret intersectional political dynamics they had honed during the war.

Black Americans were correct that short-term setbacks would bring long-term gains. Many moderate Republicans initially opposed to black suffrage and a progressive Reconstruction policy joined Radical Republicans in remaking Southern society and protecting black rights. By the end of 1866, Johnson's lenient policies, the Black Codes, the ease with which former rebels came to dominate Southern politics, and racist violence in New Orleans and Memphis that targeted black veterans convinced many moderates to support fundamental change.

During the late 1860s, congressional Republicans codified many of the changes African Americans demanded as rewards for black troops' service. In 1866, Congress passed first a civil rights act recognizing black citizenship and then a new amendment—ratified in 1868—that codified national birth-right citizenship, guaranteed Americans the equal protection of the law, and forbade states from abridging citizens' privileges and immunities. In March 1867 Congress required Southern states to write new state constitutions enfranchising African American men. Finally, in 1869 Congress passed the Fifteenth Amendment. The measure prevented states from abridging suffrage on the basis of race, color, or previous condition, and it became law the following year.[60] African Americans reacted jubilantly to this legislative revolution: at an 1870 celebration in Portland, Oregon, commemorating the amendment's ratification, Joseph Beatty called the amendment the "last spike in the construction of true liberty in America," and the meeting's attendees resolved that the government's "extension . . . [of] the privileges of citizenship" left them "duty bound to conform to all the laws of the land."[61]

In pushing this landmark legislation through Congress—key pieces of what Rogers M. Smith has called "the most extensive restructuring of American citizenship laws in the nation's history, apart from the adoption of the Constitution itself"—Civil War–era African Americans fundamentally changed United States citizenship. By appealing to black military service, they forced white Republicans to embrace their vision of enacting the Declaration of Independence's equality clause and defining black men and women as citizens.[62] Xi

Wang has identified the "idea of equality as pronounced by the Declaration of Independence [as] the main ideological source for Reconstruction politics."[63] In their efforts to enact the Declaration's equality, white Republicans often appealed to the need to reward black service. In January 1865, Pennsylvania's William D. Kelley lectured the House of Representatives on rewarding African Americans' military contributions with manhood suffrage, asking that the "brave man who [had] periled his life, and mayhap lost his limb . . . in defense of our Constitution and laws" be given the "protection" suffrage afforded.[64]

Congressional Republicans appealed to black service while moving the Fifteenth Amendment through Congress and into the 1870s as they continued to push for civil rights legislation. In 1874, Benjamin Butler, now a Massachusetts representative, told his colleagues that his experience leading black troops had changed his attitude toward black rights. He recalled how, in late September 1864, African American men under his command had assaulted a Confederate redoubt near New Market Heights and fought valiantly despite the "very fire of hell" the Southern troops "pour[ed] upon them." During the course of the assault, 543 black troops fell, and Butler remembered looking on their "bronzed faces, upturned in the shining sun to heaven as a mute appeal against the wrongs [of] that country for which they had given their lives." In that moment, he said, he swore an oath to defend their rights, declaring himself "with them against all comers" until they had secured legal equality.[65] Arguments like Butler's helped spur Congress to pass in 1875 a new civil rights bill that, though shorn of a dearly sought provision that would have outlawed school segregation, banned discrimination in a range of public places and accommodations. Into the early 1890s, Republican congressmen like Henry Cabot Lodge used black service rhetorically when pushing for legislation to protect black voters in the South.[66]

We might dismiss the ever-opportunistic Butler's words as rhetorical bombast, and it is likely that some Republicans who argued for rewarding black service did so not out of sincere conviction but simply because they sensed they had a winning argument. It is impossible to know how much moral conviction motivated white Republicans versus how much they were influenced by political pragmatism. They knew that by enfranchising millions of black Southerners they would create a new voting bloc that would in all likelihood increase their electoral might. A mix of principle and pragmatism always lay at the heart of Republicans' postwar push for legislation recognizing African American rights and citizenship. And, in truth, attempting to discern which concern motivated Republicans more misses the point.[67] Whatever their motivations, the changes Republicans enacted brought American law into greater harmony with the Declaration of Independence than ever before. As such, one must rate African Americans' Civil War–era campaign to use black service to win black citizenship a qualified success.

The black recruiters who in 1863 urged black Northerners to enlist immediately rather than hold out for terms were correct that large-scale service in a war that threatened the United States' existence could bring African Americans the changes they sought. It is hard to imagine white Americans enacting the sweeping legislation that followed the war had not African Americans insisted, even prior to the government's adoption of black enlistment, that legal change must follow black service and then kept agitating on that point after the war. African Americans' involvement in the military increased the political leverage they could exert on the white leaders who controlled national politics. Moreover, it also gave black men a claim on the nation that white politicians could not ignore, and it provided white Republicans with valuable rhetorical justification for expanding black rights and citizenship.

It might be argued that had Andrew Johnson not pursued an incredibly lenient course of Reconstruction, and had the former Confederate states not taken such defiant stances in the war's immediate aftermath, congressional Republicans might not have pushed through the postwar amendments and other measures relating to black rights. In such a scenario, black Northerners who had embraced delayed enlistment might have had cause to castigate the immediate-enlistment camp. But this is counterfactual speculation. Black Northerners who urged immediate enlistment correctly interpreted the political dynamics of the wartime North, correctly anticipated the political dynamics that would take shape following a Northern victory, and parlayed large-scale black service into government recognition of black citizenship, suffrage, and civil rights. They sought a new Union, and they won it.

As congressional Republicans authored this legislative revolution, black veterans remained politically active, although their efforts to organize collectively around their veteranhood ended rather abruptly. No trace of the Colored Soldiers' and Sailors' League exists past the early 1870s; the organization ceased to operate, an apparent victim of the success of African Americans' political agenda. Many black veterans embarked on political careers, but they were actually underrepresented in the ranks of Reconstruction-era black officeholders: about 10 percent of black officeholders from 1867 to 1877 had served, whereas black veterans accounted for around 16 percent of the black male population. The majority held office in states where Union armies had heavily recruited newly freed slaves—especially Louisiana, Mississippi, and North and South Carolina—but some held federal office, serving in the House of Representatives and a variety of appointed posts.

Once black veterans gained suffrage and citizenship, Donald Shaffer has found, they stopped organizing collectively as veterans, and their service stopped influencing their political behavior. Socioeconomic status, not veteranhood, dictated the political positions African American officeholders took. Comparatively comfortable in material terms, former servicemen declined to support radical measures like land confiscation. Like antebellum black Northern leaders, they sought to shore up their rights within the existing political system and gave little attention to the material challenges ex-slaves faced. The political positions black veterans took during Reconstruction, Shaffer has written, were "unremarkable, and their political behavior showed little discernible difference from that of nonveterans."[68]

Black veterans did not form a radical leadership cadre during Reconstruction, but they and their nonveteran brethren made significant state-level gains that augmented the success of their agenda at the federal level and in the South. African Americans in the North pushed for desegregation in the region's public schools, winning gains in states like Connecticut, New Hampshire, and Minnesota by the late 1860s. They continued this desegregation battle into the 1870s, and by decade's end no Northern state prohibited black children from attending school, and numerous states had banned school segregation. African American Northerners also continued the fight for equal access to public accommodations. Black Philadelphians still led on this issue, and by 1867 they had convinced state legislators to outlaw discrimination on state public transit facilities. With the passage of the 1875 federal civil rights bill, black Northerners in California, Illinois, New York, Indiana, Pennsylvania, New Jersey, and other states brought suit to defend their equal access to public accommodations. Sometimes they succeeded. But as judges and other government officials grew reluctant to rule or argue in favor of African American civil rights, the already-formidable obstacles that accompanied legal action increased. Congress had attempted to protect black civil rights, but as Reconstruction failed in the South black Northerners got the "message," according to Hugh Davis, "that they should not expect to be treated as the equals of whites."[69]

Indeed, the tragedy of black military service is that rights and citizenship for the race faded so quickly after having been bought so dearly—African American servicemen won a new Union, but one that continued to fall short of the nation's founding ideals. Black service had changed the law, but even after the passage of the Civil War amendments, it remained an open question whether it would compel white officials at the local and federal levels to enforce the law as it related to black rights and citizenship. As Frances Ellen Watkins Harper put it in 1875, the question was "whether . . . there [would be] strength enough in democracy . . . to deal justly with four millions of people."[70] Federal Reconstruction collapsed in the mid-1870s as a result of white Southerners' violent hostility and white Northerners' racism, apathy, and discomfort.

White Southerners gave up military efforts to found a new nation based on slavery in the spring of 1865 but never stopped fighting for white supremacy. By 1877, through a combination of intimidation, brutal paramilitary violence, white political solidarity, and legal chicanery, white Democrats had retaken Southern state governments. Nor was white violence limited to the South. Whites in the North and West sometimes attacked black voters: in 1871, Democratic thugs assassinated Octavius Catto and two other black Philadelphians attempting to vote, and city officials never prosecuted anyone for these slayings.[71] Judicial conservatism abetted white efforts to restrict black rights as, in a series of 1870s and 1880s decisions, federal judges emasculated the postwar amendments and restricted the federal government's power to protect black rights from state-level infringement.[72]

Neither Reconstruction nor black political participation ended overnight; black men voted in several Southern states into the 1890s, and they acted shrewdly to combine with white political movements that challenged Democratic power.[73] But the mid-1870s witnessed the beginning of a process by which white Southerners slowly built a Jim Crow system that divided public life into separate and unequal white and black spheres, canceling the equality for which African Americans had fought, and disenfranchised black Southerners through both formal and informal methods. By the early twentieth century, Reconstruction's slow death had made the United States, Philip A. Klinker and Rogers Smith have written, "what in one way or another it had almost always been—a regime elaborately committed to white supremacy."[74]

Late nineteenth-century African Americans were acutely aware of the limitations to the citizenship black soldiers' wartime service had won. Few whites could "realize," asserted "X.," a correspondent of the *Weekly Louisianan*, in 1881, "what it is to be a negro in the United States," or know "the withering effects" of "the iron of proscription on account of color."[75] Laws could recognize black men and women as citizens and afford them equal rights, but laws were useless if the federal government did not force the Southern states to abide by them. "Is There Any Law for the Negro?" asked the black-run *New York Globe* in 1883. The government recognized black Southerners' citizenship, but, the sheet lamented, "The states say they shall not enjoy the privileges of citizenship and the national government has shown in a thousand instances that it had no power to coerce the states." Although African Americans possessed citizenship and equality before the law in theory, the *Globe* further asserted that "at no time since the close of the war [had they] enjoyed that immunity of life, liberty and the pursuit of happiness which are guaranteed to [Americans]."[76]

Black Northerners' antebellum protest had been inspired by their recognition that they lived in a country that proclaimed fealty to certain principles but only secured enjoyment of those principles to some of its inhabitants, and the *Globe* recognized that black Southerners faced a distressingly similar situation. "We are Negroes in America, with our citizenship 'on paper,'" wrote the Reverend J. G. Robinson in 1893, but paper citizenship did not equal the "free enjoyment of every right and privilege guaranteed [African Americans] by the constitution of the United States."[77] By the late nineteenth century, many black Americans suffered the same frustrations antebellum black Northerners had endured: though free, they lacked legal equality and vital political rights.

African Americans in the late nineteenth century found themselves subject to discriminatory laws and customs that varied from place to place and state to state, a situation that recalled the patchwork pattern of discrimination in the antebellum United States. As a result, the language late nineteenth-century black Americans used to describe their situation echoed antebellum black protest rhetoric. When the AME bishop Thomas M. D. Ward in 1888 used the term "aliened Americans," he used the same phrase favored by newspaperman William H. Day, who had founded his *Aliened American* in 1853. Ward was born in 1823; he would have remembered the antebellum period and might have known Day's paper, and he doubtlessly used this term purposefully.[78]

Not twenty years after hundreds of thousands of black soldiers helped quell an internal rebellion that nearly destroyed the United States, the black minister J. F. Thomas told a convention of Kansas black leaders that "if the United States did not protect her citizens, the colored people would seek some other country and fight under her flag." Knowingly or not, Thomas echoed the antebellum leader H. Ford Douglas, who had in 1854 held that his lack of citizenship permitted him to enlist in a foreign army.[79] As the nineteenth century closed, according to the black minister William H. Heard, black men were "m[en] without being allowed to enjoy manhood . . . citizen[s] without enjoying citizenship; law-abiding without being protected . . . taxpayer[s] without representation." Antebellum black leaders' tactic of using revolutionary rhetoric—"taxpayer[s] without representation"—to protest the rights they were denied remained relevant as the twentieth century approached, a depressing comment on how the postwar situation African Americans faced resembled their antebellum circumstances. Reconstruction legislation had failed to create a citizenship African Americans could enjoy, Heard argued, and it had also failed to fulfill the bare terms of citizenship as described by Edward Bates in December 1862. State and local governments, wrote Heard, "demand of [the black man] allegiance but do not guarantee him protection of life, or property."

Black service helped kill slavery and erect, in Eric Foner's words, "a framework of legal rights enshrined in the Constitution" that served as "a vehicle for future federal intervention in Southern affairs" during the South's second Reconstruction in the twentieth century. Reconstruction was, Foner wrote, "America's unfinished revolution"; black service played a key role in that revolution, and in bringing about the legislative changes later generations of African Americans would use to move it forward. Black soldiers' wartime service, to use Evelyn Nakano Glenn's formulation, won formal citizenship for African Americans. But for many, especially black Southerners, formal citizenship did not by the 1880s and 1890s translate into substantive citizenship—that is, the ability to actually exercise rights, like the vote, associated with citizenship.[80] This reality led some to conclude that the war and black service had changed little.

The Civil War, according to Henry McNeal Turner, had proved that the United States had learned how "how to let the negro die in defence of her government," but it had not forced the country to learn "how to preserve to the negro his rights of citizenship."[81] As a result, some black Americans, as in the late antebellum years, embraced emigration as a strategy for finding the freedom the United States denied them. Some, known to history as the Exodusters, looked to Kansas and newer western states to, as a convention of black Louisianans put it, "obtain Christian independence and citizenship in the broadest sense." Black veterans figured prominently in the Exoduster movement.[82] Others, including former soldiers like Turner and Martin Delany— in 1864 commissioned a major in the U.S. Army—turned their eyes abroad, urging African Americans to leave the land of their birth to find freedom.[83] Many scorned emigration and responded to the crisis of the late nineteenth century by continuing to agitate for black rights and equality where they stood. Others, however, warmed to the doctrine of Booker T. Washington, who counseled black men to forgo politics and concentrate on economic suc-cess, a seeming admission that the struggle for African American rights and citizenship had failed.[84]

As the nineteenth century closed, black veterans remained revered mem-bers of black communities North and South, "often lionized," according to Donald Shaffer, for their wartime exploits.[85] They were determined to force the nation to remember their service. In response to early white historians' tendency to bypass African American troops' achievements, former recruiter William Wells Brown and former soldiers Joseph T. Wilson and George Wash-ington Williams became black Civil War soldiers' first historians.[86] But when it came time to assess black service's accomplishments, black veterans had to admit its limitations. As Christian Fleetwood, a sergeant major with the Fourth USCT and Medal of Honor recipient, observed in 1895, the nation had forsaken its African American defenders. "After each war, of 1776, of 1812, and of 1861," Fleetwood wrote, "history repeats itself in the absolute effacement of remembrance of the gallant deeds done for the country by its brave black defenders and in their relegation to outer darkness."[87]

The crisis of the Civil War had moved the nation into closer harmony with American founding principles. But black service had not required the federal government to enforce the laws passed in the war's wake, and as a result many African Americans found themselves, to use Henry McNeal Turner's term, "decitizened." In these circumstances, it might have seemed to many African Americans that black Civil War soldiers, though valiant and worthy of celebra-tion, had—despite their best efforts to prevent this outcome—repeated the disappointments of earlier generations by fighting for a nation that ceased to care for them once the fight had ended.

CONCLUSION

N HIS 1935 *Black Reconstruction*, W. E. B. Du Bois encapsulated black Southerners' experience of the dramas of the Civil War and Reconstruction in a famous phrase: "The slave went free, stood a brief moment in the sun; then moved back again toward slavery."[1] This study might depict black service as having produced a brief interlude in the long history of U.S. racism and legal discrimination in which black Americans won gains that proved reversible. It might conclude by observing that military service helped achieve many of the legal changes African Americans sought and that, although these legal changes failed for many decades to matter because white Americans flagrantly violated them, they remained momentous and provided a basis for later black agitation. Such an observation contains much truth, but it does not tell the full story of how black service changed American citizenship, nor does it reveal the possibilities and limitations of military service as a means of winning citizenship.

African Americans' campaign to use their contributions to the armed forces to win citizenship irrevocably changed U.S. citizenship; Civil War–era black activists forced otherwise unwilling white officials to specifically define black men and women as American citizens, and to clarify the protections available to citizens. While black service helped encode black citizenship in the Constitution, however, it did not allow all African Americans to enjoy the status and rights they gained in the war's wake. Although black service helped win formal citizenship for all African Americans, black Southerners' substantive citizenship was abridged by state regimes that retained the power to effectively nullify federal legislation in spite of the war's verdict of federal supremacy. For some African Americans, however, the Civil War did result in both formal and substantive citizenship; black Americans outside the South enjoyed something like legal equality in many places. Additionally, black Americans who had served the federal government as soldiers enjoyed substantial equality within the federal purview, experiencing in large measure the legal equality they had described as integral to citizenship.

When the last USCT unit disbanded in August 1867, it did not signal the end of the black presence in the U.S. Army. After Appomattox, federal officials needed troops to occupy the defeated South and deal with "hostile" Indians on the western frontier, and military necessity caused U.S. officials to recruit black soldiers once again. In 1866, Congress authorized the formation of six black regiments, four of infantry and two of cavalry, later consolidating the four infantry units into two. From the late 1860s through the early twentieth century, black troops assisted in the extension of effective American sovereignty over the vast lands of the West and enjoyed a far greater degree of equality than did black Southerners as Reconstruction came undone.[2]

The black regulars, often called "buffalo soldiers," who served on the American frontier confronted racism in myriad ways. They served in segregated regiments under almost exclusively white commissioned officers, some of whom were violently prejudiced. Military regulations did not forbid enlisted black soldiers from rising to commissioned office, but from 1866 through 1898 none did. While white regiments transferred back and forth regularly between the sparsely settled frontier and more populous areas, African American units remained on the frontier, enduring rough living conditions and brutal weather. Black troops frequently faced racist violence from white civilians, especially in Texas.[3] Decades of black service had not erased white convictions about black inferiority; even white officers who praised black soldiers' performance, historians William A. Dobak and Thomas D. Phillips have written, considered them "dependent and incapable of initiative."[4] The African American regulars, Dobak and Phillips conclude, "could never [escape] reminders that many observers, military and civilian, considered them second-class soldiers."[5]

Despite these indignities and obstacles, in many ways black regulars enjoyed formal equality with white troops. They received the same pay, rations, supplies, and housing as white troops, and when they received substandard fare, it was the result of armywide policy, not institutional racism. African American soldiers often received fairly evenhanded justice from military tribunals, which admitted black testimony more readily than some civilian courts. Army life on the frontier was surprisingly integrated, especially in comparison to the segregation slowly developing in the South. Black units often served at segregated posts but were as likely to serve at integrated facilities, where they performed guard and fatigue duty alongside white troops, recuperated in integrated hospitals, and practiced marksmanship in integrated rifle teams. Black and white troops socialized together at times, playing on integrated athletic squads, performing in integrated musical groups, and attending integrated worship services. On the frontier, Dobak and Phillips write, black soldiers inhabited a world in which "a general fairness . . . prevailed on the institutional level against a background of individual bigotry." The U.S. Army was one of the most "impartial institutions of the day," one that "needed [black troops'] services and could not afford to discriminate against them."[6]

Federal service allowed black regulars to experience to a relatively high degree the legal equality they associated with citizenship; there is thus striking irony in the fact that their military activities helped define members of other groups—Indians, Mexicans, immigrant laborers—as beyond the pale of American citizenship. Black soldiers conducted cross-border raids that violated Mexican sovereignty, helped establish the United States–Mexico border's reality by defining Mexicans on the other side of it as outside the bounds of citizenship, and destroyed Indian villages. They moved members of both groups out of the way of white settlement, serving as "voluntary participants in the violent subjugation of Indian and Hispanic peoples throughout the West."[7] In the 1890s black servicemen served as strikebreakers during labor disputes in places like Coeur d'Alene, Idaho. Henry McNeal Turner complained in 1890 that African Americans had been "decitizenized," and by that point many could not vote or enjoy legal equality.[8] But on the nation's borders, according to historian James Leiker, black troopers derived from their service both citizenship and a sense of "American-ness" while defining others as "foreign."[9]

Black leaders occasionally gloried in black troops' effectiveness at dealing with striking miners of European descent, contrasting black troopers' American identities with recent immigrants' devotion to class interests and countries of origin.[10] African Americans, declared the Reverend William H. Yeocum, had always fought for the United States and, unlike "the alien who comes to this country," did not embrace radical political ideologies or foment labor unrest. "The colored American citizen does not go on strike and to carry his point resort to the deadly dynamite or the torch," insisted Yeocum, "There are no Anarchists and Communists found among the colored people, nor is their love and interest divided between this and any other country."[11] Black regulars represented calm and order and acted in the national interest. Theophilus G. Steward, the black chaplain of the Twenty-Fifth Infantry, proudly told the *Christian Recorder* how his regiment had helped break the Pullman Railroad Strike of 1894, and he pronounced the black regulars "the ideal American trooper[s]."[12]

By this point, all African Americans were citizens, but black soldiers in the federal army enjoyed a better quality of citizenship than black Southerners—that is, black servicemen had better assurance that they could actually enjoy the rights they in theory possessed than did black civilians without a tie to the federal army. Black soldiers' status as Americans, however, came at the expense of members of other groups, including Indians, whom Henry McNeal Turner in 1863 labeled black Americans "co-sufferer[s]."[13] Black troopers helped subdue groups that threatened white expansion and the capitalist socioeconomic order, affirming their own American citizenship and identity in the process: as James Leiker put it in his study of black troopers' activities along the Rio Grande, "Black soldiers approached the Rio Grande and its people as American citizens."[14] Historically, U.S. citizenship has been defined as much by its exclusions as its inclusions.[15] That black troopers' relatively robust quality of citizenship depended on their oppression of other groups on the margins of American society serves as a reminder that American citizenship, even after the Fourteenth Amendment, involves profound practical inequalities whose dynamics change based on time and location. Service in the armed forces did not change that reality, although it allowed African Americans to claim the mantle of citizen.

The black regulars were not the only African Americans who enjoyed, by virtue of military service, more equality than the average black Southerner as the nineteenth century closed. Black Civil War veterans benefited greatly from the color-blind pension and claims systems the federal government administered in the war's wake. Through the claims system black veterans received unpaid bounties and recovered lost wages, and the pension system funneled an enormous sum of money into black communities North and South. The average black veteran and his family received $3,759 in pension funds, and black veterans and their families received at least $313 million in total. Black veterans could also reside in care facilities within the National Home for Disabled Volunteer Soldiers' network. As black and white troops in the postwar army served together at integrated posts, at NHDVS homes black and white veterans lived side by side.[16]

Black servicemen's experiences with the pension system and the veterans' care facilities mirrored the black regulars' experiences on the frontier: they experienced de facto discrimination but enjoyed inclusion within a system that treated them equally on the level of institutional policy. African American veterans claiming pension funds faced obstacles that their white counterparts did not. Slaves turned soldiers, for example, who had changed their names upon obtaining freedom had difficulty establishing their identities, and racism among Pension Bureau officials plagued both formerly enslaved and freeborn veterans alike. As a result, while 92 percent of white applicants successfully obtained a pension, only 75 percent of black applicants met with success. Similarly, NHDVS facilities that accepted both black and white residents often segregated internally, which may have kept some black veterans from entering them. Still, as segregation proliferated in the late nineteenth century, it was significant that these facilities were integrated at all. "In an era that offered little hope for their race," Donald Shaffer has written, African American veterans "grasped at all chances of inclusion, however much the reality fell short of the ideal."[17]

African American soldiers also prized their inclusion in the Grand Army of the Republic (GAR), the primary Union veterans' fraternal organization.[18] Founded in 1866, many of the GAR's white members believed that loyalty trumped color and welcomed black veterans into the fold. Black men who joined the organization enjoyed numerous practical benefits. GAR membership was helpful in securing pension funds, and posts generally guaranteed their members honorable burials and often raised relief funds for them and their families. Some black veterans achieved national prominence within the organization: soldier turned historian Joseph Wilson became an aide-de-camp to the GAR's commander in chief. Into the early 1880s, black men's experiences in the GAR mirrored their experiences with the pension and veterans' care facilities systems, and any discrimination they faced was generally unofficial in nature.[19]

De jure discrimination in the GAR became a significant issue in the 1880s and 1890s, when Union veterans who had moved south following the war began opening posts in the former Confederacy. New Southern posts' refusal to admit black veterans became a national issue, and the organization's national white leadership mandated integration; but when public attention abated, GAR officials often allowed segregation to prevail. The controversy over the Southern chapters also ignored the fact that effective segregation reigned in many Northern posts as well. GAR departments were integrated, but most GAR activity took place at the post level, and most black veterans belonged to all-black posts. The association was not free of discrimination, but as Shaffer has written, within its confines black veterans received a "surprising degree of respect." In addition, the GAR stood as an exception to the general pattern of strict segregation that existed in this "golden age of fraternal organizations."[20] The federal custom of institutional fairness tempered by individual racism prevailed even in the unofficial realm of Civil War remembrance, affecting the group that most prominently symbolized Union veterans' service.

African Americans whose military service created a relationship between themselves and the U.S. government could expect something approaching equal treatment when they came under direct federal purview. Black Civil

War soldiers' insistence on serving the nation in a manner consistent with citizenship forged an enduring institutional equality that, despite white racism, impacted the lives of the buffalo soldiers and black Civil War veterans. Many black veterans and their families, of course, lived in the South and likely experienced relatively equal treatment in their dealings with federal officials and profound inequality in their states of residence simultaneously. But in many ways, African American men and women with a military tie to the federal government enjoyed both formal and substantive citizenship.

Elizabeth Leonard concludes her 2012 study of black military service and citizenship by speculating that, had Frederick Douglass been alive in 1937, he "would have been deeply grieved to learn that the quality of 'citizenship' black Americans, even black veterans, then enjoyed was so little improved."[21] She therefore determined that Douglass's 1863 prediction—that once black soldiers donned the federal uniform, "no power on earth" could "deny that [they had] earned the right of citizenship in the United States"—was sadly incorrect.[22] Leonard is likely right that Douglass would have been disappointed in the state of black citizenship in 1937, but her conclusion regarding black service's inability to win black citizenship is too sweeping. We must be a bit more cautious in evaluating black service's efficacy as a tool for winning citizenship.

Military service helped make black men and women Americans in a constitutional sense, changing citizenship and reshaping the relationship between African Americans and the United States. Black soldiers helped keep the war from ending in a stalemate that would have amounted to Confederate victory, an outcome that would have been disastrous for black freedom, let alone black citizenship. African Americans' efforts in the military proved a compelling justification for the passage of the Fourteenth Amendment; the citizenship black soldiers won was limited but superior to that which African Americans would have enjoyed had the United States lost the war or black men abstained from fighting. Black service also created a personal relationship between the national government and hundreds and thousands of black soldiers, and when they came under federal purview, black soldiers, veterans, and their kin received relatively equal treatment even after Reconstruction's demise. In realms where the U.S. government possessed unambiguous authority, federal officials constructed institutional systems that treated African American soldiers and veterans equally.

Historians like Drew Gilpin Faust, Melinda Lawson, and Heather Cox Richardson have shown in recent years that the Civil War created a new bond between Americans and the federal government. After the war, U.S. citizens felt a new sense of ownership over their government. Northerners, Richardson has observed, "had died for their government, sacrificed for it, benefited from it, and had its money in their pocket." As a result, she states, "The government literally belonged to the people."[23] Union soldiers fought and died in massive numbers to preserve the nation, and the government was obligated to care for them in death and postwar life. Its attempt to identify the Union dead and its creation of national cemetery and pension systems represented, according to Faust, "a dramatically new understanding of the relationship of the citizen and the state" in which the government recognized citizens as "the literal lifeblood of the nation."[24] Neither the black men who fought for the United States nor their kinfolk were left out of this new relationship. The personal relationship black veterans created between themselves and the government, however, did not cause federal officials to feel a permanent responsibility to protect black citizenship, defend black male suffrage, or ensure equality for all African Americans very far beyond the war's conclusion.

African Americans needed more than inclusion in this new, personal government-and-citizen relationship if all it translated to was benefits to veterans and their kin. They needed federal officials to see that they possessed a duty to shield black citizenship and rights from white Southerners who sought to reestablish white supremacy and control black labor. Initially hesitant to move beyond the Thirteenth Amendment, congressional Republicans responded to white Southerners' postwar defiance by passing positive legislation to provide such a shield, and for a short time, federal officials vigorously protected black Southerners from white wrath. But by the mid-1870s federal efforts flagged, and, as a consequence, so did black Southerners' possession of substantive citizenship. It was never black Northerners' intention, as they debated service, to use it to win citizenship only for veterans and their families; they had meant for service to win lasting gains for all African Americans. In realizing this goal, military service proved tragically limited, as did the Fourteenth Amendment black Americans had worked so hard to win.

Why did the Fourteenth Amendment not result in both formal and substantive citizenship for all African Americans? The answer lies with a combination of factors: white racism, the survival of some antebellum conceptions of citizenship, and devotion to local control. The Civil War and black military service changed American citizenship laws and federal institutional practices but did not kill white racism. Many white Americans, even those who favored black rights, continued to harbor racialized assumptions about black inferiority in the war's aftermath. Although they respected black soldiers, George Fredrickson has observed, white Northerners "approached Reconstruction with their basic racial prejudices largely intact," many still viewing African

Americans as inherently submissive and inferior.[25] The depressing truth may be that, in the late nineteenth-century United States, white racism dictated that the fullest citizenship African Americans could practically enjoy was a formal equality limited by individual localized racism, and in de facto terms this type of citizenship is precisely what black soldiers achieved.

Black service also failed to totally transform Americans' conceptual thinking about citizenship. In her recent study of Reconstruction-era Washington, D.C., Kate Masur has demonstrated that some antebellum notions about citizenship survived into the postwar period despite the passage of new relevant laws. Antebellum Americans, she writes, had embraced a "vision of hierarchical citizenship" in which citizenship and its rights were distributed according to individuals' community standing and "hierarchies of race, sex, and wealth."[26] Despite the Fourteenth Amendment's injunction that citizens enjoy equality, many Americans continued in the postwar period to see citizenship as dependent on ascriptive identity and community standing, accepting a vision of citizenship in which gradations in rights and privileges could exist.

After the war, Americans black and white evinced an understanding of citizenship under which different groups might enjoy different arrays of rights. Black leaders often spoke of "full" citizenship, implying that other degrees of citizenship existed with which they would not be satisfied. California's C. M. Wilson evoked a view of citizenship as consonant with gradations in rights and status in January 1869, when he told a meeting of black Californians that the civil rights and citizenship legislation Congress had already passed had conferred on black Americans "all the minor degrees of citizenship." African Americans would hold American citizenship's "Master's Degree," he said, when the nation enfranchised black men, as then they "[would] be recognized, by every one as American citizens in every sense of that term."[27] African American men's willingness to forsake women's suffrage to win voting rights for themselves demonstrated their acceptance of the principle that different groups of Americans could possess different rights.

White Americans saw citizenship in the same terms. Many Republican framers of the Fourteenth Amendment did not believe the amendment conferred a set of absolute rights on all citizens. Rather, they believed it allowed states to regulate citizens' rights so long as they did so on the basis of some "reasonable" rationale rather than on the basis of "arbitrary" characteristics like race and color. This standard of sensible regulation left room for gradations to exist between the rights available to different classes of citizens. No one doubted women's citizenship, but states could continue to disenfranchise them, many legislators believed, because the argument that politics was a male realm unfit for female participation met the test of reasonableness.[28] White Americans did not doubt that African Americans were citizens under the new constitutional definition of the term, but with time many Americans came to believe that black citizenship did not need to imply black political rights.[29]

In winning legislation that gave U.S. citizenship a constitutional definition and identified black men and women as citizens, Civil War–era African Americans changed American citizenship fundamentally, but they did not completely alter the way Americans thought about citizenship. Americans remained comfortable with a citizenship that afforded all of its bearers certain basic protections, like property and contract rights, but recognized gradations between those who enjoyed "full citizenship," including the rights to vote and hold office, and those who did not.[30] In addition, Americans still linked the possession of full citizenship to community standing and stewardship. While this view prevailed, given the reality that the nation had only conceded blacks' citizenship and rights out of dire necessity in the first place, blacks' rights and standing as Americans remained vulnerable.

As long as white Northerners remained convinced of the need to protect black Southerners, and as long as black service remained in the forefront of their minds, black rights and citizenship received federal protection. By the 1870s, though, the crisis of the war had faded. As many Northerners came to sympathize with white Southerners' critiques of Republican state governments and black political participation, they acquiesced in Reconstruction's undoing. As Reconstruction unraveled, African Americans lost access to legal equality and voting rights, gradually slipping into second-class citizenship. From the late 1870s onward, federal officials accepted Southern segregation while continuing to oversee institutional structures that, on their face, treated black soldiers and veterans equally with their white counterparts.[31] That black service changed national laws governing citizenship without totally changing Americans' thinking about citizenship partially explains why Reconstruction's radical potential was undermined so quickly.

Americans' concerns about the proper scope of federal authority also survived the war, and by the mid-1870s superseded their commitment to equality. Racist assumptions about African Americans' ability to fulfill free-labor ideals inspired white Northerners' abandonment of Reconstruction, but so did concerns about federal-state relations.[32] On some level, white Northerners had been uncomfortable with federal interference in Southern affairs all along; many held reservations about the expansive use of federal power and countenanced federal involvement in the former Confederacy only as a temporary expedient necessary to confirm the war's outcome.

Once slavery was dead, African Americans were citizens by statute, and black men could vote, many white Northerners felt the government had done enough for black Southerners. Blithely ignoring the material realities that hampered black Southerners' efforts to achieve economic self-sufficiency, they insisted that as good free laborers black men and women needed to succeed or fail by their industry alone. As Appomattox receded from view, even white soldiers and officers who manned the army tasked with occupying the postwar South grew uncomfortable with the use of federal power on the state level. These servicemen equated their continued occupation of the former Confederate states with the threat to civil liberties posed by the existence of a standing army, which had loomed large in the minds of Americans since the nation's founding.[33] After the war, Americans still harbored grave doubts about the expansive use of federal power on the state level, which caused them to withdraw support for federal efforts to protect black citizenship in the South as the 1870s progressed.[34]

In addition to white racism and Americans' continued acceptance of antebellum notions about citizenship, Americans' postwar desire to check federal power helps explain why African Americans' ability to enjoy substantive citizenship varied according to personal circumstance and geography. In arenas where the federal government possessed clear authority, black veterans and their kin could expect something approximating equal treatment. Where the federal government's power to intervene was contested in cases involving state and private violations of individual civil and political rights, federal officials—judges, legislators, presidents—proved all too willing to bow to local preferences. Local control did not always spell the end of substantive citizenship for African Americans; seeing the futility of further federal-level agitation, black leaders in the 1880s turned to their states and convinced eighteen state legislatures in the North and west to pass civil rights laws. Discrimination by custom continued to undermine black equality in these states, but local control did not negate black citizenship.[35] However, local control did spell the doom of substantive citizenship for millions of black Southerners. White Americans' devotion to local authority trumped their devotion to life, liberty, and the pursuit of happiness, and many watched silently as white Southerners constructed a new order premised on white supremacy and racial segregation.

The Constitution's framers created a federal system believing that national and state governments each had vital functions to perform in the work of governing. Local control is an important principle of American government, one not to be dismissed lightly. But black Southerners, many of whom had fought in the war that preserved the United States, faced systematic, brutal oppression at the hands of white Southerners in part because of white Americans' squeamishness about the active use of federal authority. That fact should serve as a reminder that concerns over local jurisdiction should not supersede concerns over justice. Americans seeking to preserve inequality have often cited concerns related to local control to legitimate their positions. Before the Civil War, white Southerners opposed the use of federal power to restrict slavery because they knew that power could lead to abolition. Concerns about local control subsequently helped preserve the Jim Crow South for decades, and more recently, fidelity to state control of voting regulations has led the U.S. Supreme Court to overturn key portions of the landmark 1965 Voting Rights Act.[36] As they watched the white South reestablish racial supremacy in the late nineteenth and early twentieth centuries, black veterans of the Civil War learned dearly the tragic cost of Americans' devotion to local control and continued to hope that in time the United States might live up to its founding principles.

Black Civil War soldiers fought valiantly, but they did not achieve a United States that lived up to its founding ideals. As a result, in the twentieth century, some African Americans formally defined as citizens who have failed to *feel* like citizens have questioned whether they should fight for the United States and felt solidarity with nonwhite foreign peoples. In 1903, W. E. B. Du Bois described a "double consciousness" that African Americans constantly felt, an unresolvable tension between two conflicting identities, one American and one black. "One ever feels his twoness—an American, a Negro; two souls, two thoughts, two unreconciled strivings; two warring ideals in one dark body, whose dogged strength alone keeps it from being torn asunder."[37] Without so naming it, David Walker recognized this double consciousness when he defended black Americans' right to remain in the land of their birth but addressed them as "colored citizens of the world," and black Northerners dealt with it when they considered the conditions under which fighting for the United States made sense for them as African Americans. In spite of Northern victory and Reconstruction, black Americans entered the twentieth century aware that they were not citizens in the same way white Americans were. Thus, the question of why an African American should put on the uniform of the United States remained relevant.

In America's wars of the twentieth century, some black Americans have supported enlistment in the U.S. Army, praising the country's willingness to give black soldiers "the right to fight"; others have opposed enlistment and questioned why they should shoulder arms for the United States. African Americans divided over whether to support American involvement in the First World War, which President Woodrow Wilson claimed would make the world safe for democracy. In July 1918, Du Bois urged African Americans to "close ranks" behind the war effort. Other black voices argued that black Americans' first duty was to fight for justice at home and make the nation safe for democracy. Southern lynch law, observed members of the black press like William Monroe Trotter, the son of a member of the Fifty-Fourth Massachusetts, posed a greater threat to African Americans than the kaiser.[38]

Facing knotty dilemmas regarding enlistment in subsequent American wars, some African Americans have tried, as did black soldiers in the Civil War, to use military service to improve their domestic position. Others, however, have rejected fighting for the United States and felt solidarity with the country's nonwhite enemies. During the Second World War African Americans embraced a "Double V" campaign, seeking victory over fascism abroad and racism at home.[39] James G. Thompson coined the term "Double V" after searching his soul and asking himself whether the "kind of America" he knew "was worth defending," and whether after the war it would be a "true and pure democracy." Thompson loved his country and was willing to die for it. But he would only do so as part of a campaign that sought to destroy the United States' "enemies from without . . . [and] . . . within" who were seeking to "destroy [American] democratic forms of government just as surely as the Axis forces."[40] Hundreds of thousands of African Americans embraced the Double V campaign; but others had developed strong pro-Japanese sympathies, seeing the Japanese people as a nonwhite ally and Japan's twentieth-century rise as an antidote to white supremacy. After Pearl Harbor, Marc Gallicchio has written, "the powerful emotions unleashed by Japan's humbling of whites produced a brief moment of divided loyalties" for some African Americans.[41] Malcolm X remembered that when he received "Uncle Sam's Greetings" in 1943, he started "noising around that [he] was frantic to join . . . the Japanese army" to increase his chances of rejection.[42]

From World War II onward, the conviction that fighting nonwhite peoples abroad made little sense while discrimination persisted at home inspired some black Americans to resist the call to serve. It has also dogged African Americans who have enlisted. In 1952, when FBI agents asked Malcolm X why he had failed to register for the Korean War draft, he replied that he was a conscientious objector: "When the white man asked me to go off somewhere and fight and maybe die to preserve the way the white man treated the black man in America, then my conscience made me object."[43] During the Vietnam War, Muhammad Ali took a similar stance when government officials targeted him for induction: "I ain't got no quarrel with them Viet Cong," he proclaimed in 1966. Ali decided that his identity as a black man prevented him from fighting despite his country's designation of the North Vietnamese as a national enemy. "All I know is that [the Viet Cong] are considered as Asiatic black people, and I don't have no fight with black people."

Black troops served in Vietnam in disproportionately high numbers, and during the war's later stages, tensions between black and white troops increased as many black soldiers adopted attitudes, symbols, and dress informed by the domestic Black Power movement. African American soldiers who replaced their standard-issue headgear with black berets "acquired . . . an ominous presence as a segregated paramilitary within the military" and gave rise to the "widespread fear that the Black Panther Party had organized secret cells in the military."[44] Some soldiers came to value their consciousness as black men at least as highly as their consciousness of being American.

In 1973, military historian Russell F. Weigley suggested that combat was no longer useful to the United States in a national strategic sense: "At no point on the spectrum of violence does the use of combat offer much promise for the United States today." Warfare no longer served American goals. The United States possessed the technological capability to win a nuclear war, but the damage that would accompany this course of action would destroy so much of society that it was hardly an option. The record of "nonnuclear limited war in obtaining acceptable decisions at tolerable cost [was] also scarcely heartening," and so, Weigley argued, "the history of usable combat may at last be reaching its end."[45] American military adventures since Weigley made this contention suggest that he might have been right, but the use of combat to serve national goals is not the concern of this study. Weigley's insight about warfare's limitations as a means of bringing about a desired end, though, relates to this study's central theme. If there is a limit to combat's effectiveness in achieving national strategy, there must be a limit to the extent to which groups of Americans can use combat to achieve their domestic goals as well. That a similar dilemma regarding enlistment, along with ambivalence about fighting for the United States, has persisted in the aftermath of the Civil War suggests that black veterans of that conflict might have found that limit.

Black service in the Civil War proved that by enlisting in the U.S. Army and fighting for the United States, U.S. soldiers could advance a legislative agenda. Black Northerners enlisted, and their persistent agitation, combined with help from white allies and some fortuitous developments, won nearly all of the legislative changes they sought. They changed U.S. citizenship and laws, achieving a kind of new Union, but not one that reached their aspirations. In every society, a gap exists between law and lived reality. That gap continued to be wide for many African Americans because their service could not combat the potent postwar combination of virulent white racism, continued adherence to antebellum assumptions about citizenship, and devotion to local control. As the Civil War receded from view, black military service did not force enough white Americans to care about the ideals of equality and citizenship that animated U.S. politics for a brief moment after the war. African Americans in subsequent generations have thus found themselves asking questions about military service to similar those that black Northerners asked from 1861 through 1863. Americans may decide as members of a social group to enlist in the U.S. Army in the hope that their service will yield legislative change that collectively benefits their group. But black soldiers' experience suggests that group military service is far less effective in altering the social attitudes and political beliefs that determine how legislation is enforced and administered.

During the early stages of the Civil War, black Northerners considering enlistment asked, in effect, "What do we get in return?" During the twentieth century, African Americans have repeated this question but added a new one as well: "Why should I, a black American, go fight and kill other nonwhite people? What did they ever do to me?" African Americans never asked this question during the Civil War; they fought a virtually all-white enemy, and they knew all too well what white Confederates had done to them. This question, though, highlights the danger inherent in the United States' historical tendency to honor its founding principles in the breach. It also highlights the limitations of formal citizenship. Americans like Malcolm X and Muhammad Ali who asked why they should fight for the United States were unquestionably American citizens, but their experiences with racism, segregation, and discrimination left them with little feeling of their citizenship. They felt their color, and when it came to military service, they identified with other nonwhite peoples more than their countrymen. Black Civil War service helped make these men citizens in a formal sense, but because different classes of citizens continued to enjoy different arrays of rights, privileges, and immunities in the war's aftermath, they and many other African Americans have not felt like citizens. The fault line between what military service can and cannot achieve lies squarely on the line between what Evelyn Nakano Glenn has described as formal citizenship and substantive citizenship, and this reality has influenced black Americans' thinking about military service into the twentieth century.

Black Northerners debated the question of joining the armed forces because they wanted at last to live in a nation in which they enjoyed the freedoms spoken of in the Declaration of Independence. They fought, and they changed the nation; they helped bring American laws into greater harmony with the nation's founding principles than they had ever been before. Despite their efforts, in the war's aftermath many African Americans found their ability to enjoy life, liberty, and the pursuit of happiness limited by disenfranchisement, segregation, and brutal racist violence.

Like all nations, the United States has failed to fully embody its founding ideals: freedom, equality, liberty. These goals are lofty and this failure is likely inevitable. African Americans' debates over service and their campaign to turn it into citizenship can serve as reminders for all Americans of the need to take a critical look at their country and the ways in which its everyday reality fails to live up to its promise, and to think about how that promise might be realized. History does not move in a straight line. Much as we might like to believe otherwise, the story of the American nation has not seen the United States move progressively toward greater fidelity to its founding principles— the election of Donald Trump on a platform of bigotry and xenophobia is only the latest example of this unfortunate truth. Despite black service in the Civil War, despite the postwar amendments and black citizenship, despite the momentous civil rights legislation of the 1960s, the names Trayvon Martin, Jordan Davis, Eric Garner, Philando Castile, Tamir Rice, and Michael Brown remind us that in the twenty-first century United States, one's skin color still plays a large part in determining one's ability to live, enjoy liberty, and pursue happiness. Black soldiers won citizenship, but that citizenship did not allow all black Americans to enjoy these "unalienable rights" in the Civil War's aftermath. Citizenship is not worthless, but as a legal category it has proved too weak to guarantee Americans' ability to live their lives to their fullest potential. It remains for current and future generations to figure out how to strengthen citizenship as part of an ongoing effort to make the United States what it ought to be.

NOTES

ABBREVIATIONS

CMA Commonwealth of Massachusetts Archives
CR   *Christian Recorder*
DM   *Douglass' Monthly*
FDP   *Frederick Douglass' Paper*
HSP   Historical Society of Pennsylvania
LOC   Library of Congress
MHS Massachusetts Historical Society
NOT   *New Orleans Tribune*
PA   *Pacific Appeal*
PP   *Pine & Palm*
WAA *Weekly Anglo-African*

INTRODUCTION

1. Blatt, "*Glory*"; McPherson, "*Glory* Story," 22.

2. For this insight, I am indebted to Hannah Rosen, as a conversation with her in the fall of 2010 helped me think about this scene and its relevance to my project.

3. *Glory*.

4. Brown, *Negro in the American Rebellion*; Du Bois, *Black Reconstruction in America*. For studies of black service that offer full treatments of the topic in the manner described above, see Berlin, Reidy, and Rowland, *Black Military Experience*; Cornish, *Sable Arm*; Grant and Reid, "Fighting for Freedom"; Hargrove, *Black Union Soldiers*; Izeksohn, *Slavery and War*, chapter 4; Mays, *Black Americans and Their Contributions*; McPherson, *Negro's Civil War*; Quarles, *Negro in the Civil War*; Smith "Let Us All Be Grateful." The other articles in Smith's edited volume deal mainly with the military and battlefield aspects of black service, as does Noah Andre Trudeau's 1998 *Like Men of War*, which provides the most thorough description of the major engagements in which black soldiers fought. See also Westwood, *Black Troops, White Commanders, and Freedmen*. In recent decades, historians have moved away somewhat from narrative histories of black service and focused tightly on topics like histories of particular regiments, the relationship between black soldiers and their white officers, Confederate atrocities against black soldiers and the resulting reprisals, and black troops' medical care. See Egerton, *Thunder at the Gates*; Glatthaar, *Forged in Battle*; Humphreys, *Intensely Human*; Urwin, *Black Flag over Dixie*. For other recent

works dealing with specific facets of black Civil War service, see Gannon, *Won Cause*; Ramold, *Slaves, Sailors, Citizens*; Tomblin, *Bluejackets and Contrabands*; Wilson, *Campfires of Freedom*.

5. James M. McPherson, for instance, spends six pages of his three-hundred-plus-page book on black Americans during the Civil War considering the process of enlistment and black Northerners' reasons for objecting to volunteering. See McPherson, *Negro's Civil War*, 175–81. A few authors of short, article-length, or chapter-length works have considered black Northerners' debate over service in more detail, but these works' brevity has limited their ability to fully elucidate this debate and trace its significance. See Gallman, "In Your Hands"; Kynoch, "Terrible Dilemmas"; Martin, "Black Churches and the Civil War"; Walker, *Rock in a Weary Land*.

6. Smith, *Lincoln and the U.S. Colored Troops*, 110.

7. Manning, *What This Cruel War Was Over*, 125–26.

8. Cornish, *Sable Arm*, 291.

9. See, for instance, Cullen, "'I's a Man Now'"; Manning, *What This Cruel War Was Over*.

10. Mary Frances Berry's 1977 *Military Necessity and Civil Rights Policy* connects African Americans' postwar attainment of citizenship with black service but focuses on white officials' debates about black enlistment and citizenship. On multiple occasions, Joseph P. Reidy has written about the black campaign to turn service into citizenship with helpful insight, but he has not highlighted the reality that black Northerners disagreed about *how* to parlay their service into citizenship. See Reidy, "African American Struggle for Citizenship Rights"; Reidy, "Broadening Both the Letter and Spirit of the Law." More recently, Christian Samito has explained how black service helped make the Union Army a "primary site" for rethinking citizenship as a universal concept entailing rights and implying equality. But Samito likewise pays scant attention to black Northerners' debates over service. See Samito, *Becoming American under Fire*. Stephen Kantrowitz has provided the most thorough discussion of black Northerners' debate over service. While his 2012 *More than Freedom* does not concentrate centrally on black service, it devotes sustained attention to black Bostonians' disagreement over enlistment and acknowledges that the prospect of service presented black Northerners with a difficult dilemma. David Blight also devotes attention to the fact that Douglass had to deal with arguments against enlisting or countenancing delaying enlistment in 1863. See Blight, *Frederick Douglass' Civil War*, 159–69.

11. On the crucial roles these institutions played in antebellum black communities, see Dann, *Black Press*; Quarles, *Black Abolitionists*; Rael, *Black Identity and Black Protest*; Reed, *Platform for Change*; Tate, "Antebellum Black Communities."

12. Anderson discusses newspapers' role in fostering nationalism through the creation of "imagined communities." See Anderson, *Imagined Communities*, 60–65. On the importance of black newspapers to fostering a sense of national community for black Northerners, see also Williams, *"Christian Recorder,"* 12–13.

13. This study defines as "Northern" all states and districts that did not secede. Maryland, Kentucky, Missouri, Delaware, and Washington, D.C., could easily be depicted as Southern given their geographical situations, their commitment to slavery, and the pro-Confederate sympathies of large portions of their populations. Black citizens of

these states frequently corresponded with Northern black newspapers. In so doing, these individuals evinced their belief that they were part of a larger Northern black community that remained loyal to the Union and considered the terms under which they would fight for it. This point is the salient one for this study.

14. *Population of the United States in 1860*, ix.

15. Berlin, Reidy, and Rowland, *Black Military Experience*, 12.

16. While black women participated in the public debates that are the subject of this study, they did not often write to black newspapers about military service. This circumstance likely results from the fact that, as Jane Dabel has noted, national questions such as black service and pay policies were generally considered male provinces within the wartime black community. See Dabel, *Respectable Woman*, 129–30.

17. On Sumner and Lincoln, see Donald, *Lincoln*, 321–22.

18. Sinha, "Allies for Emancipation?," 168–69, 173, 180–82.

19. Douglass quoted in Heller, *Portrait of an Abolitionist*, 156. On this meeting, see also McFeely, *Frederick Douglass*, 227–30.

20. On the growth of American civil society and the American public sphere, see Barker and Burrows, *Press, Politics, and the Public Sphere*; Brooke, *Columbia Rising*; Koschnik, *"Let a Common Interest Tie Us Together"*; McCarthy, *American Creed*; Neem, *Creating a Nation of Joiners*; Waldstreicher, *In the Midst of Perpetual Fetes*.

21. Free and enslaved black Southerners possessed some civil-society institutions as well, including churches, lyceums, and benevolent societies. These were clustered in Southern cities like Norfolk and Richmond and did not enjoy the freedom to discuss the war, black war aims, and black enlistment possessed by their Northern counterparts. See Ernest, *Nation within a Nation*, 16–17.

22. "Honor to the Brave," *Colored Citizen*, Nov. 7, 1863.

23. Egerton, *Thunder at the Gates*, 7.

24. John Andrew to Francis G. Shaw, Jan. 30, 1863, box 11, folder 5, John A. Andrew Papers, MHS, Boston, Mass.

25. *New York Tribune* quoted in McPherson, *Negro's Civil War*, 191. The editorial appeared on September 8, 1865, and was likely written by the *Tribune*'s editor, Horace Greeley.

26. Jones, *Birthright Citizens*, 12–13.

27. Manning, *Troubled Refuge*, 14–16. Manning emphasizes the fact that, as black men enlisted and fought in the Union army, black women performed tasks for the Union army that helped cement the wartime alliance between African Americans and the federal government. This alliance is key to Manning's definition of Civil War–era citizenship.

28. See Smith, *Civic Ideals*.

29. Shklar, *American Citizenship*, 28.

30. Novak, "Legal Transformation of Citizenship." On citizenship in the nineteenth-century United States, see Kettner, *Development of American Citizenship*.

31. Scholars focusing on the historical experiences of American women or immigrants to the United States have developed a robust literature that looks at how members of these groups sought the possession of full citizenship, and their work, alongside the work of scholars focused on black citizenship, informs this study. For works

dealing, at least in part, with women's legal rights and fights for suffrage and citizenship during the latter portion of the nineteenth century, see, for instance, Chused, "Late-Nineteenth Century Married Women's Property Law"; DuBois, *Feminism and Suffrage*; DuBois, "Outgrowing the Compact"; Flexner and Fitzpatrick, *Century of Struggle*; Isenberg, *Sex and Citizenship*; Kerber, *No Constitutional Right*; Keysaar, *Right to Vote*; Kugler, *From Ladies to Women*; Lebsock, "Radical Reconstruction and the Property Rights of Southern Women"; Sachs and Wilson, *Sexism and the Law*; Smith, *Civic Ideals*; Smith, "'One United People.'" Works dealing with immigration policy and its implications for U.S. citizenship during and after the Civil War include Archdeacon, *Becoming American*; Bennett, *American Immigration Policies*; Henkin, "Constitution and United States Sovereignty"; Higham, *Strangers in the Land*; Jacobson, *Whiteness of a Different Color*; King, *Immigration, Race, and the Origins of the Diverse Democracy*; Miller, *Unwelcome Immigrant*; Park, *Elusive Citizenship*; Salyer, *Laws as Harsh as Tigers*.

32. For a discussion of freedom rights versus ascriptive citizenship, see Vorenberg, "Citizenship and the Thirteenth Amendment."

33. Shklar's argument depends on an extension of Edmund Morgan's argument about the connection between colonial Virginians' obsession with liberty and proximity to slavery. See Morgan, *American Slavery, American Freedom*.

34. Shklar, *American Citizenship*, 27.

35. Kantrowitz, *More than Freedom*, 9.

36. See Masur, *An Example for All the Land*; Vorenberg, "Citizenship and the Thirteenth Amendment."

37. See Shklar, *American Citizenship*, chapter 2.

38. "Eloquent Gratitude," *Davenport (Iowa) Gazette*, reprinted in *Elevator*, Dec. 25, 1868.

39. Alfred F. Young's work on Boston Tea Party participant and patriot George Robert Twelves Hewes may further illustrate this point. Hewes participated in events of great historical importance. But in the final analysis, he went into the American Revolution poor, and his condition did not alter much as a result of the momentous changes he helped foment; he stayed poor his whole life. Yet in the 1830s, when authors learned of Hewes's role in the Revolution and asked him to tell his story, he did not bitterly complain that his youthful militancy had availed him little. He talked instead of the incidents from his revolutionary career that meant the most to him, of times when he and his comrades asserted rights and saw their superiors respect them, and of incidents in which figures of great stature who were his social betters treated him with regard. Hewes cared little that his wartime service did little for him financially or materially. For him, the war was about a feeling of equality with other Americans and of his possession of rights, and these feelings stayed with him all his life. See Young, "George Robert Twelves Hewes."

40. Du Bois, *Black Reconstruction in America*, 104.

41. See Emberton, "'Only Murder Makes Men.'"

42. Ibid., 372.

43. Smith, *Lincoln and the U.S. Colored Troops*, 76–77.

CHAPTER ONE

1. On Newby, see C. S. F., "Colored Men of California, No. II; William H. Newby," *PA*, June 20, 1863; Gardner, *Unexpected Places*, 102–7, 210; Lapp, *Blacks in Gold Rush California*, 100–101, 223–26, 263.

2. "Proceedings of the Second Annual Convention of the Colored Citizens of the State of California Held in the City of Sacramento, Dec. 9th, 10th, 11th, and 12th, 1856," in Foner and Walker, *Proceedings of the Black State Conventions, 1840–1865*, Foner and Walker, 2:140–44.

3. For instance, Northern states rarely enforced statutes barring black emigrants, and they passed laws freeing slaves whose owners voluntarily brought them within state borders. See Finkelman, "Prelude to the Fourteenth Amendment."

4. See Jones, *Birthright Citizens*.

5. Berry, *Military Necessity and Civil Rights Policy*, 1–5; Foner, *Blacks in the American Revolution*, 8; Nash, *Red, White, and Black*, 164; Smith, *Civic Ideals*, 63. On slavery's codification in Virginia, see Brown, *Good Wives, Nasty Wenches, and Anxious Patriarchs*; Morgan, *American Slavery, American Freedom*.

6. Smith, *Civic Ideals*, 53, 63–66.

7. Foner, *Blacks in the American Revolution*, 4–10; Gilbert, *Black Patriots and Loyalists*, 63–65; Horton and Horton, *In Hope of Liberty*, 52–53. On the role of African Americans in the waterfront culture of Northern cities and revolutionary-era agitation, see Linebaugh and Rediker, "Many-Headed Hydra."

8. On black sailors, see Bolster, *Black Jacks*.

9. Foner, *Blacks in the American Revolution*, 15–16, 52–60; Gilbert, *Black Patriots and Loyalists*, xiii, 62–65; Horton and Horton, *In Hope of Liberty*, 64–69.

10. Frey, *Water from the Rock*, 45, 114, 137–38, 172–82; Gilbert, *Black Patriots and Loyalists*, 177. See also Pybus, *Epic Journeys of Freedom*. On British fidelity to the black men and women who entered their lines, see Gosse, "As a Nation, the English Are Our Friends," 1010–11.

11. See Horton and Horton, *In Hope of Liberty*, 183–85. On black participation in the War of 1812 more generally, see Litwack, *North of Slavery*, 32–33; Mullen, *Blacks in America's Wars*, 14–17; Taylor, *Internal Enemy*.

12. Smith, *Civic Ideals*, 88, 97–106.

13. Oakes, "'Compromising Expedient,'" 2035, 2043–46; Smith, *Civic Ideals*, 115–16, 124, 126, 133. On the framers, the Constitution, and slavery, see also Fehrenbacher, *Slaveholding Republic*, 28–47.

14. Deyle, *Carry Me Back*, 20–22; Wilentz, *Rise of American Democracy*, 220. On U.S. expansion and slavery in the Old Southwest, see Rothman, *Slave Country*.

15. Horton and Horton, *In Hope of Liberty*, 83, 110–14, 119–21; Nash, *Forging Freedom*, 143. On the growth of the black middle class, see Winch, *Philadelphia's Black Elite*. On Richard Allen, see Newman, *Freedom's Prophet*. On James Forten, see Winch, *Gentleman of Color*. On James McCune Smith, see Stauffer, *Black Hearts of Men*. Stauffer charts the alliance between Smith, Frederick Douglass, Gerrit Smith, and John Brown. Recently, Stephen Hahn has described the Northern black communities that coalesced during this period as "historically specific variants of the broad

phenomenon" of maroon communities. He contends that free black communities in the North resembled maroon communities for several reasons: because they included many African Americans who had experienced or fled slavery; because black Northerners tended to live in residential clusters that served as "beacons" for runaway slaves; because black communities contained their own leadership cadres, social structures, institutions, and cultural practices; and because they were anomalous in a nation that equated blackness with slavery and whose courts and legislatures often conceded slaveholders' claims to property. Northern black communities' anomalous status also called for self-defense organizations, another commonality with maroon communities. See Hahn, *Political Worlds*, 27–40.

16. "Report of the Proceedings of the Colored National Convention, Held at Cleveland, Ohio, on Wednesday, September 6, 1848," in Bell, *Minutes of the Proceedings of the National Negro Conventions*, 18.

17. On Douglass, see McFeely, *Frederick Douglass*.

18. Fredrickson, *Black Image in the White Mind*, 60–61; Horton and Horton, *In Hope of Liberty*, 106; Litwack, *North of Slavery*, 65, 68–72, 75–83, 93–97.

19. On the confused nature of citizenship law prior to the Civil War, see Novak, "Legal Transformation of Citizenship."

20. Horton and Horton, *In Hope of Liberty*, 101–2; Litwack, *North of Slavery*, 31–38, 50–54; Smith, *Civic Ideals*, 175–81. Martha Jones has recently demonstrated that, despite the legal limitations on black rights and citizenship, African Americans in Baltimore participated in legal actions in local and state courts, thereby exercising rights, such as the protection of person and property before the law, that "would come to be recognized as one of citizenship's hallmark civil rights." At least in Baltimore, black citizens often "looked more [like] rights-bearing people than the degraded subjects they were intended to be." Jones's work highlights the need for similar studies of local jurisprudence and courthouse culture in other antebellum cities, and it shows that African Americans possessed the legal acumen, resources, and determination to overcome discriminatory legislation and practices. See Jones, *Birthright Citizens*, 70, 88.

21. On at least two occasions, though, black men obtained full-fledged passports. Pennsylvania abolitionist Robert Purvis received a passport in 1834, and New York minister Peter Williams received one two years later. These two anomalies became apparent in 1849, when controversy arose over the passport application of black Pennsylvanian Harry Hambleton. State Department officials hastily explained that Williams's passport was the result of a bureaucratic error, because his application had not specified his skin color. Purvis's case was more complicated. Purvis applied once and received the special certificate usually given to black travelers. When he applied again with a note from prominent white lawyer and abolitionist Roberts Vaux testifying to his considerable wealth and light complexion, Purvis received a regular passport. Secretary of State John Clayton's response to the existence of Purvis's passport highlighted the inconsistency of State Department policy on this issue. Because Purvis was "a gentleman, a man of property, of scarcely perceptible African descent," Clayton explained, the State Department had issued him a passport, "but not," he added, "as a colored man." See Amos G. Beman to Frederick Douglass, *FDP*, Sept. 15, 1854; "Passports to People of Color," *North Star*, Sept. 7, 1849; Robertson, *Passport in America*, 132–33.

22. Robertson, *Passport in America*, 131–34, 143–48. On passports and black sailors

during the antebellum period, see Jones, *Birthright Citizens*, chapter 3. Jones traces the experience of a free black sailor from Baltimore, George Hackett, who sailed aboard the USS *Constitution*, a journey that allowed led him to develop new insights regarding race and the law.

23. Berry, *Military Necessity and Civil Rights Policy*, 22–25, 31–34; Horton and Horton, *In Hope of Liberty*, 263–64.

24. At least they did not have to fear legally sanctioned reenslavement. Black Northerners, freeborn individuals and runaway slaves alike, lived constantly with the fear that they might be kidnapped and sold South as slaves. See Wilson, *Freedom at Risk*.

25. Rael, *Black Identity and Black Protest*, 25–27, 38–41; Ernest, *Nation within a Nation*, 107–11. On the growth and development of black churches, benevolent societies, and conventions and of the black press, see Reed, *Platform for Change*; Tate, "Antebellum Black Communities." On whites' attitudes toward African Americans and assumptions of black inferiority during this period, as well as the development of a new form of racism allegedly based on scientific understanding, see Fredrickson, *Black Image in the White Mind*, chapters 1–3.

26. "Memorial by Charles W. Gardner and Frederick A. Hinton," Jan. 6, 1838, in Ripley et al., *Black Abolitionist Papers*, 3:252, 254. For a similar linkage of black revolutionary service to black rights, see "Minutes of the State Convention, of the Colored Citizens of Ohio, Convened at Columbus, Jan. 15th, 16th, 17th and 18th, 1851," in Foner and Walker, *Proceedings of the Black State Conventions, 1840–1865*, 1:271.

27. Robert Purvis, "Appeal of Forty Thousand Citizens, Threatened With Disfranchisement, to the People of Pennsylvania," 1837, in Lapsansky, Newman, and Rael, *Pamphlets of Protest*, 140. On Purvis, see Ripley et al., *Black Abolitionist Papers*, 3:81–82n.

28. Quarles, "Black History's Antebellum Origins," 92.

29. "W.," "Colored Men Citizens," *FDP*, Aug. 25, 1854.

30. Nell, *Colored Patriots*, 378.

31. Quarles, "Black History's Antebellum Origins," 90–99; Kantrowitz, *More than Freedom*, 220–22.

32. Kantrowitz, *More than Freedom*, 235–36. For a summary of the Dorr War, see Wilentz, *Rise of American Democracy*, 539–45.

33. Rael, *Black Identity and Black Protest*, 281–83.

34. "Proceedings of the Colored National Convention, Held at Rochester, July 6th, 7th and 8th, 1853," in Bell, *Minutes of the Proceedings of the Negro National Conventions*, 8. On black Northerners' embrace of American principles, see also "Minutes of the National Convention of Colored Citizens: Held at Buffalo, on the 15th, 16th, 17th, 18th and 19th of August, 1843 for the Purpose of Considering Their Moral and Political Condition as American Citizens," in Bell, *Minutes of the Proceedings of the Negro National Conventions*, 6. On Vashon, see Ripley et al., *Black Abolitionist Papers*, 3:321–22n.

35. See William Wells Brown, "The History of the Haitian Revolution," in Lapsansky, Newman, and Rael, *Pamphlets of Protest*, 253. On Brown, see Farrison, *William Wells Brown*.

36. Benjamin Banneker to Thomas Jefferson, 1791, in Aptheker, *Documentary History of the Negro*, 1:22, 25.

37. Newman, *Freedom's Prophet*, 147; "Petition of Absalom Jones and Seventy-Three

Others to the President, Senate, and House of Representatives," Dec. 30, 1799, in Aptheker, *Documentary History of the Negro*, 1:331. See also James Forten, "Series of Letters by a Man of Color," 1813, in Lapsansky, Newman, and Rael, *Pamphlets of Protest*, 59–60.

38. Armitage, *Declaration of Independence*, 90–95.

39. "Minutes of the State Convention, of the Colored Citizens of the State of Michigan, Held in the City of Detroit on the 26th & 27th of October, 1843, for the Purpose of Considering Their Moral & Political Condition, as Citizens of the State," in Foner and Walker, *Proceedings of the Black State Conventions, 1840-1865*, 1:187. See also "Convention of the Colored Inhabitants of the State of New York, August 18–20, 1840," in Foner and Walker, *Proceedings of the Black State Conventions, 1840-1865*, 1:9.

40. "Minutes of the State Convention, of the Colored Citizens of Ohio, Convened at Columbus, Jan. 15th, 16th, 17th and 18th, 1851," in Foner and Walker, *Proceedings of the Black State Conventions, 1840-1865*, 1:270.

41. Rael, *Black Identity and Black Protest*, 77. See "Frederick Douglass Discusses the Fourth of July," 1852, in Aptheker, *Documentary History of the Negro*, 1:334.

42. "The American Negro's Fourth of July," 1832, in Aptheker, *Documentary History of the Negro*, 1:137.

43. "Denouncing Colonization," 1831, in Aptheker, *Documentary History of the Negro People*, 1:109. Black Northerners did not refer exclusively to the Declaration of Independence, often asserting that slavery and discriminatory legislation violated the Constitution as well, but the Declaration guided their conception of what they wanted the United States to become in a way that the Constitution did not. The Constitution included several key protections for slavery and had generally been given a proslavery interpretation by federal officials. However, the Declaration remained unsullied by even veiled protections of slavery. While they sometimes denied that the Declaration's equality clause applied to African Americans, white Americans never developed a proslavery theory of the document to match their proslavery constitutional theorizing. On federal officials, constitutional interpretation, and slavery, see Fehrenbacher, *Slaveholding Republic*.

44. Armitage, *Declaration of Independence*, 93–96. See also Foner, *We, the Other People*.

45. On the transition from an older, elite-centered, deferential school of abolitionism that worked through established political institutions and dated to the revolutionary period, to the immediate-abolition energies of the 1830s and the late antebellum period, see Newman, *Transformation of American Abolitionism*. Recently, Paul J. Polgar has challenged Newman's interpretation of early abolitionism as conservative and legalistic. Polgar instead characterizes this abolitionism as a "racially progressive reform enterprise" for its emphasis on educating emancipated slaves and integrating them into the American polity as citizens. See Polgar, "'Raise Them to an Equal Participation.'" On late-antebellum abolitionism, see Stewart, *Holy Warriors*.

46. Ernest, *Nation within a Nation*, 126; Kantrowitz, *More than Freedom*, 62–64; Quarles, *Black Abolitionists*, 47–49. On black abolitionists' resentment of white abolitionists' condescension and assumptions of superiority, see Davis, *The Problem of Slavery in the Age of Emancipation*, 194–95. Davis uses an imaginative device to convey

black abolitionists' view of free black Northerners' place in American society and the abolitionist struggle: he writes a letter from the point of view of a black abolitionist.

47. Douglass, *Two Speeches of Frederick Douglass*, 21.

48. Pease and Pease, "Negro Conventions," 40; Horton and Horton, *In Hope of Liberty*, 261–62. The fullest discussion of questions and controversies such as these remains Pease and Pease, *They Who Would Be Free*.

49. See Cooper, "Elevating the Race." On scholars' perceptions of black leaders' protest thought, and on the historiography surrounding antebellum Northern black leadership, which she characterizes as the historiography of "black abolitionists," see Sinha, "Coming of Age."

50. Pease and Pease, *They Who Would Be Free*, 129–31, 287–91; Rael, *Black Identity and Black Protest*, 147, 155–56, 158–207. Quote appears on page 188. See also Rael, "Market Revolution and Market Values."

51. On the kidnapping of black freemen before and after the 1850 Fugitive Slave Law, see Wilson, *Freedom at Risk*.

52. On slavery and sectional political controversies in the 1850s, see Potter, *Impending Crisis*. On Lincoln's conspiratorial charges regarding the Slave Power, see Donald, *Lincoln*, 207–8. On slaveholders' political and economic power, see Rothman, "'Slave Power.'"

53. Smith, *Civic Ideals*, 265–68. On the *Dred Scott* decision, see also Fehrenbacher, *Dred Scott Case*.

54. Frances Ellen Watkins Harper, "Could We Trace the Record of Every Human Heart," in Foster, *Brighter Coming Day*, 100. Martha Jones has shown that, despite Taney's finding regarding black citizenship, state courts continued to recognize that African Americans possessed some relationship to their political communities, and therefore also possessed at least some rights whites were bound to respect. Taney was upset enough about state courts' defiance of his opinion, and the general criticism his decision received, that he took the unusual step of writing a supplemental opinion further explaining his reasoning, which he hoped to publish during his lifetime. See Jones, *Birthright Citizens*, 133–37.

55. On Delany, see Adeleke, *Without Regard to Race*. On Garnet, see Schor, *Henry Highland Garnet*.

56. Blight, *Frederick Douglass' Civil War*, 91–92; Brown, "History of the Haitian Revolution," 253. For Garnet's speech to the 1843 national convention and the debate over publishing it as part of the convention's proceedings, see "Minutes of the National Convention of Colored Citizens: Held at Buffalo, on the 15th, 16th, 17th, 18th and 19th of August, 1843, for the Purpose of Considering Their Moral and Political Condition as American Citizens," in Bell, *Minutes of the Proceedings of the Negro National Conventions*. On late-antebellum black colonizationist movements, see Pease and Pease, *They Who Would Be Free*, 251–76. On black Northerners' embrace of violence during the 1850s, see also Dick, *Black Protest*, 140–57.

57. Other black units formed during the 1850s included the Attucks Blues of Cincinnati; the Loguen Guards (named for the Syracuse minister and Underground Railroad operative Jermain Loguen) of Binghamton, New York; the Attucks Guards of New Bedford, Massachusetts; the Henry Highland Garnet Guards of Pittsburgh; the Attic

Guard of Morris Grove, Long Island; the Douglass Guard of Reading, Pennsylvania; the Henry Highland Garnet Guards of Harrisburg, Pennsylvania; and the National Guards of Providence. On black militia units, see Cunningham, *Black Citizen-Soldiers of Kansas*, 7–9; Ernest, *Nation within a Nation*, 19; Frederick Douglass, "Letter from the editor," *FDP*, Aug. 10, 1855; Johnson, *African American Soldiers in the National Guard*, 9–11; Horton and Horton, *In Hope of Liberty*, 265; Quarles, *Allies for Freedom*, 68–69, 154–55; Quarles, *Black Abolitionists*, 229–30.

58. Quarles, *Black Abolitionists*, 229.

59. On Walker, see Hinks, *To Awaken My Afflicted Brethren*.

60. Walker, *David Walker's Appeal*, 15, 30.

61. Walker here worked in the tradition of the black jeremiad, warning whites of the apocalyptic consequences that would result from their betrayal of American first principles. See Howard-Pitney, *Afro-American Jeremiad*; Rael, *Black Identity and Black Protest*, 266–72.

62. "Speech by Robert Purvis," May 12, 1857, in Ripley et al., *Black Abolitionist Papers*, 4:364.

63. "Speech by Charles L. Remond," in Ripley et al., *Black Abolitionist Papers*, 4:386, 388.

64. "A Public Discussion of Insurrection," in Aptheker, *Documentary History of the Negro*, 1:406.

65. Frederick Douglass to readership of *Douglass' Monthly*, *Douglass' Monthly*, Nov. 1859.

66. On Douglass's actions in the wake of Harpers Ferry, see McFeely, *Frederick Douglass*, 197–203. According to McFeely, the "deliberate, calm" tone of Douglass's letter reflected "the conscious effort Douglass had made to regain his composure" in the aftermath of the raid, when he narrowly evaded capture.

67. "Proceedings of a Convention of the Colored Men of Ohio, Held in the City of Cincinnati, on the 23d, 24th, 25th, and 26th Days of November, 1858," in Foner and Walker, *Proceedings of the Black State Conventions, 1840–1865*, 1:333; "Proceedings of the State Convention of Colored Men of the State of Ohio, Held in the City of Columbus, January 21st, 22 & 23d, 1857," in Foner and Walker, *Proceedings of the Black State Conventions, 1840–1865*, 1:324.

68. Quoted in Quarles, *Black Abolitionists*, 228. On Douglas, see Ripley et al., *Black Abolitionist Papers*, 4:78–79.

69. See Taylor, *Internal Enemy*.

70. "An Address Delivered at the African Masonic Hall," Feb. 27, 1833, in Richardson, *Maria W. Stewart*, 61.

71. Untitled letter copied from *Colored People's Press*, *The Liberator*, Apr. 1, 1842.

72. "Nubia" to editor, *Frederick Douglass' Paper*, March 16, 1855.

73. Lapp, *Blacks in Gold Rush California*, 263; Gardner, *Unexpected Places*, 210.

74. Kantrowitz, *More than Freedom*, 226–28.

75. "Comparing White and Negro Americans," 1858, in Aptheker, *Documentary History of the Negro*, 1:404.

76. "Speech of Dr. John S. Rock," *The Liberator*, Mar. 16, 1860.

77. Kantrowitz, *More than Freedom*, 199–200; Horton and Horton, *In Hope of Liberty*, 263–64; Quarles, *Black Abolitionists*, 229.

78. Crofts, *Lincoln and the Politics of Slavery*, 70–71, 88–89.

79. Sinha, "Allies for Emancipation?," 173. On Lincoln's opposition to black citizenship, see also Oakes, "Natural Rights, Citizenship Rights," 121–23. Oakes stresses that Lincoln, unlike his antagonist Stephen Douglas, did not actively *oppose* black citizenship. Lincoln, Oakes has written, included this statement about opposing black citizenship within an implicitly condemnatory summary of the *Dred Scott* decision. Oakes also points out that in Lincoln's First Inaugural, the president acknowledged black citizenship by calling for a revision of the Fugitive Slave Law of 1850 that would allow for supposed fugitives' due process rights to be protected under the Constitution's comity clause.

80. See Geffert and Libby, "Regional Black Involvement in John Brown's Raid," 2006; Geffert, "They Heard His Call." On Brown's relationship with his black allies generally, see Quarles, *Allies for Freedom*.

CHAPTER TWO

1. Immaterial, "Black Regiments Proposed," *DM*, May 1861.

2. During the secession crisis and the war's early months, Douglass was characteristically mercurial. At times, he despaired that the war and the Union cause would do little to benefit African Americans, lamenting the slowness to embrace emancipation. Mostly, though, Douglass was hopeful about the war and black men's potential to play a decisive role for the Union. He saw the war as a divine chastisement for the sin of slavery that would purge the young republic of sin and thereby allow the United States to play its ordained role in world history as a beacon of liberty and freedom. On Douglass's thinking during the war, see Blight, *Frederick Douglass' Civil War*.

3. Anonymous to editor, *WAA*, May 11, 1861.

4. In 1965, James M. McPherson wrote, "In the first weeks after the fall of Fort Sumter, Northern Negroes joined in the outburst of patriotism and offered their services to the government to help suppress the rebellion." In 2009, Christian Samito concurred: "Black men eagerly sought to participate in the patriotic wave that swept the North after the firing on Fort Sumter." See McPherson, *Negro's Civil War*, 19; Samito, *Becoming American under Fire*, 35.

5. For an example of a black man who joined a white unit, see H. Ford Douglas to Frederick Douglass, Jan. 8, 1863, in Ripley et al., *Black Abolitionist Papers*, 5:166–67. Douglas, a light-skinned black man, enlisted in the Ninety-Fifth Illinois, and might not have been questioned about his race at first. Eventually, Douglas's comrades discovered his ancestry but continued to treat him with respect. He eventually transferred to a black unit, where he became one of the few black men to rise to the level of commissioned officer, serving as captain of the Independent Battery, U.S. Colored Light Artillery. See Berlin, Reidy, and Rowland, *Black Military Experience*, 311.

6. Glenn David Brasher, Mark Grimsley, and Kristopher Teters have shown that early Confederate victories and the war's protracted length did help convince many Northerners to support harsher measures against the Confederacy, including military emancipation, and to support black participation in the Union war effort. See Brasher, *Peninsula Campaign and the Necessity of Emancipation*, especially chapter 8; Grimsley, *Hard Hand of War*, 67–78, 136–41; Teters, *Practical Liberators*, 62–64.

7. "Better Than Peace," *CR*, Apr. 27, 1861.

8. Frederick Douglass, "How to End the War," *DM*, May 1861.

9. Alfred M. Green, "Letter from Pennsylvania," *PP*, May 25, 1861. On Green, see Ripley et al., *Black Abolitionist Papers*, 5:125–27n; Wayman, *Cyclopaedia of African Methodism*, 68–69.

10. Ripley et al., *Black Abolitionist Papers*, 3:448–49n.

11. Cunningham, *Black Citizen-Soldiers of Kansas*, 8; "Sentiments of the Colored People of Boston," *The Liberator*, Apr. 26, 1861.

12. "Meeting of Colored Citizens," *The Liberator*, May 3, 1861. On Hayden, see Kantrowitz, *More than Freedom*.

13. "Equal Rights," *The Liberator*, Nov. 22, 1861; Green and Whitman, *Letters and Discussions on the Formation of Colored Regiments*, 3; McPherson, *Negro's Civil War*, 19–20; "Meeting of Colored Citizens," *The Liberator*, May 3, 1861; "Meeting of Colored Citizens in New Bedford," *The Liberator*, Oct. 18, 1861; "No Proscription of Citizens," *The Liberator*, May 17, 1861; "Petition," *The Liberator*, Nov. 22, 1861.

14. McPherson, *Negro's Civil War*, 21–22.

15. David A. Gerber, "Peter Humphries Clark," 173–80.

16. Clark, *Black Brigade of Cincinnati*, 2–3.

17. See Thomas Bayne, "Letter from Brother Bayne," *CR*, July 20, 1861; "Goodelle," "Letter from Syracuse," *PP*, June 6, 1861; T. M. D. Ward, "Letter from California," *CR*, Sept. 7, 1861; "Meeting of Colored Citizens in New Bedford," *The Liberator*, Oct. 18, 1861. On Powell, see Ripley et al., *Black Abolitionist Papers*, 3:302–3n.

18. Ernest, *Nation within a Nation*, 179–80; Jackson, "Cultural Stronghold"; Reed, *Platform for Change*, 117–19.

19. Weaver voluntarily left the editor's chair in July 1861 in favor of A. L. Stanford, but he returned at the start of 1862.

20. Gardner, *Unexpected Places*, 56.

21. Ernest, *Nation within a Nation*, 182; Reed, *Platform for Change*, 119–20; Williams, *"Christian Recorder,"* 12, 15–16. On Weaver and the *Recorder*, see ibid., 54–70, 75–83.

22. "Sentiments of the Colored People of Boston upon the War," *The Liberator*, Apr. 26, 1861.

23. "Celebration of the First of August, at Island Grove, Abington," *The Liberator*, Aug. 15, 1862. Henry McNeal Turner also acknowledged that Northern defeats were helping the cause of black freedom. "The truth is," he wrote on July 9, "every victory the Southerners gain tends to loosen the chains of slavery, and every one the Northerners gain tends only to tighten them, and it will be so till the North is brought to her senses. And God's plan of teaching her sense is through Southern victories." See Henry McNeal Turner to editor, *CR*, July 19, 1862.

24. "Where Hope Rests," *PP*, May 25, 1861.

25. For other examples of black commentators predicting that Northern defeats or a long, painful war would cause the Union to enlist black soldiers and embrace emancipation, see Inquirer, "Letter from Philadelphia," *PP*, Nov. 2, 1861; "Frederick Douglass on the Crisis," *DM*, June 1861; "George E. Stephens to editor, *Weekly Anglo-African*," in Yacovone, *Voice of Thunder*, 151–53.

26. On Cameron's dismissal, see McPherson, *Battle Cry of Freedom*, 357–58; Quarles, *Negro in the Civil War*, 108–9.

27. Lincoln quoted in Foner, *Fiery Trial*, 228; Oakes, *Freedom National*, 90, 104. V. Jacque Voegeli has demonstrated that, in 1861 and 1862, antislavery Republicans from midwestern states often coupled their advocacy for antislavery measures with white supremacist rhetoric. They asserted white Northerners' superiority to black Northerners and pandered to white midwesterners' fears that emancipation would entail massive black migration to the North. John Sherman of Ohio could thus proclaim that though the "great mass" of midwesterners were "opposed to slavery—morally, socially and politically"—they were yet "opposed to having many negroes among them." Sherman also argued that African Americans were "spurned and hated all over the country North and South." Sherman quoted in Voegeli, *Free but Not Equal*.

28. On appropriations for colonization in congressional legislation, see Oakes, *Freedom National*, 280. On Republicans' embrace of colonization and continued white supremacist rhetoric, see Voegeli, *Free but Not Equal*, 19–29.

29. "The War—Its Prosecution," *WAA*, 4 Jan. 1862.

30. Oakes, *Freedom National*, 138–45, 156–63, 175, 213–17.

31. George E. Stephens to editor, *WAA*, Feb. 13, 1862, in Yacovone, *Voice of Thunder*, 181.

32. "Speech of John S. Rock, Esq., at the Annual Meeting of the Massachusetts Anti-Slavery Society, Thursday Evening, Jan. 23," *CR*, Feb. 22, 1862.

33. "Bobb'n Around," "Colored Americans and the War," *PP*, May 25, 1861. For other instances in which black commentators expressed dissatisfaction with Union policy toward slavery, see "Progress of Opinion," *CR*, Nov. 23, 1861; "What Are We Fighting For?" *PP*, 2 June 1861.

34. "The Fatal Step Backward," *WAA*, Sept. 9, 1861.

35. Wesley W. Tate, "Letter from a Colored Frontiersman," *PP*, Nov. 23, 1861. For other examples of black men discouraged by Union policy toward slavery and African Americans, see Jabez P. Campbell, untitled article, *CR*, Oct.12, 1861. Campbell argued that President Lincoln did not include black men when he spoke of the American nation, citing the president's and other officials' repeated assertions that they were not fighting an antislavery war. Campbell also noted citations of the *Dred Scott* decision as law, the president's revocation of Fremont's proclamation, the government's refusal to enlist black soldiers, and the War Department's order barring black laborers from wearing the federal uniform. All these circumstances provided evidence that, as he stated, "[Lincoln] does not recognise black men, neither expressly nor impliedly to be a part and parcel of this nation."

36. "Inquirer," "Letter from Philadelphia," *PP*, Aug. 24, 1861.

37. N. B. Harris, "Letter from Oberlin," *PP*, Aug. 24, 1861.

38. Richard McDaniel to editor, *Anglo-African Magazine*, Aug. 26, 1865.

39. William C. Nell, "Matters and Things," *The Liberator*, Dec. 5, 1862; William Parham to Jacob C. White Jr., Sept. 7, 1862, box 115-2, Jacob C. White Collection, Moorland-Spingarn Research Center, Manuscript Division, Howard University, Washington, D.C.

40. Clark, *Black Brigade of Cincinnati*, 9–10. Cincinnati black men's labor may have

inspired their brethren in Louisville, for a call for one thousand black men to work on city entrenchments in advance of Confederate forces' arrival appeared in the September 27 issue of the *Christian Recorder*. See B. L. Brooks, "From Louisville, KY," *CR*, Sept. 1862.

41. Nell, "Matters and Things," *The Liberator*, Dec. 5, 1862. Both quotations are extracts from letters written by black Cincinnatians to Nell. Nell did not name either man.

42. "Aleph" to editor, *CR*, Sept. 20, 1862; Elisha Weaver, "Editorial Correspondence," *CR*, Sept. 20, 1862.

43. "The Colored Preachers of Philadelphia—No. III.—Rev. Wm. Douglass," *PP*, Dec. 14, 1861.

44. William E. Walker, "Baptist Convention at New Bedford," *WAA*, Oct. 12, 1861.

45. "The Glorious First," *PP*, Aug. 24, 1861.

46. See "Emancipation Day at Drummondsville, Canada West," *The Liberator*, Aug. 23, 1861; "W. J. Watkins on the American Revolution," *The Liberator*, July 26, 1861.

47. William J. Watkins, "A Few Notes By the Way," *PP*, Oct. 5, 1861. Around this same time, AME minister Henry McNeal Turner also talked about how he had his mind changed about African Americans' stake in the Union war effort. Initially, he had disagreed with his fellow AME clergyman Jabez P. Campbell that the "colored man . . . had no interests for which the administration contemplated any idea of benefiting." The prejudiced manner in which Northern newspaper correspondents, even those sympathetic to emancipation, described African Americans, persuaded Turner otherwise. He also expressed frustration with what he perceived as Northern slowness to strike at slavery: "Every person knows, that the national strife now agitating this country, is about the thraldomized condition of the colored man, and yet its unpopularity palsies the tongue of its clearest perceivers, and they will wise in, and wise out, and wise all around the theme, and never wise into it." See Henry McNeal Turner to editor, *CR*, Nov. 30, 1861.

48. N. A .D., "How We Stand," *PP*, May 25, 1861.

49. J. H. W., "Letter from Ohio," *PP*, May 25, 1861. On Parham, see Joe William Trotter, *African American Urban Life*, 78.

50. On White, see Ripley et al., *Black Abolitionist Papers*, 4:138–39.

51. William Parham to Jacob C. White Jr., Oct. 12, 1861, box 115–2, Jacob C. White Collection.

52. "'Arming the Slaves,'" *WAA*, Mar. 23, 1861.

53. "The Star-Spangled Banner, and the Duty of Colored Americans to the Flag," *CR*, Apr. 27, 1861.

54. "Have We a War Policy?" *WAA*, Apr. 27, 1861. For another black correspondent making an argument that used the example of unrewarded black service in earlier wars to oppose immediate enlistment, see J. N. S., "A Word from the Country," *PP*, May 25, 1861.

55. On citizenship in the antebellum United States, see Kettner, *Development of American Citizenship*; Novak, "Legal Transformation of Citizenship"; Smith, *Civic Ideals*. On distinctions between natural, political, civil, and social rights, see Foner, *Reconstruction*, 231.

56. Henry Cropper, "Note from Philadelphia," *PP*, May 25, 1861. The Frank Johnson Guards took their name from Francis Johnson, a popular black composer, musician, and bandleader who hailed from Philadelphia. On Johnson, see Jones, *Francis Johnson*.

57. J. N. S., "Word from the Country," *PP*, May 25, 1861.

58. "Fighting Rebels With Only One Hand," *DM*, Sept. 1861.

59. "Argo," "Letter from Washington," *CR*, May 4, 1861.

60. "Colored Men and the War," *The Liberator*, May 10, 1861.

61. R. H. V.'s identity is impossible to establish with certainty. Both Debra Jackson and Maxwell Whitman identify him as a member of the Vashon family, but neither indicates how they know this piece of information. See Jackson, "Cultural Stronghold," 349–50; "Alfred M. Green and the Controversy over Black Men as Soldiers in the Civil War, a Bibliographical Note by Maxwell Whitman," in Green and Whitman, *Letters and Discussions on the Formation of Colored Regiments*. But C. Peter Ripley speculates that R. H. V. is Robert H. Vandyne, "a frequent New York City contributor to the *Weekly Anglo-African*." See R. H. V., "Formation of Colored Regiments," Sept. 28, 1861, in Ripley, *Witness for Freedom*, 211–15.

62. R. H. V., "Formation of Colored Regiments," *WAA*, Sept. 28, 1861.

63. Alfred M. Green, "Colored Regiments," *WAA*, Oct. 12, 1861.

64. R. H. V., "Formation of Colored Regiments," *WAA*, Oct. 26, 1861.

65. Green replied again to R. H. V. in November; see Alfred M. Green, "Formation of Colored Regiments," *WAA*, Nov. 23, 1861. See also Green and Whitman, *Letters and Discussions on the Formation of Colored Regiments*.

66. Ernest, *Nation within a Nation*, 107–12.

67. See Jabez P. Campbell and L. R. Seymour to editor, *CR*, Sept. 6, 1862; "Great Meeting in Shiloh Church," *The Liberator*, May 22, 1863; "Sentiments of the Colored People of Boston upon the War," *The Liberator*, Apr. 26, 1861; "War Meeting in Brooklyn," *WAA*, 21 Mar. 21, 1863.

68. "Meeting of Colored Citizens," *The Liberator*, June 27, 1862; "Meeting of Colored Citizens in New Bedford," *The Liberator*, Oct. 18, 1861; "War Meeting in Massachusetts," *WAA*, Mar. 21, 1863.

69. Nash, *Forging Freedom*, 277–78.

70. "Lecture on the 'Crisis,'" originally published in *Philadelphia Inquirer*, reprinted in *DM*, Apr. 1863; "Meeting of Colored Citizens," *The Liberator*, June 27, 1862; "War Meeting in Ward Six—Our Colored Citizens in Council," *The Liberator*, Dec. 11, 1863.

71. Charles Berry and Daniel B. Landin, "A War-Meeting in New Jersey," *WAA*, Apr. 25, 1863.

72. Henry McNeal Turner to editor, *CR*, Aug. 9, 1862.

73. "War Meeting in New Bedford," *WAA*, Feb. 28, 1862.

74. Ernest, *Nation within a Nation*, 113; Rael, *Black Identity and Black Protest*, 54–65.

75. Berry and Landin, "War-Meeting in New Jersey," *WAA*, Apr. 25, 1863.

76. On Gloucester, see Ripley et al., *Black Abolitionist Papers*, 4:380.

77. Johnson, *African American Soldiers in the National Guard*, 7. On Wilson, see Ripley et al., *Black Abolitionist Papers*, 4:145.

78. "Bobb'n Around," "Colored Americans and the War," *PP*, May 25, 1861.

79. On Wears, see Ripley et al., *Black Abolitionist Papers*, 4:318-19n.

80. "Veritas" to editor, *WAA*, Nov. 2, 1861.

81. "Inquirer," "Letter from Philadelphia," *PP*, Nov. 23, 1861. On Smith, who was responsible for organizing the AME Church in Chester, Pennsylvania, see Ripley et al., *Black Abolitionist Papers*, 4:316-17; Wayman, *Cyclopaedia of African Methodism*, 35.

82. On Catto, see Biddle and Dubin, *Tasting Freedom*.

83. John A. Williams and A. M. Green, "Meeting in Relation to Colored Enlistment," *PA*, Sept. 27, 1862. Around this same time, the AME Church's Genesee Conference resolved a similar debate differently, expressing opposition to enlisting without certain guarantees. Those at the meeting resolved the following: "That we, as ministers, advise our brethren to take no part in this war on either side until they can do it as men, as freemen, and citizens. When that time comes, as come it must, let them be ready to prove themselves true lovers of God and liberty, nobly acting their part." It is possible this meeting took place after Lincoln's preliminary Emancipation Proclamation was released, but it seems unlikely. The proclamation likely would have been enumerated among a list of measures that cheered the gathering, including D.C. abolition and the new confiscation legislation. The ministers also resolved on the circumstances under which the war should end: "[Not] until it uses up slavery root and branch, and fully restores to the colored man all his God-given rights." See "The Genesee Conference—Concluded," *CR*, Oct. 4, 1862.

84. Dittmer, "The Education of Henry McNeal Turner," 253.

85. Henry McNeal Turner, "Washington Correspondence," *CR*, Aug. 9, 1862.

86. On Loguen, see Hunter, *To Set the Captives Free*; Ripley et al., *Black Abolitionist Papers*, 4:87-88.

87. Jermain W. Loguen to editor, *WAA*, Sept. 14, 1861.

88. "The Colored People of Cleveland on the War," *WAA*, Nov. 9, 1861.

89. Gallagher, *Union War*; Manning, *What This Cruel War Was Over*, 39-44; James McPherson, *For Cause and Comrades*, 17-19.

90. On this period of the war, see McPherson, *Battle Cry of Freedom*, 392-437, 454-62.

91. On Anderson, see Ripley et al., *Black Abolitionist Papers*, 5:185-86n; Lapp, *Blacks in Gold Rush California*, 219-20.

92. "The Events of the Day," *PA*, Apr. 5, 1862.

93. "Review of the Past Year," *CR*, Apr. 26, 1862.

94. Oakes, *Freedom National*, 257-74.

95. Frederick Douglass to Charles Sumner, Apr. 6, 1862, reel 25, Charles Sumner Papers, Manuscript Division, LOC, Washington, D.C. For accounts of references to celebrations of D.C. emancipation in Northern cities, see "The Celebration [Calif.]," *PA*, Aug. 2, 1862; "The Jubilee Meeting [New Haven, Conn.]," *CR*, May 10, 1862; "The Late Emancipation Act [Terre Haute, Ind.]," *CR*, 17 May 1862; "Meeting of Colored Citizens [Buffalo, N.Y.]," *The Liberator*, June 27, 1862; "Newark, N.J.," *CR*, June 28, 1862. For other positive comments on D.C. emancipation in the black press, see "Observer," "Sketches from Washington," *CR*, Apr. 5, 1862; Sacer, "The Great Prospect," *CR*, Apr. 5, 1862.

96. Guelzo, *Lincoln's Emancipation Proclamation*, 161-62; Oakes, *Freedom National*, 264-65, 285-89; Robertson, *Passport in America*, 129.

97. "Colored Citizenship," *CR*, Sept. 14, 1861. For another instance in which a black leader emphasized the importance of the passport issue and its link to black citizenship, see "Martin's Farewell to England," *The Liberator*, Feb. 28, 1862.

98. On white abolitionists' reactions to their newfound popularity and abolitionism's sudden respectability in the North, see McPherson, *Struggle for Equality*, 81–86; Sinha, "Allies for Emancipation?," 179–80.

99. Sacer, "District of Columbia Correspondence," *CR*, Jan. 25, 1862. See also "Wendell Phillips," *CR*, 29, 1862.

100. Sacer, "District of Columbia Correspondence," *CR*, Mar. 22, 1862.

101. John S. Rock, for instance, addressed the issue at two public meetings in early 1862, though the scenario he contemplated involved a war between Great Britain and the United States, which at that point seemed possible. See "Speech of John S. Rock, Esq., at the Annual Meeting of the Massachusetts Anti-Slavery Society, Thursday Evening, Jan. 23," *CR*, Feb. 22, 1862; E. D. B., "Lectures by John S. Rock, Esq.," *CR*, Apr. 19, 1862.

102. Of course, not all black commentators were cheered by the aforementioned developments in the spring of 1862. For continued skepticism about Lincoln and the Union war effort, see "Essex Co. Anti-Slavery Convention and Pic-nic," *The Liberator*, July 25, 1862; Henry McNeal Turner, "The Plagues of This Country," *CR*, July 12, 1862; J. W. P., "Colored Men in the Revolution and in the War of 1812," *CR*, May 10, 1862; untitled article, *PA*, June 14, 1862; untitled article, *PA*, June 21, 1862. William J. Watkins, who had soured on the Union war effort, had not warmed to the prospect of black service by the summer of 1862. McNeal Turner reported on Watkins's view of black service:

> [African Americans] might sing[,] "In Dixie's land we take our stand, We will live and die in Dixie's land." But living and dying is about all we ever would do in this country. We might stay to fight it out, as many had said, but how men could fight without arms he could not see, and he knew the colored people had none in this country. He stated that many who had claimed to be the colored man's friend, were actuated with a desire to rid the country of the negro, and that there were not five leading men in this country who desired to see the negro on an equality with the white, and that one thousand years would not secure one colored man the nomination for President. (See Henry McNeal Turner, "Letter from Washington," *CR*, June 28, 1862.)

103. On this period of the war, see McPherson, *Battle Cry of Freedom*, 463–80, 490–94, 511–37.

104. Sanger, *U.S. Statutes at Large*, 12:592, 599.

105. Untitled editorial, *PA*, July 19, 1862.

106. "Arming of the Colored People, and the Confiscation Bill," *CR*, July 19, 1862.

107. Henry McNeal Turner to editor, *CR*, July 19, 1862.

108. Frederick Douglass, "What the People Expect of Mr. Lincoln," *DM*, Aug. 1862.

109. "War.—Mobs," *CR*, Aug. 9, 1862.

110. On colonization appropriations in these acts, see Oakes, *Freedom National*, 280. On Republicans' embrace of colonization and continued white supremacist rhetoric, see Voegeli, *Free but Not Equal*, 19–29, and on midwestern racial violence, 34–35.

On complaints about mistreatment in Kentucky, see "An Observer," "Letter from Kentucky," *CR*, Apr. 5, 1862. Black Northerners complained at various times during 1862 of black civilians being mistreated by Union soldiers. Racism among Union soldiers incensed Henry McNeal Turner. On September 19, 1862, he wrote,

> The latest round of Union recruits are all the time cursing and abusing the infernal negro, as some say, nigger. In many instances you may see a regiment of soldiers passing along the street, and knowing them to be fresh troops, you may (as it is natural) stop to take a look at them, and instead of them thinking about the orders of their commanders, or Jeff. Davis and his army, with whom they must soon contend, they are gazing about to see if they can find a nigger to spit their venom at. And I believe it is to kill off just such rebels as these that this war is being waged for, one in rebellion to their country, and the other in rebellion to humanity, for that man who refuses to respect an individual because his skin is black, when God himself made him black, is as big a rebel as ever the devil or any of his subalterns were. (See Henry McNeal Turner, "Affairs in Washington," *CR*, Sept. 27, 1862.)

111. Henry McNeal Turner, "Washington Correspondence," *CR*, Aug. 30, 1862.

112. On this meeting, see Foner, *Fiery Trial*, 224–26; Masur, "African-American Delegation," 135. In November 1862, E. J .J., a black correspondent of the *Pacific Appeal*, remembered how African Americans in New Bedford, Massachusetts, had felt prior to the ministers' meeting with the nation's chief executive. "We looked and felt hopeful," he wrote. "We were sure of a welcome, for we were invited guests. The air we breathed seemed to be impregnated with humanity and love. The sun shone brighter and the birds sang more sweetly as we wended our way to the interview." See E. J .J., "Acts of the Present Administration," *PA*, Dec. 6, 1862.

113. Foner, *Fiery Trial*, 224–25. Some historians think Lincoln was putting on an act here, especially in light of the fact that he had already told his cabinet about his plans to issue an emancipation proclamation. Lincoln was, in this interpretation, trying to soften up white Northern opinion concerning emancipation; that is, he might have believed that white Northerners would be amenable to emancipation if they thought it would be paired with colonization. For analyses of Lincoln's conduct at this meeting, see Donald, *Lincoln*, 367–68; Oakes, *Freedom National*, 308–10.

114. Frederick Douglass, "The President and His Speeches," *DM*, Sept. 1862.

115. George B. Vashon to Abraham Lincoln, *DM*, Oct. 1862. On black Washingtonians' enthusiasm for emigration to Chiriqui in modern-day Panama, see Masur, "African-American Delegation," 138–40. On Vashon, see Ripley et al., *Black Abolitionist Papers*, 3:321n. Other protests relating to Lincoln's colonization plan and the meeting with the D.C. black delegation include "Mrs. Frances E. Watkins Harper on the War and the President's Colonization Scheme," *CR*, Sept. 27, 1862; "Reply to the President, by the Colored People of Newtown, L.I.," *The Liberator*, Sept. 12, 1862; A. P. Smith to Abraham Lincoln, *DM*, Oct. 1862. In the October issue, Douglass also included his own correspondence with Montgomery Blair in which he opposed colonization. See "Postmaster General Blair and Frederick Douglass," *DM*, Oct. 1862.

116. On federally supported colonization efforts, see McPherson, *Battle Cry of Freedom*, 508–9; McPherson, *Struggle for Equality*, 155–56. Lincoln actually signed a

contract with Bernard Kock, whom McPherson describes as a "fly-by-night promoter," for a colonization venture on the small island of Ile-de-Vache off Haiti, but it attracted little support and failed dismally. Lincoln admitted the failure and sent a ship to return the expedition's survivors in 1864. Black leaders opposed to colonization confronted an acute threat in 1862 when certain segments of the free black population were talking enthusiastically of colonization at the same time that the administration was touting it as policy. For instance, when in March the *Recorder's* D.C. correspondent "Sacer" learned that Rev. Alexander Crummell, a prominent advocate of black emigration to Liberia, was visiting the District, he hoped Crummell would "say just as little about Africa, at this present time, as he [could]." Sacer declared, "When a strong party is forming in the nation to banish from the shores of America the colored man, because there is a prospect of his chains falling off, it is no time to lend directly or indirectly any aid to the scheme of sending the colored people out of the country." See Sacer, "District of Columbia Correspondence," *CR*, Mar. 22, 1862. It seems certain that some enthusiasm for colonization nevertheless remained. Henry McNeal Turner reported hearing William J. Watkins advocate emigration to Haiti before a cheering audience, though he noted that this same crowd had cheered John Rock when he had spoken against emigration the week prior. See Henry McNeal Turner, "Letter from Washington," *CR*, June 28, 1862. McNeal Turner also reported enthusiasm for colonization in October. See Henry McNeal Turner, "Our Washington Correspondence," *CR*, Nov. 1, 1862.

117. "The War," *CR*, Aug. 16, 1862.

118. J. P. Campbell and L. R. Seymour to editor, *CR*, Sept. 6, 1862.

119. "An Appeal in Behalf of the Persecuted Colored Citizens of the Free States," *The Liberator*, Aug. 22, 1862.

120. J. M. W. to editor, *PA*, Aug. 9, 1862.

121. J. C. J. to editor, *PA*, Aug. 16, 1862.

122. Hofstadter, *American Political Tradition*, 132.

123. In so doing, Allen Guelzo has argued, it committed the federal government to supporting a slave insurrection. See Guelzo, *Lincoln's Emancipation Proclamation*, 174. Frederick Douglass seems to have understood this section of the Emancipation Proclamation in precisely this way. At a rally in Chicago in February 1863, he said that "the President's proclamation had given the slaves the *legal* right to liberty. Now they could obtain their personal freedom without trampling upon civil laws. Instead of rising up as insurrectionists, in opposition to law, they could rise up in obedience to law." See "Fred. Douglass in Chicago, His Lecture Last Evening," *DM*, Feb. 1863.

124. Untitled article, *CR*, Sept. 27, 1862.

125. Henry McNeal Turner, "A Call to Action by Rev. H. M. Turner," *CR*, Oct. 4, 1862.

126. McPherson, *Struggle for Equality*, 118–19.

127. Turner, "Call to Action."

128. William Parham to Jacob C. White Jr., Oct. 6, 1862, box 6, folder 18, Jacob C. White Papers, Leon B. Gardiner Collection of American Negro Historical Society Records, 1790–1905, HSP, Philadelphia, Pa.

129. See "Remarks to a Deputation of Western Gentlemen," *New York Tribune*, Aug. 5, 1862, in Basler, *Collected Works of Abraham Lincoln*, 5:357; Smith, *Lincoln and the U.S. Colored Troops*, 14–15.

130. On Johnson, see C. N. B., "Colored Men of California, No. IV: Dr. E. R. Johnson,"

PA, July 18, 1863; Winch, *Gentleman of Color*, 88; Grover, *Fugitive's Gibraltar*, 133, 136–38, 276.

131. E. R. J. [Ezra R. Johnson], "Liberty Bells Are Ringing," *PA*, Oct. 4, 1862.

132. E. R. J. [Ezra R. Johnson], "The North and the South," *PA*, Nov. 1, 1862.

133. E. J .J., "Acts of the Present Administration," *PA*, Nov. 1, 1862. It is possible that this "E. J. J." was in fact E. R. J. and that a typo accounts for the different middle initial in this case. This is unlikely, as E. R. J.'s articles were usually numbered with Roman numerals and billed as part of a series, but the possibility remains.

134. Continuing its prewar policy of enlisting black sailors, the Union navy welcomed black recruits, free and enslaved. From the war's earliest days, slaves reached Union ships and naval installations and enlisted alongside white and free black sailors. Black men in the Union navy dealt with racism in the ranks but often enjoyed substantial equality with white sailors, usually serving in integrated crews, receiving equal pay, benefits, and living conditions, and enjoying access to promotion. Black enlistment, Steven J. Ramold has written, was a "godsend" to Navy Secretary Gideon Welles, who faced the formidable task of establishing an effective blockade of Confederate ports and rivers. The navy's policy elicited little comment. This silence likely stemmed from the fact that the prewar navy had enlisted black men. Black sailors spent long periods at sea or in a small number of eastern naval yards and were literally not as visible to the Northern public as black infantry troops later would be; this fact, combined with Americans' low estimation of the navy and those who served in it, quieted criticism. See Ramold, *Slaves, Sailors, Citizens*, 4–5, 36–43, 82–83. William H. Johnson was another black man who fought in white regiments, the Second and Eighth Connecticut, during this period of the war. After seeing action at First Bull Run, Johnson actually wrote to the *Pine & Palm* to oppose black service, though later in the year he wrote to his friends at the Banneker Institute in Philadelphia to urge them to enlist. Johnson was one of a handful of black men already serving in the Union army in 1861. Despite Union officials' determination to keep their armies segregated, these pioneer black Civil War soldiers enlisted in white regiments, either passing as white men or simply gaining acceptance for their courage and bearing despite their ancestry. William H. Johnson of Connecticut was one of these early black soldiers; in the summer of 1861, he joined the Second Connecticut as an "independent man"—records do not indicate what this term meant—and served with it for ninety days before transferring to the Eighth Connecticut. Johnson fought at the First Battle of Bull Run and participated in the capture of New Bern and Roanoke Island, North Carolina. See William H. Johnson, "Negroes in the Southern Army," *PP*, Aug. 2, 1861; William H. Johnson to the Banneker Institute, 18 Dec. 1861, box 5G, Records of the Banneker Institute (1853–1865), Leon B. Gardiner Collection of American Negro Historical Society Records, 1790–1905, HSP; Redkey, *Grand Army of Black Men*, 10.

135. H. Ford Douglas to Frederick Douglass, Jan. 8, 1863, in Ripley et al., *Black Abolitionist Papers*, 5:166–67.

136. On these 1862 efforts to raise black troops, see Berlin, Reidy, and Rowland, *Black Military Experience*, 37–45. For primary documents relating to these efforts, see pages 46–73. See also Cornish, *Sable Arm*, 37–84.

137. McPherson, *Struggle for Equality*, 119–22.

CHAPTER THREE

1. Guelzo, *Lincoln's Emancipation Proclamation*, 200–207, 293–95. Guelzo's work includes a helpful appendix containing the various drafts of Lincoln's preliminary and final Emancipation Proclamations.

2. Ibid., 203, 293–95.

3. "Great Meeting in Shiloh Church," *The Liberator*, May 22, 1863.

4. The white abolitionist who posed the question was Norwood P. Hallowell. See Stearns, *Cambridge Sketches*, 264.

5. Robert Purvis to anonymous, Feb. 18, 1863, accessed Mar. 10, 2014, http:// bap .chadwyck.com. The editors of the *Black Abolitionist Papers'* online archive simply list this letter as "Purvis, Robert to [?]," and in the letter Purvis gave no indication of who the "Dear Friend" he was writing to was.

6. P. B. Randolph to John Andrew, Jan. 16, [1863], vol. 57a, Executive Letters Collection, CMA, Boston, Mass. The letter is actually dated "1862" in Randolph's hand, but it is marked "1863" in someone else's hand and filed with other letters from January 1863. It is a reminder that, in 1863 as in 2019, it takes some time to adjust to the dawning of a new calendar year.

7. On Stevens, see Trefousse, *Thaddeus Stevens*.

8. *Congressional Globe*, 37th Cong., 3rd sess., pt. 1, pp. 282, 689–90, 695; Cornish, *Sable Arm*, 98–99.

9. For opposition to Stevens's bill, see speeches made by H. B. Wright (Pennsylvania), William Allen (Ohio), C. A. White (Ohio), and James S. Rollins (Missouri). All can be found alongside Crittenden's speech in *Congressional Globe*, 37th Cong., 3rd sess., appendix.

10. "Speech of Hon. J. J. Crittenden, in the House of Representatives, January 29, 1863, on the Bill of the House (No. 675) to Raise Additional Soldiers for the Service of the Government," *Congressional Globe*, 37th Cong., 3rd sess., appendix, pp. 72–75.

11. "Speech of Hon C. A. Trimble, of Ohio, January 31, 1863, in the House of Representatives, the House Having Under Consideration the Bill to Raise Additional Soldiers for the Service of the Government," *Congressional Globe*, 37th Cong., 3rd sess., appendix, pp. 77–79.

12. "Speech of Hon T. Stevens, of Pennsylvania, in the House of Representatives, February 2, 1863. The House Having Under Consideration the Bill to Raise Additional Soldiers for the Service of the Government," *Congressional Globe*, 37th Cong., 3rd sess., appendix, pp. 79–81.

13. Cornish, *Sable Arm*, 98–99.

14. Henry McNeal Turner to editor, *CR*, March 7, 1863. On Turner's observations of the congressional debates, see also Henry McNeal Turner to editor, *CR*, Jan. 10, 1863; Henry McNeal Turner to editor, *CR*, Jan.31, 1863; Henry McNeal Turner to editor, *CR*, Feb. 14, 1863.

15. H. Ford Douglas to Frederick Douglass, *DM*, Feb. 1863; Frederick Douglass, untitled, *DM*, Feb. 1863.

16. "Frederick Douglass at the Cooper Institute—The Proclamation and a Negro Army," *DM*, Mar. 1863.

17. Ibid.; Frederick Douglass, "Condition of the Country," *DM*, Feb. 1863.

18. "Frederick Douglass at the Cooper Institute," *DM*, Mar. 1863.

19. Berlin, Reidy, and Rowland, *Black Military Experience*, 74–75.

20. "Occasional" to editor, *CR*, May 9, 1863. On Jones, see Garb, "Political Education of John Jones."

21. Thomas H. C. Hinton to editor, *CR*, Aug. 22, 1863. On Hinton, see Ripley et al., *Black Abolitionist Papers*, 5:271.

22. Berlin, Reidy, and Rowland, *Black Military Experience*, 74–76. On Stearns and his role in black enlistment, see Heller, *Portrait of an Abolitionist*, 143–67.

23. George Stearns to John Andrew, Apr. 30, 1863, folder 21B, Executive Letters Collection; John Mercer Langston to George Stearns, May 21, 1863, vol. 84, Executive Letters Collection.

24. George Stearns to John Andrew, Apr. 30, 1863, folder 21B, Executive Letters Collection.

25. "Meeting at Shiloh Church," *DM*, June 1863. Joel Schor has described Garnet's words on April 20 as a "trial balloon" Garnet floated after having agreed to assist in recruiting efforts. This interpretation is a bit hard to square with the newspaper article describing this meeting. Speaking after John V. Givens, who endorsed immediate enlistment in unabashed terms, Garnet began by stating that "he did not arise to speak entirely in support of the remarks of the able and eloquent advocate on the enlistment of colored men." After concluding his own remarks, Garnet invited anyone who wanted to speak with him on the subject of black enlistment to come forward and do so, seemingly challenging those present to disagree with his analysis. None took him up on his offer. These objections to enlistment might have been a "trial balloon" intended to gauge black New Yorkers' opinion on enlistment and prepare them for the idea of enlisting under unequal terms of service. It seems more likely that Garnet's words at this meeting were sincere. In addition, it is likely that his back-and-forth thinking about the wisdom of enlistment in the spring of 1863—he would endorse enlistment at a similar meeting only a week later—reflects his soul-searching on this question and the real dilemma it presented black Northerners. See Schor, *Henry Highland Garnet*, 189–90.

26. "New England Anti-Slavery Convention," *The Liberator*, June 5, 1863.

27. George L. Stearns to John Andrew, Feb. 27, 1863, folder 21B, Executive Letters Collection.

28. John S. Rock to John Andrew, Feb. 24, 1863, vol. 57A, Executive Letters Collection.

29. "Call for Colored Soldiers. Will They Fight? Should They Fight?" *CR*, Feb. 14, 1863.

30. "The Present—And Its Duties," *WAA*, Jan. 17, 1863.

31. "Military Tactics," *PA*, Feb. 21, 1863.

32. Bates, *Opinion of Attorney General Bates*, 3, 14–15, 27; Oakes, *Freedom National*, 356. On Bates's opinion, see also McClure, Johnsen, Norman, and Vanderlan, "Circumventing the *Dred Scott* Decision."

33. James Oakes has argued that Bates's opinion cleared the way for black enlistment, and in a theoretical sense it did. Since the late eighteenth century, military service had been linked to citizenship, and the 1792 Militia Act that barred black men from the federal army had limited its membership to white male citizens. The 1862

Militia Act had removed freedom and whiteness as qualifiers for army service, but it kept the stipulation that soldiers must be citizens. Bates's finding that free black men born in the United States were citizens—and, by implication, that citizenship attached to native-born slaves once they were freed—was a legally necessary concomitant to the large-scale black enlistment that began in 1863. Using this reasoning, Oakes has argued that, because the Emancipation Proclamation authorized black enlistment, black citizenship must be viewed as one of the document's hidden assumptions. If black leaders understood the combined implications of Bates's opinion and Lincoln's proclamation in exactly these terms, to the author's knowledge they did not say so. Oakes, *Freedom National*, 360–62.

34. Bates, *Opinion of Attorney General Bates*, 7, 24.

35. That black Northerners saw great significance in Bates's opinion is confirmed by the frequency with which mentions or discussions of the opinion appeared in the black and abolitionist press in 1863. See Philip A. Bell, "Lecture and War Meeting," *PA*, June 6, 1863; Frederick Douglass, "Citizenship of Colored Americans," *DM*, Feb. 1863; Frederick Douglass, "Negro Citizenship," *DM*, Jan. 1863; Frederick Douglass, "Why Should Colored Men Enlist?" *DM*, Apr. 1863; W. J. Davis to editor, *CR*, Mar. 21, 1863; "Frederick Douglass at the Cooper Institute," *DM*, Mar. 1863; "Hear Ye, My People," *CR*, Feb. 21, 1863; Junius to editor, *CR*, May 23, 1863; Junius to editor, *CR*, Oct. 10, 1863; Junius to editor, *CR*, Nov. 14, 1863; "Louisville Correspondent" to editor, *CR*, Jan. 31, 1863; "Our Relation to the Government," *PA*, Apr. 11, 1863; "Proceedings of a Meeting of the Colored Citizens of Shasta County, in Relation to the Call for a Formation of a Colored Regiment," *PA*, July 25, 1863; "War Meeting in Chicago," *WAA*, May 2, 1863.

36. "Emancipation Day in Boston," *The Liberator*, Jan. 16, 1863.

37. "Meeting at Bridge Street Church, Brooklyn," *WAA*, Mar. 7, 1863. For similar public statements linking Bates's opinion on black citizenship with enlistment, see "Guerre" to editor, *CR*, Mar. 7, 1863; "Thirtieth Annual Meeting of the American Anti-Slavery Society," *The Liberator*, May 22, 1863.

38. "The Negro Regiment—Meeting of Colored Citizens," *The Liberator*, Feb. 20, 1863.

39. John Mercer Langston to William Seward, June 28, 1863, William Seward Papers, University of Rochester, accessed Mar. 22, 2014, http://bap.chadwyck.com. See also John Mercer Langston to John Andrew, June 28, 1863, vol. W100, Executive Letters Collection.

40. "Duty of Colored Men," *DM*, Aug. 1863.

41. Frederick Douglass, "Men of Color, to Arms!" *DM*, Mar. 1863.

42. "War Meeting in New Bedford," *WAA*, Feb. 28, 1863. For similar words from Brown on this topic, see also "Meeting at the Metropolitan Assembly Room," *WAA*, Mar. 7, 1863.

43. E. R. J. [Ezra R. Johnson], "The War and Passing Events," June 6, 1863. For other sources in which black leaders emphasized the need for black men to strike for black rights while the opportunity presented itself, see "Flag Presentation at Camp William Penn," *CR*, Sept. 5, 1863; John Leekin to editor, *CR*, Mar. 7, 1863; "Our Colored Soldiers," *CR*, May 23, 1863; "War Meeting in Massachusetts," *WAA*, Mar. 21, 1863.

44. "Hope" to editor, *WAA*, Apr. 4, 1863.

45. Thomas H. C. Hinton to editor, *CR*, July 25, 1863. For other expressions of

willingness to wait for change in the postwar period, or confidence that black service would bring change in time, see John H. Dickson Jr., to editor, *PA*, July 18, 1863; "Guerre" to editor, *CR*, May 16, 1863; John Mercer Langston, "Colored Soldiers of Ohio," *WAA*, July 25, 1863; "Our Colored Soldiers," *WAA*, Apr. 4, 1863; "Tomahawk" to editor, *WAA*, Apr. 11, 1863; the speech of "Rev. Mr. Girdwood," in "War Meeting in Massachusetts," *WAA*, Mar. 21, 1863. Brooklyn's Junius, who in February counseled black men to wait to enlist, eventually came around to this view as well. In September, referring to the rewards of land and freedom he believed black men would receive in return for their service, Junius wrote, "We are not very technical on that point just now, as we know that all these 'constitutional' questions cannot be settled while the country is in such an unsettled condition." See Junius to editor, *CR*, Sept. 5, 1863.

46. In April 1863, Douglass did include concerns related to citizenship among a list of reasons why black men should enlist. He did not say that, as citizens, black men owed service to the nation; rather, he argued that their refusal to serve would justify white Americans' long tendency to treat African Americans as noncitizens. Douglass wrote, "You have hitherto felt wronged and slighted, because while white men of all other nations have been freely enrolled to serve the country, you a native born citizen have been coldly denied the honor of aiding in defense of the land of your birth. The injustice thus done you is now repented of by the Government and you are welcomed to a place in the army of the nation. Should you refuse to enlist now, you will justify the past contempt of the Government towards you and lead it to regret having honored you with a call to take up arms in its defense. You cannot but see that here is a good reason why you should promptly enlist." Frederick Douglass, "Why Should a Colored Man Enlist?" *DM*, Apr. 1863.

47. Frederick Douglass, "Men of Color, to Arms!" *DM*, Mar. 1863; "Faith," "Spirited War Meeting in Ithaca," *WAA*, May 23, 1863.

48. See Furstenberg, "Beyond Freedom and Slavery."

49. See, for instance, "Governor of Ohio to a Northern Black Recruiter," May 16, 1863, in Berlin, Reidy, and Rowland, *Black Military Experience*, 92–93.

50. Frederick Douglass, "Men of Color, to Arms!" *DM*, Mar. 1863.

51. "Great Meeting in Shiloh Church," *The Liberator*, May 22, 1863.

52. "Great Meeting at Shiloh Church, Continued," *The Liberator*, May 29, 1863; John Andrew to George T. Downing, *WAA*, Apr. 18, 1863. The *Anglo-African* printed a similar affirmation of the basic equality of the daily treatment black and white troops would receive from Pennsylvania representative William D. Kelley. G. W. J. Bagwell of Philadelphia had requested that Kelley inform him of the conditions under which black men could serve; Kelley replied that, although they would not have access to promotion initially, "as to food, clothing, pay, and the right to pension, [black soldiers would] be on the footing of all other national troops." See G. W. J. Bagwell to William D. Kelley, *WAA*, Apr. 11, 1863; William D. Kelley to G. W. J. Bagwell, *WAA*, Apr. 11, 1863. For other promises of equal rights as soldiers during this period, see "Colored Men Soldiers for the War, and the 54th Mass. Regiment," *CR*, Apr. 4, 1863; "Our Colored Regiment," *CR*, Apr. 18, 1863.

53. The War Department's June 1863 announcement that black soldiers would receive less monthly pay than white soldiers put officials like Andrew, who had promised black troops equality, in an awkward position. "My statement, declaring [black

soldiers'] position as to pay and all the rights of soldiers—save that I could not promise promotions to the place of commissioned officers, were promulgated by a speech in print. And there men enlisted in the faith of these representations," the governor wrote to John Wilder in May 1863 upon learning of the pay issue. His embarrassment and anger at having his promises undermined surely influenced Andrew's vehement efforts to secure equal pay for black troops later in the war. See John Andrew to John Wilder (copy), May 23, 1863, vol. W100, Executive Letters Collection.

54. See Berlin, Reidy, and Rowland, *Black Military Experience*, 303-7; McPherson, *Negro's Civil War*, 176-77; Smith, *Lincoln and the U.S. Colored Troops*, 51-52. In commissioning black officers in his Kansas regiment, James Lane had acted without official authorization, limiting the value of his black officers as precedent setters. In Louisiana, the situation was a bit more complicated. The men of the Louisiana Native Guards were members of New Orleans's free black elite class, the *gens de coleur*, and many claimed descent from the black men who had fought with Andrew Jackson during the War of 1812. While he commanded the Department of the Gulf, Benjamin Butler allowed the black officers of the Native Guard regiment to serve. But when Nathaniel Banks took command of the department in December 1862, he began through a combination of intimidation, bureaucratic chicanery, and racist invective to force the black officers under his command to resign. A few black officers survived what the scholars of the Freedmen and Southern Society Project refer to as Banks's "purge" of black officers from his ranks. However, Banks's hostility to black commissioned officers and the mass resignations it occasioned limited the value of black commission holding in the Louisiana regiment to set a general precedent. For more on the Louisiana Native Guards, see Hollandsworth, *Louisiana Native Guards*.

55. "War Meeting in New Bedford," *WAA*, Feb. 28, 1863. Wendell Phillips echoed this point. A *Liberator* correspondent reported, "[Phillips] showed several reasons why white officers will be better for them [black soldiers] at present, and among others, the fact that they would be more likely to have justice done them, than if commanded by men of their own race, and the prejudice against them would be more surely overcome." See "Negro Regiment—Meeting of the Colored Citizens," *The Liberator*, Feb. 20, 1863.

56. "War-Meeting in Chicago," *WAA*, May 2, 1863.

57. "Our Colored Soldiers," *WAA*, Apr. 4, 1863.

58. Berlin, Reidy, and Rowland, *Black Military Experience*, 567-93; Cornish, *Sable Arm*, 163-68; Davis, Kirkley, Lazelle, Perry, and Scott, *War of the Rebellion*, series 2, vol. 5, pp. 940-41.

59. "Emancipation Day in Boston," *The Liberator*, Jan. 16, 1863.

60. "Black Soldiers," *WAA*, May 30, 1863.

61. Douglass was not the only immediate-enlistment advocate to brand as cowards black men who remained hesitant to enlist. See, for instance, "Colored Men Must Fight," *WAA*, May 16, 1863; H. A. Thompson's remarks in "War Meeting at the Metropolitan Assembly Room," *WAA*, Mar. 7, 1863; "Index" to editor, *WAA*, May 16, 1863.

62. "Ohio Congressman to the Secretary of War, Enclosing a Letter from a Black Recruiter to the Secretary of War; and a Reply from the Bureau of Colored Troops to the Recruiter," Mar. 28, 1865, in Berlin, Reidy, and Rowland, *Black Military Experience*, 346-47.

63. Langston, *From the Virginia Plantation*, 201.

64. "Speech of John S. Rock," *The Liberator*, June 12, 1863.

65. Berlin, Reidy, and Rowland, *Black Military Experience*, 362; Cornish, *Sable Arm*, 188.

66. Berlin, Reidy, and Rowland, *Black Military Experience*, 76; Cornish, *Sable Arm*, 142–56; McPherson, *Negro's Civil War*, 180. For more information on black troops' performance in these engagements, see Trudeau, *Like Men of War*.

67. This decision also violated the March 1863 conscription law subjecting black men to the draft and directing that all conscripts receive the same wages. Berlin, Reidy, and Rowland, *Black Military Experience*, 362–64; Cornish, *Sable Arm*, 184–87; McPherson, *Negro's Civil War*, 200–201.

68. Newman, *Freedom's Prophet*, 200–207.

69. Masur, "African American Delegation," 135–36, 144.

70. Junius's identity is difficult to establish. Carol Faulkner and Judith Wellman have argued that that Junius was "probably" Junius C. Morel (sometimes spelled "Morrell"), a public-school principal from Brooklyn. See Faulkner, *Women's Radical Reconstruction*; Wellman, *Brooklyn's Promised Land*, 61. Mitchell A. Kachun, on the other hand, claims that "Junius" was the "nom de plume" for New York minister and future congressman Richard H. Cain. See Kachun, *Festivals of Freedom*, 281. In his correspondence of November 21, 1863, Junius wrote that the Reverend R. H. Cain had been called to answer for some unpopular words from one of Junius's columns. Junius responded by saying that the "Rev. Gentleman so charged . . . had no part nor lot in the matter." This statement is unfortunately also inconclusive. It could be interpreted as evidence either of Morel's authorship or Cain's desire to protect his anonymity. Either way, Junius was a prominent member of Brooklyn's black community.

71. "Junius" to editor, *CR*, Feb. 14, 1863.

72. "Box" to editor, *WAA*, Feb. 28, 1863. For other examples of black men advocating delaying black enlistments until black soldiers received equal treatment or saying they would only enlist under terms of equality, see M. S. D. to editor, *CR*, Aug. 15, 1863; W. J. E. Jennings to editor, *CR*, April 4, 1863; "Our Future," *WAA*, Feb. 14, 1863; "Philadelphia Conference of the A. M. E. Zion Church," *CR*, May 16, 1863; Charles Satchell to editor, *PA*, June 20, 1863. Additionally, doubts that black and white Americans could live together on terms of equality continued. For opposition to service based on this fear, see J. W. Menard to Frederick Douglass, *DM*, Apr. 1863.

73. Frisby J. Cooper to editor, *CR*, July 25, 1863; Frisby J. Cooper to editor, *CR*, Aug. 8, 1863. Black men in the Colorado Territory also hoped that the draft would not apply to them. On July 5, a G. W. T. reported, "Those who were afraid of the draft begin to breathe easier now. Since the defeat of the rebels in Pennsylvania, and the fall of Vicksburg, as they believe, there will now be no need of enforcing the draft in this Territory." See G. W. T. to editor, *CR*, Aug. 1, 1863. A week later, after lamenting the mob violence that had recently terrorized New York City's black community, G. W. T. informed the *Recorder*'s readership that talk of forming a local regiment had been laid aside, though he did not imply direct causation between the Draft Riots and the ceasing of black Coloradans' martial planning. See G. W. T. to editor, *CR*, Aug. 8, 1863.

74. Frisby J. Cooper to editor, *CR*, Aug. 29, 1863. Black men in Maryland also manifested their desire to serve only under the same terms the government extended to

whites. See John Kline and Samuel Perkins to editor, *New York Tribune*, reprinted in *WAA*, July 11, 1863.

75. Thomas H. C. Hinton to editor, *CR*, Aug. 1, 1863. Back in February, members of Philadelphia's Banneker Institute had considered a closely related question: "Will the enlistment of colored men advance their political and social rights?" No record survives of the arguments or which position prevailed. See "Philadelphia Items," *CR*, Feb. 14, 1863.

76. Thomas H. C. Hinton to editor, *CR*, Aug. 22, 1863.

77. Turner's observation appeared in a letter written by Hinton including the text of a sermon preached by Turner that had originally been published in the *National Republican*. See Thomas H. C. Hinton to editor, *CR*, Aug. 29, 1863; Thomas H. C. Hinton to editor, *CR*, Sept. 5, 1863. During this same period, two *Anglo-African* correspondents also reported refrains of "What are black men to fight for?," substitute hunting by black men, and resistance to the draft within the D.C. black community. See "Bob Logic" to editor, *WAA*, Aug. 1, 1863; "Bob Logic" to editor, *WAA*, Aug. 15, 1863; "Tom Peeper" to editor, *WAA*, Sept. 19, 1863. For other references to anxiety over the draft or black men expressing unwillingness to serve or a desire to look for substitutes, see "Approximate" to editor, *WAA*, Aug. 8, 1863; Thomas H. C. Hinton to editor, *CR*, Dec. 26, 1863; A. W. W. [Alexander W. Wayman] to editor, *CR*, Dec. 12, 1863; "Wide Awake" to editor, *WAA*, Dec. 12, 1863.

78. N. N., "A Grand Emancipation Demonstration at Harrisburg; The First Response to the Black Soldier Bill," unidentified newspaper clipping. The envelope that accompanies the clipping is marked February 5, 1863, and it seems likely that the meeting took place at some point during mid-January when Congress was debating Thaddeus Stevens's black-soldier bill. folder 21b, Executive Letters Collection.

79. "Recruiting Soldiers for the War," *WAA*, Mar. 21, 1863.

80. On Pennington, see Stone, *African American Connecticut*, 125–28.

81. "Hope" to editor, *WAA*, Apr. 4, 1863.

82. J. W. C. Pennington to editor, *WAA*, Apr. 18, 1863. For commentary on hesitancy to enlist among black Philadelphians, see Parker T. Smith, "Philadelphia Department," *WAA*, July 11, 1863; Parker T. Smith, "Philadelphia Department," *WAA*, July 25, 1863. On black recruitment in Philadelphia during the summer of 1863, see Gallman, "In Your Hands."

83. "State Central Committee of the Michigan State Convention," *WAA*, Mar. 7, 1863.

84. "L'Occident," "Cincinnati Affairs," *WAA*, May 2, 1863.

85. William Parham to Jacob C. White Jr., Mar. 28, 1863, box 115-2, Jacob C. White Collection, Moorland-Spingarn Research Center, Manuscript Division, Howard University, Washington, D.C.

86. William Parham to Jacob C. White Jr., Aug. 7, 1863, box 115-2, Jacob C. White Collection.

87. "L'Occident," "Cincinnati Affairs," *WAA*, Nov. 7, 1863. On black Ohioans' objections to Union pay policy, see "Governor of Ohio to the Secretary of War and Subsequent Correspondence," in Berlin, Reidy, and Rowland, *Black Military Experience*, 370–71. In a note to Edwin Stanton, Ohio governor David Tod complained, "The item of pay [was] a most serious obstacle in my way" and pleaded to be allowed to raise a regiment on the basis of equal pay.

88. Mitchell S. Haynes to John Andrew, Mar. 27, 1863, vol. 57a, Executive Letters Collection.

89. On Grimes, see Ripley et al., *Black Abolitionist Papers*, 4:184–85. Prominent white and black recruiters agreed that service inequalities were responsible for hesitancy to enlist. See "Chairman of the Pennsylvania Committee for Recruiting Colored Regiments to the Secretary of War," July 30, 1863, in Berlin, Reidy, and Rowland, *Black Military Experience*, 372; J. M. Forbes et al. to John Andrew, Nov. 11, 1863, vol. W103, Executive Letters Collection; "Petitioners to the Secretary of War," Jan. 1865, in Berlin, Reidy, and Rowland, *Black Military Experience*, 340–41.

90. C. J. Grimes to John Andrew, ca. Aug. 1863, vol. W103, Executive Letters Collection.

91. Blight, *Frederick Douglass' Civil War*, 166–67; McPherson, *Battle Cry of Freedom*, 794. Lincoln never made good on this proclamation, though it retained symbolic importance for its acknowledgment that black and white Union troops ought to be treated equally.

92. Frederick Douglass to George L. Stearns, *DM*, Aug. 1863. Douglass excoriated Lincoln separately in a piece that appeared in his monthly newspaper's final issue. See "The Commander-in-Chief and His Black Soldiers ," *DM*, Aug. 1863.

93. Frederick Douglass, "Duty of Colored Men," *DM*, Aug. 1863.

94. McFeely, *Frederick Douglass*, 227–30.

95. Ibid.

96. George Stearns to John Andrew, Mar. 28, 1863, vol. 57a, Executive Letters Collection. See also Zenas W. Bliss to John Andrew, Oct. 27, 1863, vol. W100, Executive Letters Collection.

97. Lewis Hayden to John Andrew, Dec. 24, 1863, box 12, folder 16, John A. Andrew Papers, MHS, Boston, Mass.; Stephen Myers to John Andrew, Mar. 19, 1863, vol. 57A, Executive Letters Collection. On Myers, see Ripley et al., *Black Abolitionist Papers*, 3:378–79n.

98. "Superintendent of Maryland Black Recruitment to the Bureau of Colored Troops, Enclosing a Writ by a Justice of the Peace," Aug. 26, 1863, in Berlin, Reidy, and Rowland, *Black Military Experience*, 206–7.

99. On black recruitment in the Border States, see, Berlin, Reidy, and Rowland, *Black Military Experience*, chapter 4.

100. Ibid., 5, 8–9, 74–75; "Governor of Iowa to the General-in-Chief of the Army," Aug. 5, 1862, in Berlin, Reidy, and Rowland, *Black Military Experience*, 85.

101. Quoted in McPherson, *For Cause and Comrades*, 126–27. On white soldiers' reactions to black enlistment, see also Manning, *What This Cruel War Was Over*, 95–96.

102. George Stearns to John Andrew, Apr. 3, 1863, folder 21b, Executive Letters Collection. See also Norwood P. Hallowell to John Andrew, Dec. 14, 1863, vol. W100, Executive Letters Collection.

103. "Circular of the Supervisory Committee on Colored Enlistments," American Negro Historical Society Records, box 10G, folder 15, Leon B. Gardiner Collection of American Negro Historical Society Records, 1790–1905, HSP, Philadelphia.

104. *Report of the Committee of Merchants*, 7.

105. McPherson, *Battle Cry of Freedom*, 610–11; McPherson, *Negro's Civil War*, 71. For a full treatment of the Draft Riots and discussion of their place in state and national politics, see Bernstein, *New York City Draft Riots*.

106. John Rock to John Andrew, July 20, 1863, vol. W103, Executive Letters Collection.

107. Untitled article, *CR*, July 25, 1863. See also Junius to editor, *CR*, July 25, 1863.

108. "Junius Albus," "Colored Soldiers Will Fight," *CR*, Aug. 1, 1863.

109. Junius to editor, *CR*, Aug. 1, 1863.

110. "Sea Side" to editor, *CR*, Aug. 8, 1863.

111. See, for example: C. W., "Colored Enlistments in Chester," July 17, 1863, *Delaware County Republican*; "Enlistment Meeting at Providence," *The Liberator*, Mar. 13, 1863; "Enthusiastic War Meeting in Washington," *The Liberator*, June 12, 1863; W. H. Gibson to editor, *CR*, May 23, 1863; Occasional, "Two Weeks in Chicago," *CR*, May 9, 1863; "War Meeting in New Bedford," *WAA*, Feb. 28, 1863; "A War-Meeting in New Jersey," *WAA*, Apr. 25, 1863.

112. Blight, *Frederick Douglass' Civil War*, 167–69.

113. Davis, Kirkley, Lazelle, Perry, and Scott, *War of the Rebellion*, series 3, vol. 3, pp. 1111–13. This figure omits the 1,600 black soldiers who had by that point enlisted in Kansas, most of whom would've joined a year prior as part of James Lane's previously discussed regiment. This figure also omits the 1,800 black men who had enlisted in Maryland, as many of them were likely slaves who gained their freedom by enlisting. Thus these soldiers were not likely inspired by the types of arguments black recruiters used to convince free black Northerners to enlist.

114. This figure is based on the data provided by the scholars of the Freedmen and Southern Society Project, which they compiled using 1860 U.S. census data and figures given in *War of the Rebellion* delineating how many black troops had been credited to each state. This study, however, defines as Northern all states that did not secede from the Union. Determining the percentage of black men free before the war in all of the states that remained within the Union during the Civil War is problematic because the scholars' data does not make clear what percentage of black troops from Maryland, Kentucky, Delaware, and Missouri were free before their enlistment. Nor does the information show how many gained freedom as a result of their enlistment. Most of the 954 black soldiers from Delaware would have been free when they joined the military, as the state contained only 289 slaves in 1860. In 1860, Maryland's free and enslaved black populations were roughly equal, so it seems fair to assume that a substantial portion of the 8,718 black soldiers from that state gained their freedom prior to enlisting. Missouri and Kentucky both had very small free black populations relative to their populations of enslaved black men, making it likely that the vast majority of black soldiers from those states gained their freedom through military service. The distinction here is important; whereas slaves could be motivated to enlist by the desire for personal freedom, free black men did not possess this impetus. Thus by freedmen's rate of enlistment can we best judge the performance of the black recruiters who argued the correctness of the immediate-enlistment position. See Berlin, Reidy, and Rowland, *Black Military Experience*, 12.

115. Glatthaar, "Black Glory."

116. Freehling, *South vs. The South*, 154. Andrew Lang has shown that many nineteenth-century Americans saw garrison duty as incompatible with the citizen-soldier ideal that was central to American military culture. Citizen-soldiers left their homes and occupations to answer a crisis and returned to peacetime pursuits when the crisis had passed. On the other hand, troops engaged in garrison duties, inhabited stagnant, static spaces far from the field of battle, and seemed to many nineteenth-century Americans to embody all the evils associated with the improper use of military power that had made many uncomfortable with the existence of a standing U.S. Army. During the era of the Mexican-American War and Civil War, many Americans came to view garrison troops as "permanent, powerful arbiters of military government . . . embodiment[s] of a standing, bureaucratic army, which aroused great suspicion and dismay" and which "seemed to threaten the very republican principles they had volunteered to defend." Lincoln's Emancipation Proclamation authorized black service but explicitly envisioned black soldiers serving as garrison troops. In this way it suggested that African Americans were second-class citizens properly relegated to "second-class wartime roles." See Lang, *In the Wake of War*, 12–13, 130–32.

117. Lang, *In the Wake of War*, 159, 160–81.

118. Freehling, *South vs. The South*, 146.

119. McCurry, *Confederate Reckoning*, 310–57.

120. On Confederate attempts to enlist black soldiers at the war's end, see Levine, *Confederate Emancipation*.

121. Foner, "Lincoln, Colonization," 46–47.

122. A. M. Taylor to editor, *CR*, Nov. 28, 1863.

123. Parker T. Smith to editor, *WAA*, Sept. 19, 1863.

124. Alexander T. Augusta to editor, *National Republican*, May 15, 1863, in Ripley et al., *Black Abolitionist Papers*, 5:205–11. On the changed state of things in Baltimore by the middle of 1863, see also A. W. W. [Alexander W. Wayman] to editor, *CR*, Oct. 10, 1863.

125. On Hall, see Lapp, *Blacks in Gold Rush California*, 222.

126. W. H. Hall, "Patriotic Colored Men," *PA*, Apr. 25, 1863. Frederick Douglass echoed this language in his February speech at New York's Cooper Union Institute, claiming, "[January 1 will] henceforth . . . take rank with the Fourth of July. [Applause.] Henceforth it becomes the date of a new and glorious era in the history of American liberty." He also replied to complaints that Lincoln's Emancipation Proclamation was "only an ink and paper proclamation" by observing that "our own Declaration of Independence was at one time but ink and paper." See "Frederick Douglass at the Cooper Institute—The Proclamation," *DM*, Mar. 1863. Douglass recognized that the war gave black men a chance to strike for their freedom analogous to the colonists' struggle during the Revolutionary War, writing in April, "The white-man's soul was tried in 1776. The black-man's soul is tried in 1863. The first stood the test, and is received as genuine—so may the last." See Frederick Douglass, "Another Word to the Colored Men," *DM*, Apr. 1863.

127. "The Fourth of July, 1863," *PA*, July 4, 1863. See also "The Ensuing Fourth of July," *PA*, June 27, 1863.

128. P. Johnson Jr., "War and Its Causes," *PA*, Aug. 8, 1863.

129. "Anniversary of the Association for the Relief of Contrabands in the District of

Columbia," *CR*, Aug. 22, 1863. For another example of a black speaker linking black participation in the war to the American Revolution, see William C. Nell's comments in "Emancipation Day in Boston," *The Liberator*, Jan. 16, 1863.

130. S. T. Johnson to editor, *WAA*, April 25, 1863.

131. See Chandra Manning's work on Northern soldiers' understanding of the war's cause and purpose. She argues persuasively that many Northern soldiers, for a variety of reasons, became convinced by the conflict's close of the need to end slavery, and that some went further than this and recognized the need to purge the nation of racism and racial discrimination as well. See Manning, *What This Cruel War Was Over*.

132. For the various drafts and versions of Lincoln's Gettysburg Address, including the "Final Text" quoted here, see "Address Delivered at the Dedication of the Cemetery at Gettysburg," Nov. 19, 1863, in Basler, *Collected Works of Abraham Lincoln*, 7:18–23.

133. Wills, *Lincoln at Gettysburg*, 45. On the Gettysburg Address as well as Lincoln's use of the Declaration of Independence in his political rhetoric generally, see also Wilson, *Lincoln's Sword*, 198–237.

134. "New England Anti-Slavery Convention," *The Liberator*, June 5, 1863.

CHAPTER FOUR

1. Thomas H. C. Hinton to editor, *CR*, Mar. 12, 1864.

2. Loudon S. Langley to editor, *WAA*, Jan. 30, 1864.

3. William W. Grimes to editor, *CR*, Apr. 2, 1864. The Twenty-Ninth Connecticut was not the only black regiment to have its departure for the front marred by the spring 1864 pay controversy. The Twenty-Eighth USCT, raised in Indiana, was marched off under guard because of dissatisfaction over Union pay policy. See "G." to editor, *CR*, May 21, 1864. Union compensation practices caused friction within black units as well. In April, John Rock spoke with two furloughed members of the Fifth Massachusetts Cavalry, John America and John Wesley Postles, who feared returning to their regiment. These men found themselves in a "very uncomfortable position," Rock reported, because they were believed to have used promises of bounties to trick other members of their regiment into enlisting. America's and Postles's comrades had written letters home accusing the pair of "deceiv[ing] them and caus[ing] them to leave their families to suffer and threaten if they go with the Regt they will be avenged." Rock told Andrew later that the letters the men of the Fifth wrote home describing the government's refusal to award them bounties were "doing much to retard enlistments" in the unit. See John Rock to John Andrew, Mar. 18, 1864, vol. W80, Executive Letters Collection, CMA, Boston, Mass.

4. Henry McNeal Turner to editor, *CR*, June 25, 1864.

5. Oakes, "Natural Rights, Citizenship Rights," 124–25.

6. Virtually all historians of black service have covered black soldiers' campaign for equal pay. See, for instance, Berlin, Reidy, and Rowland, eds., *Black Military Experience*, 362–405; McPherson, *Negro's Civil War*, 197–207. Because none has devoted the attention to the debate over black enlistment in the North and the importance of Edward Bates's opinion to black Northerners, none has analyzed in depth how the campaign for equal pay connected to earlier debates over service, contractual principles, and concerns about black citizenship.

7. Late in 1864, John Mercer Langston, in a public speech, called Bates's opinion the "finest legal document ever written by an American." But he also characterized the opinion merely as "a step in the right direction" that "did not go far enough" toward protecting black rights by itself. See "National Equal Rights' League," *CR*, Dec. 10, 1864.

8. Junius to editor, *CR*, Nov. 14, 1863.

9. Abraham Lincoln to Charles D. Robinson, Aug. 17, 1864, in Basler, *Collected Works of Abraham Lincoln*, 7:499–501. The *New York Tribune* published a modified version of these remarks on September 10. Berlin, Reidy, and Rowland, *Black Military Experience*, 76–77; Cornish, *Sable Arm*, 248.

10. George H. W. Stewart to editor, *CR*, Jan. 23, 1864. Stewart referred to Walker as "Edward," but his description of Walker as a lawyer living in the Charlestown section of Boston all but confirms that he referred to Walker's son, Edwin. Some confusion as to Walker's first name seems to have existed. Most scholars, including Peter Hinks, refer to him as Edwin, but some scholarly works use the first name Edward. See Horton and Horton, "Affirmation of Manhood," 133.

11. Jabez P. Campbell to editor, *CR*, Mar. 12, 1864. Free black Marylanders' hesitance to enlist, reported Union officials charged with securing black volunteers, owed to Union pay policy. Maryland slaves delayed joining the military because they wanted positive legislation freeing their family members and because, as 1864 progressed, they saw that Maryland's legislature would likely abolish slavery. Freedom as an incentive to enlistment thus lost much of its luster. See Berlin, Reidy, and Rowland, *Black Military Experience*, 186. On Campbell, see Jessie Carney Smith, "Mary Ann Campbell," 80; Wayman, *Cyclopaedia of African Methodism*, 6–7. For other sources linking slowness to enlist with service inequalities in 1864, see "Colored Troops of the United States," *CR*, Apr. 2, 1864; "Justice at Last," *WAA*, May 7, 1864; "The President's Call for Five Hundred Thousand More Troops," *CR*, July 23, 1864.

12. Tunion's letter can be found in Thomas H. C. Hinton to editor, *CR*, Sept. 12, 1863.

13. George Stephens to editor, *WAA*, Sept. 19, 1863, in Yacovone, *Voice of Thunder*, 259. Stephens boldly protested the injustices he and his fellow soldiers suffered as a result of the pay policy and other grievances. Privately, he wrote to Philadelphia's William Still and appealed to Still and other black leaders to secure for himself and Frederick Johnson, a fellow member of the Fifty-Fourth, positions as drill sergeants. Citing the army's refusal to commission black officers, a return of prejudice following Robert Gould Shaw's death during the July 18 assault on Fort Wagner, excessive fatigue duty, and lack of drill, he declared, "[These are] some of the reasons which has led us to desire this new field of service. And made us lose heart with the 54th." Stephens still believed in black service's potential to bring change, but his military experiences had at least temporarily dimmed his desire to participate on the front lines. See George E. Stephens to William Still, Sept. 19, 1863, William Still Correspondence, box 9G, folder 17, Leon B. Gardiner Collection of American Negro Historical Society Records, 1790–1905, HSP, Philadelphia.

14. For other letters to newspapers from soldiers protesting Union pay policy during this period, see H. S. Harmon to editor, *CR*, Dec. 26, 1863; Theodore Tilton to editor, *Boston Journal*, Dec. 15, 1863, in Redkey, *Grand Army of Black Men*, 234. The white abolitionist Tilton included in his letter an extract from another letter authored by a black man he identified simply as "Massachusetts Soldier."

15. George E. Stephens to editor, *WAA*, Oct. 24, 1863, in Yacovone, *Voice of Thunder*, 280.

16. "Court-Martial Statement by a South Carolina Black Sergeant," Jan. 12, 1864, in Berlin, Reidy, and Rowland, *Black Military Experience*, 393.

17. Berlin, Reidy, and Rowland, *Black Military Experience*, 366–68.

18. "Pay of Colored Soldiers," *CR*, Dec. 26, 1863.

19. G. L. R. [George L. Ruffin] to editor, *WAA*, Nov. 7, 1863.

20. For examples of black soldiers and other black commentators criticizing black soldiers' protests over Union pay policy, see G. C. D. to editor, *CR*, Aug. 27, 1864; Garland H. White to editor, *CR*, Sept. 17, 1864; "Wild Jack" to editor, *CR*, Aug. 6, 1864; "Wolverine" to editor, *CR*, May 7, 1864; "Wolverine" to editor, *WAA*, May 14, 1864. Southern ex-slaves who enlisted in the Union army also sometimes criticized black Northern soldiers' protests over pay, believing their agitation hurt black soldiers' military reputation. See Wilson, *Campfires of Freedom*, 52–53.

21. Daniel Walker to editor, *CR*, Jan. 30, 1864.

22. "Barquet" to editor, *WAA*, Feb. 13, 1864.

23. J. H. Hall to editor, *CR*, Aug. 27, 1864.

24. "Colored Soldiers and the Government," *CR*, Feb. 27, 1864.

25. "A Great Moral Triumph," *WAA*, Nov. 12, 1864. For another letter from a black civilian who saw Union pay policy as a violation of an agreement between the government and black soldiers, see Thomas L. Brown to editor, *CR*, Oct. 1, 1864. See also Wilson, *Campfires of Freedom*, 47–48.

26. Edward W. Washington to editor, *CR*, May 7, 1864.

27. "Bay State" to editor, *WAA*, Apr. 30, 1864.

28. "A Sergeant of the 55th Mass." to editor, *CR*, July 9, 1864. For other examples of black soldiers using language not explicitly contractual and yet implying the existence of a relationship of mutual obligation between themselves and the government, see George O. DeCourcy to editor, *CR*, Sept. 10, 1864; Sergeant Kellies to editor, *WAA*, June 11, 1864.

29. E. D. W. to editor, *CR*, Apr. 2, 1864.

30. J. H. B. P. to editor, *CR*, June 11, 1864.

31. For other letters in which black soldiers enumerated the terms of enlistment or understandings under which they had enlisted as part of a protest regarding service inequalities, see "Bay State" to editor, *WAA*, Apr. 30, 1864; "Bellefonte" to editor, *CR*, Sept. 3, 1864; "Black Sergeant to the Secretary of War," Apr. 27, 1864, in Berlin, Reidy, and Rowland, *Black Military Experience*, 377–78; "Close Observer" to editor, *CR*, Aug. 27, 1864; D. I. I. to editor, *CR*, Aug. 6, 1864; Ferdinand H. Hughes to editor, *WAA*, Jan. 14, 1865; G. W. H. to editor, *CR*, June 25, 1864; George O. DeCourcy to editor, *CR*, Sept. 3, 1864; George E. Stephens to editor, *WAA*, Mar. 26, 1864, in Yacovone, *Voice of Thunder*, 299–300; H. I. W. to editor, *CR*, July 23, 1864; "Mon" to editor, *WAA*, May 21, 1864; "Louisiana Black Officers to the Secretary of War," Oct. 1863, in Berlin, Reidy, and Rowland, *Black Military Experience*, 381–82; "Mr. Corporal" to editor, *CR*, Oct. 8, 1864; Alexander H. Newton to editor, *WAA*, May 28, 1864; "New York and Delaware Black Soldiers to the President," Aug. 1864, in Berlin, Reidy, and Rowland, *Black Military Experience*, 680–81; "New York Black Soldier to the President," Aug. 1864, in Berlin, Reidy, and Rowland, *Black Military Experience*, 501–2; "Rhode Island" to

editor, *WAA*, Jan. 23, 1864; R. W. W. to editor, *WAA*, June 4, 1864; Sergeant Kellies to editor, *WAA*, June 11, 1864; "A Sergeant in Co. H" to editor, *WAA*, Aug. 6, 1864; "Sergeant of the 55th Mass." to editor, *CR*, July 9, 1864; Unknown to editor, *CR*, May 21, 1864; "Venoir" to editor, *WAA*, Apr. 23, 1864.

32. "From the Members of the Mass 54 Regiment That Still Lives" to John Andrew, July 27, 1863, folder 21b, Executive Letters Collection.

33. Frederic Johnson to John Andrew, Aug. 10, 1863, vol. 59, Executive Letters Collection.

34. Joseph Holloway to anonymous, Mar. 27, 1864, vol. 59, Executive Letters Collection. The letter was forwarded to Andrew by a J. W. Ritner, for whom Halloway had worked as a servant.

35. "Massachusetts Black Sergeant to the Adjutant General's Office," Jan. 14, 1864, in Berlin, Reidy, and Rowland, *Black Military Experience*, 376–77.

36. Berlin, Reidy, and Rowland, *Black Military Experience*, 308.

37. "Peaceful mutinies" is a term coined for this study and may seem contradictory, but it fits Anderson's description of New England soldiers' mutinous behavior. According to Anderson, New England servicemen's "mutinies did not resemble the classic mutiny in regard to the participants' disposition toward authority; rather than seeking to overthrow or kill their commanders, the rebellious troops apparently either behaved with respect toward them or treated them with simple indifference." Black Civil War soldiers might have expressed more rhetorical hostility toward their white superiors than did these white militiamen of earlier generations, but in their revolts and strikes they likewise displayed little desire to overthrow or kill their superiors. Anderson, "Colonial New England Soldiers," 409.

38. Ibid., 401. On New England militia units' contractual understanding of service, see also Anderson, *People's Army*, 178–94.

39. Royster, *Revolutionary People at War*, 325.

40. Rothman, *Slave Country*, 132–33.

41. Berlin, Reidy, and Rowland, *Black Military Experience*, 365–66.

42. E. W. D. to editor, *CR*, June 25, 1864.

43. Members of Company D, 55th Massachusetts Volunteers, "Petition to the President of the United States, July 16, 1864", in Trudeau, *Voices of the 55th*, 116–18.

44. On black soldiers' strategies of resistance to Union pay policy, see Wilson, *Campfires of Freedom*, 51–53.

45. "A Soldier" to editor, *WAA*, Apr. 2, 1864.

46. "Unknown" to editor, *CR*, May 21, 1864. For another example of a black soldier demanding either an end to service inequalities or discharge, see "Venoir" to editor, *WAA*, Apr. 23, 1864.

47. J. H. B. P. to editor, *CR*, June 11, 1864.

48. Outright insurrection did not take place, but violence sometimes occurred as an unintended consequence of black protests over pay. Military authorities occasionally executed leaders of black soldiers' mutinies, as in the case of William Walker. For examples of violent confrontations between black soldiers and their white officers that arose from protests over pay, see Berlin, Reidy, and Rowland, *Black Military Experience*, 366.

49. White officers often supported black soldiers' campaigns for equal pay in public

and private ways. See Glatthaar, *Forged in Battle*, 172–74; Thomas Wentworth Higginson to editor, *New York Tribune*, reprinted in *CR*, Aug. 20, 1864; Thomas Wentworth Higginson to Thaddeus Stevens, June 20, 1864, box 2, Thaddeus Stevens Papers, Manuscript Division, LOC, Washington, D.C.

50. "A Soldier" to editor, *CR*, May 21, 1864.

51. It is entirely possible that this soldier and the soldier whose letter appears in the note above were the same person. "A Soldier of the 55th Mass. Vols." to editor, *WAA*, Jan. 30, 1864.

52. J. H. Hall to editor, *CR*, Aug. 27, 1864.

53. "Massacre at Fort Pillow," *WAA*, Apr. 23, 1864.

54. "Meeting in Boston," *WAA*, July 16, 1864.

55. Despite their relative silence in the pages of black newspapers, black women took on new and vital roles in Northern black communities during the war, speaking in public about the war, fund-raising, organizing relief efforts for soldiers and ex-slaves, and acting as community leaders in the aftermath of the New York City Draft Riots. On black women's public activities before and during the war, see Dabel, *Respectable Woman*; Jones, *All Bound Up Together*.

56. Hannah Johnson to Abraham Lincoln, July 31, 1863, in Berlin and Rowland, *Families and Freedom*, 81–82; Rosanna Henson to Abraham Lincoln, July 11, 1864, in Berlin and Rowland, *Black Military Experience*, 680; Rachel Ann Wicker to "Mr. President Andrew," Sept. 12, 1864, in Berlin and Rowland, *Families and Freedom*, 88.

57. Black soldiers' wives did, however, write to Northern officials to protest their husbands' wages. See "Wife of an Ohio Black Soldier to the Governor of Massachusetts or the President," Sept. 12, 1864, in Berlin, Reidy, and Rowland, *Black Military Experience*, 402. In writing letters like this one, black soldiers' wives joined Confederate soldiers' wives, who, Stephanie McCurry has argued, developed a "politics of subsistence" in basing their requests for assistance from Confederate officials on their identity as military spouses. See McCurry, *Confederate Reckoning*, 133–77.

58. "Bay State" to editor, *WAA*, Apr. 30, 1864.

59. "Mon" to editor, *WAA*, May 21, 1864.

60. Edward J. Wheeler to editor, *CR*, Apr. 16, 1864. For other letters from black soldiers that invoked the suffering of black families to underline the injustice of Union pay policy, see S. H. B. to editor, *CR*, Sept. 17, 1864; "Bought and Sold" to editor, *CR*, Feb. 20, 1864; E. W. D. to editor, *CR*, June 25, 1864; "De Waltigo" to editor, *WAA*, Apr. 30, 1864; "Fort Green" to editor, *CR*, Sept. 24, 1864; Ferdinand H. Hughes to editor, *CR*, Jan. 14, 1865; D. I. I. to editor, *CR*, Aug. 6, 1864; Jacob S. Johnson to editor, *CR*, Nov. 12, 1864; Jacob S. Johnson to editor, *CR*, Dec. 3, 1864; William B. Johnson to editor, *CR*, May 28, 1864; William McCoslin to editor, *CR*, Aug. 27, 1864; Enoch K. Miller to *CR*, Mar. 4, 1865; Enoch K. Miller to editor, *CR*, May 6, 1865; "Rhode Island" to editor, *WAA*, Mar. 26, 1864; "Unknown" to editor, *CR*, May 21, 1865; S. A. Valentine to editor, *CR*, Aug. 27, 1864; "Venoir" to editor, *WAA*, Apr. 23, 1864; H. I. W. to editor, *CR*, July 23, 1864; T. S. W. to editor, *CR*, Aug. 20, 1864; Edward Washington to editor, *CR*, May 7, 1864.

61. Dudley T. Cornish, for example, concluded his 1966 *The Sable Arm: Negro Troops in the Union Army, 1861-1865* with the observation that, in the Civil War, "the Negro soldier proved that the slave could become a man." More recently, Chandra Manning

has recognized that "African Americans knew that slavery robbed black men of many of the nineteenth century's hallmarks of manhood, including independence, courage, the right to bear arms, moral agency, liberty of conscience, and the ability to protect and care for one's loved ones. Fighting in the Civil War offered African Americans the opportunity to display those very attributes and reclaim their identities as black men in direct defiance of proslavery ideology's insistence that blacks were children or savages rather than real men." See Cornish, *Sable Arm*, 291; Manning, *What This Cruel War Was Over*, 129. On the linkage between black service and manhood, see also Cullen, "'I's a Man Now.'"

62. On black women's labor for the Union army, see also Taylor, *Embattled Freedom*.

63. Manning, *Troubled Refuge*, 205-6, 212-18.

64. See Foster, "'We Are Men!'" Douglass's gendered vision of citizenship, Foster argues, contributed to his postwar willingness to sacrifice women's suffrage in order to gain black manhood suffrage.

65. The author of this letter was likely Richard H. Cain. R. H. C. to editor, *CR*, Apr. 30, 1864. For another example of a black civilian publicizing the need to advocate for black soldiers, see Junius to editor, *CR*, July 30, 1864.

66. E. Goodelle H— to editor, *CR*, Feb. 25, 1865.

67. R. H. B. to editor, *CR*, Sept. 17, 1864.

68. *Proceedings of the National Convention of Colored Men*, 59.

69. On this campaign, see Davis, "Pennsylvania State Equal Rights League," 614-15; Giesberg, *Army at Home*, 92-118; Still, *Brief Narrative of the Struggle*.

70. William Johnston Alston to editor, *Philadelphia Press*, reprinted in *CR*, July 23, 1864.

71. "The Enthusiastic Gathering of Colored Persons in Sansom St. Hall," *CR*, July 30, 1864. On this letter, see also Angell and Pinn, *Social Protest Thought*, 7-8. Black civilians also appealed to black service when they faced racist violence on the home front. After witnessing a race riot in Camden, New Jersey, "West Jersey" plaintively addressed white Americans. "Have ye forgotten," he asked, "that 125,000 black men have sallied forward to meet that hydra-headed monster—disunion—whose iron hand, during years past, has held the throat of the nation with a death-like grasp, while the traitor's flag proudly waves over cities and towns where once the Stars and Stripes did so majestically float?" See "West Jersey" to editor, *CR*, Oct. 1, 1864.

72. Britton Lanier to editor, *CR*, Mar. 25, 1865.

73. J. O. to editor, *WAA*, Apr. 2, 1864.

74. "Enthusiastic Gathering." For other instances in this campaign for equal rights on Pennsylvania railcars in which black correspondents or speakers referred to discriminatory policies' effects on the female relatives of black soldiers, see "Colored People and the Philadelphia City Railroads," *The Liberator*, Dec. 23, 1864; "L'Ouverture" to editor, *WAA*, Dec. 31, 1864.

75. "The Great Public Meeting in Philadelphia," *WAA*, Aug. 13, 1864.

76. On Forten, see Ripley et al., *Black Abolitionist Papers*, 5:282-83n.

77. William Forten to Charles Sumner, June 18, 1864, reel 31, Charles Sumner Papers, Manuscript Division, LOC, Washington, D.C.

78. "Mass Meeting in Boston," *WAA*, Aug. 13, 1864.

79. On Grant's Overland Campaign and Sherman's drive toward Atlanta during the spring and summer of 1864, see McPherson, *Battle Cry of Freedom*, 718-50.

80. On the Battle of the Crater, see Levin, *Remembering the Battle of the Crater*; McPherson, *Battle Cry of Freedom*, 758-60. On Lincoln's response to Confederate peace feelers in the summer of 1864, see Donald, *Lincoln*, 521-23; Foner, *Fiery Trial*, 303-7. "Mass Meeting in Boston," *WAA*, Aug. 13, 1864.

81. On the equalization of black soldiers' pay, see Berlin, Reidy, and Rowland, *Black Military Experience*, 367-68. See also Belz, "Law, Politics and Race." Belz has argued that while Bates's decision was legally dubious and unrepresentative of his true feelings on the matter, it reflected political expedience and the fact that black soldiers were serving in large numbers. Belz holds that, though morally repugnant, William Whiting's legal logic in interpreting the Militia Act of 1862 as intended to govern the enlistment of black soldiers was sound and based on Congress's intention in passing the law. In this instance, Belz contends, the normally conservative Bates took a radical position because his analysis of the case was more "political in nature than legalistic."

82. *Congressional Globe*, 38th Cong., 1st sess., pt. 3, p. 2472.

83. Ibid., pt. 1, p. 481.

84. Belz, "Law, Politics and Race," 202.

85. See Garnet, *Memorial Discourse*, 85-86.

86. McPherson, *Negro's Civil War*, 254-55, 266-70.

87. Ibid., 255-65. On black activism in California, see also Smith, *Freedom's Frontier*. On the struggle against Illinois's black laws, see Garb, "Political Education of John Jones"; Jones, *Illinois Black Laws*.

88. On abolition in these states, see Oakes, *Freedom National*, 456-68, 482. On the Thirteenth Amendment, see Vorenberg, *Final Freedom*.

89. On the Syracuse Convention and the formation of the NERL, see Davis, *Satisfied with Nothing Less*, 17-26.

90. John Mercer Langston, St. George R. Taylor, and Davis D. Turner, "The National League," *The Liberator*, Dec. 23, 1864.

91. "Africana" to editor, *CR*, Feb. 4, 1865. On the necessity of striking immediately for black rights, see also Stanford, "Action! Action! Action!" *CR*, Mar. 25, 1865.

92. "New England Anti-Slavery Convention," *The Liberator*, June 3, 1864.

93. "Frederick Douglass on President Lincoln," *The Liberator*, Sept. 16, 1864.

94. *Proceedings of the National Convention of Colored Men*, 47.

95. "Lee's Surrender—Peace," *WAA*, Apr. 15, 1865.

96. Donald, *Lincoln*, 588; Sinha, "Allies for Emancipation?," 194-95. On Booth and his murder plot, see Kauffman, *American Brutus*.

97. James Lynch, "The Word African Is Our Denominational Title," *CR*, May 6, 1865.

CHAPTER FIVE

1. Henry McNeal Turner to editor, *CR*, Aug. 5, 1865.

2. "Speech by the Hon. Henry McNeal Turner on the 'Benefits Accruing from the Ratification of the Fifteenth Amendment,' and Its Incorporation into the United States Constitution. Delivered at the Celebration in Macon, Georgia, April 19, 1870,"

in Foner and Walker, *Proceedings of the Black National and State Conventions, 1865–1900*, 417.

3. "Pastor of a Washington, D.C., African Methodist Episcopal Church to the Secretary of War," Aug. 1, 1863, in Berlin, Reidy, and Rowland, *Black Military Experience*, 358.

4. Henry McNeal Turner to B. K. Sampson, originally printed in *Memphis Appeal*, reprinted in *CR*, Dec. 13, 1883.

5. See Dittmer, "Education of Henry McNeal Turner."

6. Henry McNeal Turner to Blanche K. Bruce, *CR*, 27 Mar. 27, 1890; Shaffer, *After the Glory*, 84–85.

7. Since the late nineteenth century, several historical schools of thought regarding the Reconstruction period have achieved prominence. In the late 1800s and early twentieth century, adherents of William A. Dunning depicted the period as a tragic attempt by vindictive Republicans to punish the South, characterizing the white Southerners who overthrew Reconstruction state governments as heroes. In the late 1920s, revisionist historians challenged key Dunning assertions, such as the claims that black Southerners had dominated the region's politics and Reconstruction governments had accomplished nothing of value. W. E. B. Du Bois's 1935 *Black Reconstruction in America, 1860–1880*, disparaged by most professional historians at the time, reinterpreted the period boldly, depicting Reconstruction as a heroic attempt to establish democracy in the South. The work also defended Reconstruction governments from charges of corruption. In the 1950s, a new group of historians influenced by the civil rights movement focused on the issue of formerly enslaved men's and women's place in American society. The tragedy these historians saw in Reconstruction was its failure to achieve black equality and democracy in the South. For a statement of the neo-revisionist position, see Stampp, *The Era of Reconstruction*. Eric Foner's landmark *Reconstruction* depicts Reconstruction as a noble failure, concentrating on black Southern political activity as well as economic conflicts that caused Northerners to lose faith in the Reconstruction project. As a result of Foner's work, the study of Reconstruction "thrives less as a form of combat than as a collective building on a solid foundation." See Brown, *Reconstructions: New Perspectives on the Postbellum United States*. Recent valuable contributions to Reconstruction historiography include Hahn, *Nation under Our Feet*; Rodrigue, *Reconstruction in the Cane Fields*; Rosen, *Terror in the Heart of Freedom*; Saville, *Work of Reconstruction*; Schwalm, *A Hard Fight for We*.

8. Henry Carpenter Hoyle, "Christmas Pastime, or Carpenter's Address to the African Race," *CR*, Jan. 12, 1867.

9. On the association of military service with citizenship, see Berry, *Military Necessity and Civil Rights Policy*, ix, 2–34.

10. T. Strother to editor, *CR*, July 29, 1865.

11. "A." to editor, *CR*, July 15, 1865.

12. James H. Payne to editor, *CR*, July 15, 1865. For another black Fourth of July celebration that included an articulation of black political goals, see "The Day We Celebrate, and How We Celebrate It," *Elevator*, July 7, 1865.

13. Vorenberg, *Final Freedom*, 79, 82–86.

14. "Proceedings of the State Equal Rights Convention, of the Colored People of

Pennsylvania, Held in the City of Harrisburg, February 8th, 9th, and 10th, 1865, Together with a Few of the Arguments Presented Suggesting the Necessity for Holding the Convention, and an Address of the Colored State Convention to the People of Pennsylvania," in Foner and Walker, *Proceedings of the Black State Conventions, 1840–1865*, 1:153, 161, 164.

15. Frederick Douglass, "What the Black Man Wants: Speech of Frederick Douglass at the Annual Meeting of the Massachusetts Anti-Slavery Society at Boston," in *Equality of All Men before the Law*, 36–37.

16. On the contention that black rights not won in the war's immediate aftermath would be lost for generations, see William Nesbit, "A Cheering Word," *CR*, Aug. 19, 1865.

17. On the schism between antislavery advocates who saw abolition's work as finished with slavery's death and those who believed abolitionists needed to continue to work for black rights, see McPherson, *Struggle for Equality*.

18. William Gibson to editor, *CR*, May 27, 1865.

19. F. H. Sawyer to editor, *NOT*, Nov. 7, 1865.

20. For examples of black men assenting to race-neutral qualifications based on personal attributes like intelligence, see J. H. Payne to editor, *CR*, Aug. 19, 1865; "Letter from Idaho," *Elevator*, Dec. 27, 1867; "Proceedings of the Annual Meeting of the Pennsylvania State Equal Rights League, Held in the City of Harrisburg, August 9th and 10th, 1865," in Foner and Walker, *Proceedings of the Black National and State Conventions, 1865–1900*, 144; "National Equal Suffrage Association," *NOT*, Dec. 16, 1865.

21. "Suffrage for Our Oppressed Race," *CR*, July 1, 1865.

22. "Proceedings of the First Annual Meeting of the National Equal Rights League of the United States, Held in Cleveland, Ohio, October 19, 20 and 21, 1865," in Foner and Walker, *Proceedings of the Black National and State Conventions, 1865–1900*, 52, 63.

23. "Meeting at Economy Hall," *NOT*, May 23, 1865; "Citizenship And Suffrage," *Elevator*, Dec. 22, 1865.

24. "August First in Denver," *CR*, Nov. 18, 1865.

25. On Harper, see Stancliff, *Frances Ellen Watkins Harper*.

26. M. R. L., "Mrs. Frances Ellen Watkins Harper on Reconstruction," *The Liberator*, Mar. 3, 1865; James A. Handy, "Manhood Suffrage in Washington, D.C.," *CR*, June 15, 1867.

27. "We Are Not Theorists," *NOT*, Feb. 4, 1869.

28. For black leaders meeting or corresponding with government officials and congressmen, see, for instance, Colored Citizens of Oskaloosa, Iowa, to Charles Sumner, Jan. [9?], 1872, reel 56, Charles Sumner Papers, Manuscript Division, LOC, Washington, D.C.; Colored Citizens of York County, Pa., to Charles Sumner, Feb. 18, 1872, reel 56, Charles Sumner Papers; "Suffrage. A Delegation of Colored Men at the Executive Mansion. Their Interview with the President and His Speech," *CR*, Feb. 17, 1866.

29. Davis, *Satisfied with Nothing Less*, 26–29. On black Southerners' politics during the early postwar period, see Hahn, *Nation under Our Feet*, chapters 3–4; Hayden et al., *Land and Labor, 1866–1867*. See also "Gaining Ground," *CR*, Apr. 6, 1867.

30. "Convention of the Colored People of New England, Boston, December 1, 1865," in Foner and Walker, *Proceedings of the Black National and State Conventions, 1865–1900*, 203–4.

31. Colored Union League of Wilmington, N.C., to Charles Sumner, Apr. 29, 1865, reel 33, Charles Sumner Papers.

32. "Proceedings of the Annual Meeting of the Pennsylvania State Equal Rights League Held in the City of Harrisburg," in Foner and Walker, *Proceedings of the Black National and State Conventions, 1865–1900*, 160.

33. William C. Nell, "Crispus Attucks Celebration," *The Liberator*, Mar. 24, 1865. For other examples of black leaders' postwar use of service inequalities in their arguments for black rights, see "Appeal of the Colored Men of Virginia to the American People," *NOT*, Aug. 18, 1865; "Black Residents of Washington, D.C., to the U. S. Congress," Dec. 1865, in Berlin, Reidy, and Rowland, *Black Military Experience*, 817–18; Ruth G., "Passing Events," *CR*, Mar. 31, 1866.

34. "Convention of Colored Iowa Soldiers," *CR*, Nov. 18, 1865.

35. "Convention for Colored Soldiers and Saylors," *CR*, Oct. 13, 1866; Shaffer, *After the Glory*, 70. For another example of black veterans making a political appeal on the basis of their veteranhood, see "Petition of Kentucky Former Black Soldiers to the U.S. Congress," July 1867, in Berlin, Reidy, and Rowland, *Black Military Experience*, 822–23.

36. "Colored Soldiers' and Sailors' Convention," *CR*, Jan. 12, 1867. On the Colored Soldiers' and Sailors' Convention, see also "The Convention," *CR*, Jan. 5, 1867; G. M. Arnold, C. B. Fisher, Thomas R. Hawkins, and George D. Johnson, "The Colored Soldiers and Sailors Convention," *NOT*, Oct. 31, 1866; "A Convention of Colored Soldiers and Sailors," *NOT*, Oct. 10, 1866; G. M. Arnold, C. B. Fisher, Thomas R. Hawkins, and George D. Johnson, "National Convention of Colored Soldiers and Sailors," *CR*, Nov. 3, 1866; J. A. Galbrath, "Colored Soldiers' National League," *CR*, Aug. 25, 1866; J. R. V. Morgan, George Hart, and D.D. Turner, "Mass Meeting of Colored Soldiers and Sailors," *CR*, Nov. 17, 1866; "National Convention of Colored Soldiers and Sailors, Philadelphia, January 8, 1867," in Foner and Walker, *Proceedings of the Black National and State Conventions, 1865–1900*, 287.

37. "Proceedings of the State Convention of Colored Men, Assembled at Galesburg, October 16th, 17th and 18th, Containing the State and National Addresses Promulgated by It with a List of Delegates Composing It, October 1866," in Foner and Walker, *Proceedings of the Black National and State Conventions, 1865–1900*, 271.

38. "State Convention of the Colored People of Indiana, Indianapolis, October 24, 1865," Foner and Walker, in *Proceedings of the Black National and State Conventions, 1865–1900*, 185.

39. "The Harrisburg Celebration," *CR*, Nov. 18, 1865. For other examples of African Americans linking the change they sought to the Declaration of Independence, see Day, *Celebration by the Colored People's Educational Monument Association*, 16; Untitled article, *NOT*, July 8, 1865.

40. "The Fourth," *NOT*, July 4, 1865. For arguments that black rights had been recognized in earlier periods of history, see "An Interesting Address," *Jefferson City (Mo.) Democrat*, Dec. 18, 1865; "Citizenship and Suffrage," *Elevator*, Dec. 22, 1865; Edmund Kelly to editor, *CR*, Dec. 9, 1865; "Great Suffrage Meeting in Westley Church," *CR*, Sept. 15, 1866; "Proceedings of the Convention of Colored Citizens of the State of Arkansas, Held in Little Rock, Thursday, Friday and Saturday, Nov. 30, Dec. 1 and 2,

1865," in Foner and Walker, *Proceedings of the Black National and State Conventions, 1865-1900*, 191.

41. Douglass, "What the Black Man Wants: Speech of Frederick Douglass at the Annual Meeting of the Massachusetts Anti-Slavery Society at Boston," *Equality of All Men before the Law*, 36–37.

42. Thomas Bayne and Colored Citizens of Norfolk, Virginia, "Address by a Committee of Norfolk Blacks," June 26, 1865, accessed Mar. 7, 2014, http:// bap.chadwyck .com; John Mercer Langston, "Speech by John Mercer Langston, Delivered at the Masonic Hall, Indianapolis, Indiana," Oct. 25, 1865, accessed Mar. 7, 2014, http:// bap.chadwyck.com. For other examples of black commentators urging the political necessity of black suffrage, see "A Gala Day in Leavenworth, Kansas. Reception of the First Regiment Kansas Colored Troops," *CR*, Dec. 9, 1865; David Jenkins et al., "To the Colored People of Ohio and Indiana," *CR*, Aug. 19, 1865; John J. Moore, "Enemies of the American Republic," *Elevator*, July 14, 1865; "Opinions of Our Soldier," *Elevator*, July 14, 1865; "Petition of Kentucky Former Black Soldiers to the U.S. Congress," July 1867, in Berlin, Reidy, and Rowland, *Black Military Experience*, 822–23; "What We Should Do, and How We Shall Do It," *Elevator*, June 23, 1865.

43. Davis, *Satisfied with Nothing Less*, 50–51.

44. Varon, *Appomattox*, 3, 202, 246–48.

45. Foner, *Reconstruction*, 177–83, 190, 191, 198–200.

46. Originally printed in the *Nation*, reprinted as "Perry on Government," *Colored Tennessean*, Oct. 14, 1865.

47. "Anti-Slavery Celebration at Framingham," *The Liberator*, July 14, 1865.

48. A. Atwood to editor, *Anglo-African Magazine*, Aug. 26, 1865.

49. "Proceedings of the First Annual Meeting of the National Equal Rights League of the United States," 61. For anger over the perceived betrayal of black veterans, see also "Hannibal" to editor, *Christian Recorder*, Nov. 4, 1865.

50. Ibid., 64.

51. "Proceedings of the Convention of Colored Citizens of the State of Arkansas," 193–94.

52. Foner, *Reconstruction*, 184.

53. Kantrowitz, *More than Freedom*, 4, 73.

54. "Equal Suffrage. Address from the Colored Citizens of Norfolk, VA., to the People of the United States. Also an Account of the Agitation among the Colored People of Virginia for Equal Rights. With an Appendix Concerning the Rights of Colored Witnesses before the State Courts," in Foner and Walker, *Proceedings of the Black National and State Conventions, 1865-1900*, 86.

55. "The New Evangel," *Anglo-African Magazine*, Oct. 7, 1865.

56. Alfred M. Green, "Colored Soldiers' and Sailors' National Convention," *CR*, Jan. 12, 1867. For other examples of black commentators threatening violence if the nation refused to recognize black rights, see "Anti-Slavery Celebration at Framingham, July 4th, 1865," *The Liberator*, July 14, 1865; "First of August Celebration," *The Liberator*, Aug. 11, 1865; Henry Carpenter Hoyle to editor, *CR*, Jan. 12, 1867; Hoyle, "Christmas Pastime"; "Watcher About Town," "Black Men to Retain Their Arms," *NOT*, Aug. 31, 1865; J. W. M., "Words for the Hour," *NOT*, Sept. 13, 1866; "Vialor" to editor, *NOT*, Nov. 10, 1865.

57. "Proceedings of the Annual Meeting of the Pennsylvania State Equal Rights League, held in the City of Harrisburg, August 9th and 10th, 1865," *CR*, undated clipping, circa Aug. 1865, Pennsylvania State Equal Rights League, Executive Board Minutes, 1864–1868, vol. 1, Leon B. Gardiner Collection of American Negro Historical Society Records, 1790–1905, HSP.

58. "President Johnson and Congress," *CR*, May 19, 1866.

59. "Southern Folly Our Best Help," *NOT*, Oct. 23, 1866. For another prediction that Johnson's policies and Southern intransigence would in time work to black Americans' benefit, see "Celebration of West India Emancipation," *The Liberator*, Aug. 11, 1865.

60. Foner, *Reconstruction*, 224–27; Wang, *Trial of Democracy*, 42–46.

61. Originally printed in the *Oregonian*, Apr. 7, 1870, reprinted as "Celebration in Portland," *Elevator*, Apr. 22, 1870.

62. Smith, *Civic Ideals*, 286.

63. Wang, *Trial of Democracy*, 47. On the postwar Republican Party and Reconstruction-era politics, see also Calhoun, *Conceiving a New Republic*.

64. Kelley, "Speech of Hon. William D. Kelley, of Pennsylvania, in Support of the Proposed Amendment to the Bill 'To Guarantee to Certain States, Whose Governments Have Been Usurped or Overthrown, a Republican Form of Government,' Delivered in the House of Representatives, January 16, 1865," *Equality of All Men before the Law*, 17.

65. "A Black Brigade," *Elevator*, Jan. 31, 1874.

66. Wang, *Trial of Democracy*, 30, 189, 238.

67. Ibid., xxiv–xxv. On the convergence of principle and pragmatism in Republicans' Reconstruction efforts, see also Calhoun, *Conceiving a New Republic*.

68. Shaffer, *After the Glory*, 73–76.

69. Davis, *Satisfied with Nothing Less*, 30–31, 134–35; Douglas, *Jim Crow Moves North*, 61–122; Weaver, "The Failure of Civil Rights 1875–1883 and Its Repercussions." On black Pennsylvanians' campaign for streetcar desegregation, see Diemer, "Reconstructing Philadelphia"; Foner, "The Battle to End Discrimination against Negroes on Philadelphia Streetcars: (Part I) Background and Beginning of the Battle"; Foner, "The Battle to End Discrimination against Negroes on Philadelphia Streetcars: (Part II) The Victory."

70. Frances Ellen Watkins Harper, "The Great Problem to Be Solved," in Foster, *Brighter Coming Day*, 219.

71. Kantrowitz, *More than Freedom*, 369; Quintard Taylor, *In Search of the Racial Frontier*, 125.

72. On the *Slaughterhouse Cases, United States v. Cruikshank, United States v. Reese*, the *Civil Rights Cases*, and postwar federal jurisprudence generally, see Foner, *Reconstruction*, 529–31; Nelson, *Fourteenth Amendment*, 163–64, 174–87; Smith, *Civic Ideals*, 331–38; Wang, *Trial of Democracy*, 123–30, 212–14.

73. On black Virginians' alliance with the Readjusters, see Dailey, *Before Jim Crow*.

74. Klinker and Smith, *Unsteady March*, 105. On the decline of Reconstruction, see Richardson, *Death of Reconstruction*; Foner, *Reconstruction*; Hogue, *Uncivil War*; Perman, *Road to Redemption*; Slap, *Doom of Reconstruction*; Summers, *Dangerous Stir*; Zuczek, *State of Rebellion*. Richardson emphasizes Northerners' growing equation of black Southerners seeking government aid with labor radicalism, as well as their perception that black Southerners had violated free-labor ideals. Hogue

and Zuczek foreground white Southerners' violent opposition to Reconstruction and Republican rule, and Perman deals with white Southerners' political attempts to undermine Reconstruction and undo its achievements. Slap covers the Liberal Republican movement and the perception among some Northern elites that the use of federal power to remake the South threatened liberty. For his part, Summers argues that Reconstruction had been meant primarily to prevent another war, not remake the South. When Northerners no longer perceived the South as a threat in the early 1870s, their commitment to Reconstruction began to wane. Foner's survey offers perhaps the most judicious assessment of Reconstruction's undoing, acknowledging class conflict in the North and Northerners' growing dissatisfaction with Reconstruction, as well as white Southerners' political efforts to combat Republican rule. Ultimately, however, Foner identifies white violence as the decisive factor in Reconstruction's death.

75. "X.," "Color," *Weekly Louisianan*, Aug. 13, 1881.

76. "Is There Any Law for the Negro?" *New York Globe*, Feb. 17, 1883.

77. J. G. Robinson, "The Negro Problem," *CR*, Apr. 20, 1893.

78. Pease and Pease, *They Who Would Be Free*, 118; "Quadrennial Address—of the Board of Bishops of the A.M.E. Church, Delivered by Bishop T. M. D. Ward, to the Nineteenth Session, May 12, 1888," *CR*, June 14, 1888; Wayman, *Cyclopaedia of African Methodism*, 8.

79. "The Convention of Colored Men," *Herald of Kansas*, Apr. 16, 1880.

80. Glenn, *Unequal Freedom*, 2.

81. "Opening of the Colored Exhibit," *CR*, Mar. 12, 1885.

82. "Address of the Colored Convention," *Weekly Louisianan*, Apr. 26, 1879.

83. Hahn, *Nation under Our Feet*, 330-33. On emigration sentiment in the late 1870s, see also "Address of the Colored National Conference to the People of the United States," *Weekly Louisianan*, May 17, 1879; C. H. Pearce to editor, *CR*, July 5, 1877; Shaffer, *After the Glory*, 82-85.

84. Klinker and Smith, *Unsteady March*, 97-98.

85. Shaffer, *After the Glory*, 59.

86. See Brown, *Negro in the American Rebellion*; Williams, *History of the Negro Troops*; Wilson, *Black Phalanx*. On black veterans' perception of the need to ensure that the nation remembered black service, see Jno C. Brock, "Reunion of Colored Troops," *CR*, July 15, 1886.

87. *The Negro as a Soldier, Written by Christian A. Fleetwood, Late Sergeant-Major 4th U.S. Colored Troops, for the Negro Congress at the Cotton States and International Exposition, Atlanta GA, November 11 to November 23, 1895*, reel 17, Carter G. Woodson Papers, Manuscript Division, LOC, Washington, D.C.

CONCLUSION

1. Du Bois, *Black Reconstruction in America*, 30.

2. Leonard, *Men of Color to Arms!*, 38-41, 48-50, 78-79. On the postwar black regiments, see also Leckie and Leckie, *Buffalo Soldiers*; Schubert, *Buffalo Soldiers, Braves, and the Brass*.

3. Dobak and Phillips, *Black Regulars*, 247-56; Leonard, *Men of Color to Arms!*, 59-65; Taylor, *In Search of the Racial Frontier*, 165, 174-77.

4. Dobak and Phillips, *Black Regulars*, 263.

5. Ibid., 245. On black cadets at West Point during the nineteenth century, see Leonard, *Men of Color to Arms!*, 124–74.

6. Dobak and Phillips, *Black Regulars*, 85–88, 194–203, 280. On black soldiers' treatment in the postwar U.S. Army, see also Kevin Adams, *Class and Race in the Frontier Army*. Adams disagrees with Dobak and Phillips on some points. He concedes that supply issues were the result of army policy rather than institutionalized racism, and he agrees that individual racism among white enlisted men and officers was one of the most daunting issues with which black soldiers had to contend. Adams, however, holds that black soldiers did not always receive equal justice from military courts. At integrated posts they were court-martialed more often than white soldiers, and they sometimes received harsher sentences. Adams also emphasizes these servicemen's segregation in black regiments, and he notes that only a small number of them rose to the ranks of commissioned officers over the day-to-day equality in pay, rations, clothing, and supplies that black soldiers enjoyed. Charles Kenner has also found evidence of institutional racism in his work on the enlisted men and officers of the Ninth Cavalry stationed at Fort Robinson, Nebraska. See Kenner, *Buffalo Soldiers and Officers of the Ninth Cavalry*. Monroe Lee Billington tends to echo Dobak and Phillips's emphasis on day-to-day equality and formal fairness. See Billington, *New Mexico's Buffalo Soldiers*. This study agrees with the view offered by Dobak and Phillips not because it disputes Adams's and Kenner's conclusions, but because it does not exactly view the patterns of racial discrimination these two authors reveal as evidence of institutionalized racism. Both authors argue compellingly that black soldiers faced unequal justice in the army. But that does not change the fact that this irregular justice was not the result of written army policy—there was no statute that ordered trying black soldiers more often and sentencing them to longer terms—but the result of racist white officers applying the system differently to black troops. The same observation holds for Kenner's point about the unequal distribution of duties at Fort Robinson and Adams's point about the small number of black officers. Finally, Adams emphasizes black soldiers' segregation in all-black units; Dobak and Phillips underscore their day-to-day equality. Day-to-day equality was what mattered to black Civil War servicemen far more than segregated units, which Henry McNeal Turner thought gave these men an advantage, so this study continues to privilege this aspect of their service.

7. Leiker, *Racial Borders*, 15; Taylor, *In Search of the Racial Frontier*, 186–87.

8. Henry McNeal Turner to Blanche K. Bruce, *CR*, Mar. 27, 1890.

9. Leiker, *Racial Borders*, 15–17, 47–49, 176–77.

10. Leiker ascribes black newspapers' tendency to ignore the black regiments to the bourgeois values of their editors, who looked down on those who made their living in the army. See ibid., 96–97.

11. William H. Yeocum, "Encourage the Negro," *CR*, Aug. 9, 1888.

12. Theophilus G. Steward to editor, *CR*, Aug. 9, 1894.

13. Henry McNeal Turner to editor, *CR*, Jan. 31, 1863.

14. Leiker, *Racial Borders*, 17.

15. Glenn, *Unequal Freedom*, 1, 24; Smith, *Civic Ideals*, 1–3, 6.

16. Shaffer, *After the Glory*, 119–22, 133, 137–40.

17. Ibid., 136, 139, 142. See also Shaffer, "'I Do Not Suppose.'"

18. On the Grand Army of the Republic, see McConnell, *Glorious Contentment*.

19. Fleche, "'Shoulder to Shoulder as Comrades Tried,'" 292, 296–97; Shaffer, *After the Glory*, 144–45, 156–58.

20. Shaffer, *After the Glory*, 143, 145, 149–50, 152.

21. Leonard, *Men of Color to Arms!*, 247.

22. "Speech of Frederick Douglass," *The Liberator*, July 24, 1863.

23. Richardson, *West from Appomattox*, 28.

24. Faust, *This Republic of Suffering*, xiv, 268–69. See also Lawson, *Patriot Fires*.

25. Fredrickson, *Black Image in the White Mind*, 174.

26. Masur, *An Example for All the Land*, 4–5, 220–21.

27. "Sixth Anniversary of President Lincoln's Emancipation Proclamation," *Elevator*, Jan. 8, 1869. For other examples of postwar black commentators talking about citizenship in this manner, see G. M. Arnold, C. B. Fisher, Thomas R. Hawkins, and George D. Johnson, "The Colored Soldiers and Sailors Convention," *NOT*, Oct. 31, 1866; "Second Letter to Our Colored Fellow Citizens," *CR*, Oct. 26, 1867. Even black leaders who genuinely supported women's rights, like Frederick Douglass, supported Reconstruction legislation that defined voting as a male right, rupturing a decades-old feminist-abolitionist alliance. On the alliance between abolitionists and first-wave feminists and its postwar rupture, see DuBois, *Feminism and Suffrage*.

28. Additionally, Reconstruction-era white politicians in Washington and numerous other cities who launched "citizens'" and "taxpayers'" campaigns seized on an antebellum vision of citizenship that associated citizens' rights with community standing. The architects of these campaigns depicted themselves as sober community stewards capable of wielding citizenship's responsibilities. They also portrayed newly enfranchised black men and other lower-class voters as ignorant, easily led tools of corrupt politicians. Many white Southerners had always opposed black voting due to their general belief in black inferiority, but as the 1870s wore on many white Northerners began to think in similar terms, embracing racially tinged notions about the potential danger of black voting. See Richardson, *Death of Reconstruction*. Richardson argues that many white Northerners in the 1870s began to see black Southerners' requests for government aid as appeals for "class legislation," and to equate black Southerners' political activity with the labor strife then brewing in Northern cities and in Europe. Those in the North began to accept stereotypes of black Southerners as lazy and unwilling to work to support themselves, and to sour on black suffrage.

29. Nelson, *The Fourteenth Amendment*, 110–16; Masur, *An Example for All the Land*, 176–77, 220–21, 254.

30. Nelson, *Fourteenth Amendment*, 163–64.

31. On the birth of the Jim Crow South, see Ayers, *Promise of the New South*, 132–59; Klarman, *Unfinished Business*, 75–92; Packard, *American Nightmare*; Klinker and Smith, *Unsteady March*, 91–105.

32. On white Americans' changing perceptions of black Southerners and their withdrawal of support from federal Reconstruction, see Richardson, *Death of Reconstruction*.

33. See Lang, *In the Wake of War*, chapters 8 and 9.

34. On Americans' postwar discomfort with the expansive use of federal power, see Richardson, *West from Appomattox*. See also Slap, *Doom of Reconstruction*.

35. Davis, *Satisfied with Nothing Less*, 146–47.

36. Adam Liptak, "Supreme Court Invalidates Key Part of Voting Rights Act," *New York Times*, June 25, 2013; Shelby County v. Holder, 570 U.S. (2013).

37. Du Bois, *Souls of Black Folk*, 9.

38. On African Americans, black service and World War I, see Jordan, "'The Damnable Dilemma,'" 1562–83; Lentz-Smith, *Freedom Struggles*; Williams, *Torchbearers of Democracy*.

39. On African American service and protest during the Second World War, see James, *The Double V*; Knauer, *Let Us Fight as Free Men: Black Soldiers and Civil Rights*; Wynn, *African American Experience*.

40. James G. Thompson, "Should I Sacrifice to Live," *Pittsburgh Courier*, Jan. 31, 1942, in Wynn, *African American Experience*, 110–11.

41. Gallicchio, "Memory and the Lost Found Relationship," 265.

42. Malcolm X as told to Haley, *Autobiography of Malcolm X*, 108.

43. Ibid., 207.

44. Phillips, *War! What Is It Good For?*, 223.

45. Weigley, *American Way of War*, 477.

BIBLIOGRAPHY

PRIMARY SOURCE COLLECTIONS

Boston, Mass.
  Commonwealth of Massachusetts Archives
    Executive Letters Collection
  Massachusetts Historical Society
    John A. Andrew Papers
Philadelphia, Pa.
  Historical Society of Pennsylvania
    Leon B. Gardiner Collection of American Negro Historical Society
      Records, 1790–1905
Washington, D.C.
  Howard University, Moorland-Spingarn Research Center
    Jacob C. White Collection
  Library of Congress, Manuscript Division
    Thaddeus Stevens Papers
    Charles Sumner Papers
    Carter G. Woodson Papers

NEWSPAPERS AND PUBLICATIONS

Anglo-African Magazine
Christian Recorder
Colored Citizen
Colored Tennessean
Congressional Globe
Crisis
Douglass' Monthly
Elevator
Frederick Douglass' Paper
Herald of Kansas
The Liberator
National Principia
New Orleans Tribune
New York Globe
New York Times
North Star
Pacific Appeal
Pine & Palm
Weekly Anglo-African
Weekly Louisianan

PUBLISHED PRIMARY SOURCES

Aptheker, Herbert, ed. *Documentary History of the Negro People in the United States.* Vol. 1. New York: Citadel Press, 1951.

Basler, Roy P., Lloyd A. Dunlap and Marion Dolores Pratt, eds. *The Collected Works of Abraham Lincoln.* 8 vols. New Brunswick: Rutgers University Press, 1953.

Bates, Edward. *Opinion of Attorney General Bates on Negro Citizenship.* Washington, D.C.: Government Printing Office, 1863.

Berlin, Ira, Joseph P. Reidy, and Leslie Rowland, eds. *Freedom: A Documentary History of Emancipation 1861–1867.* Vol. 2, *The Black Military Experience.* Cambridge: Cambridge University Press, 1982.

Berlin, Ira, and Leslie S. Rowland, eds. *Families and Freedom: A Documentary History of African-American Kinship in the Civil War Era.* New York: New Press, 1997.

Bell, Howard Holman, ed. *Minutes of the Proceedings of the National Negro Conventions, 1830–1864.* Reprint, New York: Arno, 1969.

Clark, Peter H. *The Black Brigade of Cincinnati.* Cincinnati, Ohio: Joseph B. Boyd, 1864.

Dann, Martin E., ed. *The Black Press, 1827–1890: The Quest for National Identity.* New York: Putnam, 1971.

Davis, George B., Joseph W. Kirkley, H. M. Lazelle, Leslie J. Perry, and Robert N. Scott, eds. *The War of the Rebellion: A Compilation of the Official Records of the Union and Confederate Armies.* 70 vols. Washington, D.C.: Government Printing Office, 1880–1901.

Day, William H. *Celebration by the Colored People's Educational Monument Association in Memory of Abraham Lincoln, on the Fourth of July, 1865, in the Presidential Grounds, Washington, D.C.* Washington, D.C.: McGill and Witherow, 1865.

Douglass, Frederick. *Two Speeches of Frederick Douglass: One on West India Emancipation, Delivered at Canandaigua, Aug. 4th, and the Other on the Dred Scott Decision, Delivered in New York, on the Occasion of the Anniversary of the American Abolition Society, May 1857.* Rochester, N.Y.: C. P. Dewey, 1857.

———. *The Life and Writings of Frederick Douglass.* Edited by Philip S. Foner. 5 vols. New York: International Publishers, 1950–75.

Douglass, Frederick, William Heighton, William D. Kelley, Wendell Phillips, and Elizur Wright. *The Equality of All Men before the Law Claimed and Defended; in Speeches by Hon. William D. Kelley, Wendell Phillips, and Frederick Douglass, and Letters from Elizur Wright and Wm. Heighton.* Boston: George C. Rand and Avery, 1865.

Foner, Philip S., ed. *We, the Other People: Alternative Declarations of Independence by Labor Groups, Farmers, Women's Rights Advocates, Socialists, and Blacks, 1829–1975.* Urbana: University of Illinois Press, 1976.

Foner, Philip S., and George E. Walker, eds. *Proceedings of the Black State Conventions, 1840–1865.* 2 vols. Philadelphia: Temple University Press, 1980 and 1986.

———, eds. *Proceedings of the Black State and National Conventions, 1865–1900.* Philadelphia: Temple University Press, 1986.

Franklin, John Hope. *Mirror to America: The Autobiography of John Hope Franklin.* New York: Farrar, Straus and Giroux, 2005.

Garnet, Henry Highland. *A Memorial Discourse by Rev. Henry Highland Garnet, Delivered in the Hall of the House of Representatives, Washington City, D.C., on Sabbath, February 12, 1865.* Philadelphia: Joseph M. Wilson, 1865.

Green, Alfred M., and Maxwell Whitman, eds. *Letters and Discussions on the Formation of Colored Regiments and the Duty of Colored People in Regard to the Great Slaveholders' Rebellion, in the United States of America.* Philadelphia: Ringwalt and Brown, 1862.

Harper, Frances Ellen Watkins. *A Brighter Coming Day: A Frances Ellen Watkins Harper Reader*. Edited by Frances Foster Smith. New York: Feminist Press at the City University of New York, 1990.

Hayden, Rene, Antony E. Kaye, Kate Masur, Steven F. Miller, Susan E. O'Donovan, Leslie S. Rowland, and Stephen A. West, eds. *Freedom: A Documentary History of Emancipation, 1861–1867*. Ser. 3, vol. 2, *Land and Labor, 1866–1867*. Chapel Hill: University of North Carolina Press, 2013.

Jones, John. *The Illinois Black Laws, and a Few Reasons Why They Should Be Repealed*. Chicago: Tribune Book and Job Office, 1864.

Langston, John Mercer. *From the Virginia Plantation to the National Capitol, or, The First and Only Negro Representative from Old Dominion*. 1894. Reprint, New York: Arno, 1969.

Lapsansky, Philip, Richard S. Newman, and Patrick Rael, eds. *Pamphlets of Protest: An Anthology of Early African-American Protest Literature, 1790–1860*. New York: Routledge, 2001.

Malcolm X, as told to Alex Haley. *The Autobiography of Malcolm X*. 1964. Reprint, New York: Ballantine, 1999.

Morrow, Curtis. *What's a Commie Ever Done to Black People?: A Korean War Memoir of Fighting in the U. S. Army's Last All-Negro Unit*. Jefferson, N.C.: McFarland, 1997.

The Negro as a Soldier, Written by Christian A. Fleetwood, Late Sergeant-Major 4th U.S. Colored Troops, for the Negro Congress at the Cotton States and International Exposition, Atlanta GA, November 11 to November 23, 1895. Washington, D.C.: Howard University, 1895.

Nell, William C. *The Colored Patriots of the American Revolution, with Sketches of Several Distinguished Colored Persons: To Which Is Added a Brief Survey of the Condition and Prospects of Colored Americans*. Boston: R. F. Wallcutt, 1855.

O'Reilly, Henry. *First Organization of Colored Troops in the State of New York, to Aid In Suppressing the Slaveholders' Rebellion*. New York: Baker and Godwin, 1864.

Population of the United States in 1860; Compiled from the Original Returns of the Eighth Census Under the Direction of the Secretary of the Interior, by Joseph C. G. Kennedy, Superintendent of Census. Washington, D.C.: Government Printing Office, 1864.

Proceedings of the National Convention of Colored Men, Held in the City of Syracuse, NY, October 4, 5, 6, and 7, 1864; with the Bill of Wrongs and Rights and the Address to the American People. Boston: Avery and Rand, 1864.

Redkey, Edwin, ed. *A Grand Army of Black Men: Letters from African-American Soldiers in the Union Army, 1861–1865*. Cambridge: Cambridge University Press, 1992.

Report of the Committee of Merchants for the Relief of Colored People, Suffering From the Late Riots in the City of New York. New York: George A. Whitehorne, 1863.

Richardson, Marilyn, ed. *Maria W. Stewart: America's First Black Woman Political Writer*. Bloomington: Indiana University Press, 1987.

Ripley, C. Peter, ed. *Witness for Freedom: African American Voices on Race, Slavery and Emancipation*. Chapel Hill: University of North Carolina Press, 1993.

Ripley, C. Peter, et al., eds. *The Black Abolitionist Papers*. 5 vols. Chapel Hill: University of North Carolina Press, 1985–1992.

Sanger, George P., ed. *U.S. Statutes at Large*. Vol. 12. Boston: Little and Brown, 1863.

Stephens, George. *A Voice of Thunder: The Civil War Letters of George E. Stephens*. Edited by Donald Yacovone. Chicago: Chicago University Press, 1997.

Still, William. *A Brief Narrative of the Struggle for the Rights of the Colored People of Philadelphia in the City Railway Cars; and a Defence of William Still, Relating to His Agency Touching the Passage of the Late Bill, Etc. Read Before a Large Public Meeting in Liberty Hall, April 8th, 1867*. Philadelphia: Merrihew and Son, 1867.

Trudeau, Noah Andre, ed. *Voices of the 55th: Letters from the 55th Massachusetts Volunteers, 1861–1865*. Dayton, Ohio: Morningside, 1996.

Walker, David. *David Walker's Appeal, In Four Articles; Together With a Preamble, to the Colored Citizens of the World, but in Particular, and Very Expressly, to Those of the United States of America*. 1829. Reprint, New York: Hill and Wang, 1999.

SECONDARY SOURCES

Adams, Kevin. *Class and Race in the Frontier Army: Military Life in the West, 1870–1890*. Norman: University of Oklahoma Press, 2009.

Adeleke, Tunde. *Without Regard to Race: The Other Martin Robison Delany*. Jackson: University of Mississippi Press, 2003.

Anderson, Benedict. *Imagined Communities*. London: Verso, 1983.

Anderson, Fred. *A People's Army: Massachusetts Soldiers and Society in the Seven Years' War*. New York: W. W. Norton, 1984.

———. "Why Did Colonial New England Soldiers Make Bad Soldiers? Contractual Principles and Military Conduct during the Seven Years' War." *William and Mary Quarterly* 38, no. 3 (1981): 395–417.

Angell, Stephen Ward, and Anthony B. Pinn, eds. *Social Protest Thought in the African Methodist Episcopal Church, 1862–1939*. Knoxville: University of Tennessee Press, 2000.

Archdeacon, Thomas J. *Becoming American: An Ethnic History*. New York: Free Press, 1983.

Armitage, David. *The Declaration of Independence: A Global History*. Cambridge, Mass.: Harvard University Press, 2007.

Ayers, Edward. *The Promise of the New South: Life after Reconstruction*. New York: Oxford University Press, 1992.

Barker, Hannah, and Simon Burrows, eds. *Press, Politics, and the Public Sphere in Europe and North America, 1760–1820*. New York: Cambridge University Press, 2002.

Belz, Herman. "Law, Politics, and Race in the Struggle for Equal Pay during the Civil War." *Civil War History* 22 (1976): 197–213.

Bennett, Marion T. *American Immigration Policies: A History*. Washington, D.C.: Public Affairs, 1963.

Berlin, Ira. *Many Thousands Gone: The First Two Centuries of Slavery in North America*. Cambridge, Mass.: Belknap Press, 1998.

Bernstein, Iver. *The New York City Draft Riots: Their Significance for American Society and Politics in the Age of the Civil War.* New York: Oxford University Press, 1990.

Berry, Mary Frances. *Military Necessity and Civil Rights Policy: Black Citizenship and the Constitution.* Port Washington, N.Y.: Kennikat, 1977.

Biddle, Daniel R., and Murray Dubin. *Tasting Freedom: Octavius Catto and the Battle for Equality in Civil War America.* Philadelphia: Temple University Press, 2010.

Billington, Monroe Lee. *New Mexico's Buffalo Soldiers, 1866–1900.* Niwot: University of Colorado Press, 1991.

Blatt, Martin H. "*Glory*: Hollywood History, Popular Culture, and the Fifty-Fourth Massachusetts Regiment." In *Hope and Glory: Essays on the Legacy of the 54th Massachusetts Regiment,* edited by Martin H. Blatt, Thomas L. Brown, and Donald Yacovone, 215–35. Amherst: University of Massachusetts Press, 1994.

Blight, David W. *Frederick Douglass' Civil War: Keeping Faith in Jubilee.* Baton Rouge: Louisiana State University Press, 1989.

———. *Race and Reunion: The Civil War in American Memory.* Cambridge, Mass.: Harvard University Press, 2001.

Bolster, Jeffrey W. *Black Jacks: African-American Seamen in the Age of Sail.* Cambridge: Cambridge University Press, 1997.

Brasher, Glenn David. *The Peninsula Campaign and the Necessity of Emancipation: African Americans and the Fight for Freedom.* Chapel Hill: University of North Carolina Press, 2012.

Brennan, Denis. *The Making of an Abolitionist: William Lloyd Garrison's Path to Publishing "The Liberator."* Jefferson, N.C.: McFarland, 2014.

Brooke, John L. *Columbia Rising: Civil Life on the Upper Hudson from the Revolution to the Age of Jackson.* Chapel Hill: University of North Carolina Press, 2010.

Brown, Kathleen. *Good Wives, Nasty Wenches, and Anxious Patriarchs: Gender, Race, and Power in Colonial Virginia.* Chapel Hill: University of North Carolina Press, 1996.

Brown, Thomas, ed. *Reconstructions: New Perspectives on the Postbellum United States.* Oxford: Oxford University Press, 2013.

Brown, William Wells. *The Negro in the American Rebellion: His Heroism and His Fidelity.* Boston: Lee and Shepherd, 1867.

Calhoun, Charles. *Conceiving a New Republic: The Republican Party and the Southern Question, 1869–1900.* Lawrence: University Press of Kansas, 2006.

Chused, Richard H. "Late-Nineteenth Century Married Women's Property Law: Reception of the Early Married Property Acts by Courts and Legislatures." *American Journal of Legal History* 29 (January 1985): 3–35.

Cooper, Frederick. "Elevating the Race: The Social Thought of Black Leaders, 1827–50." *American Quarterly* 24, no. 5 (December 1972): 604–25.

Coppin, Levi Jenkins. *Unwritten History.* Philadelphia: AME Book Concern, 1919.

Cornish, Dudley T. *The Sable Arm: Negro Troops in the Union Army, 1861–1865.* New York: W. W. Norton, 1966.

Crofts, Dan. *Lincoln and the Politics of Slavery.* Chapel Hill: University of North Carolina Press, 2016.

Cullen, Jim. "'I's a Man Now': Gender and African American Men." In *Divided Houses: Gender and the Civil War*, edited by Catherine Clinton and Nina Silber, 213–42. New York: Oxford University Press, 1993.

Cunningham, Roger D. *The Black Citizen-Soldiers of Kansas, 1864–1901*. Columbia: University of Missouri Press, 2008.

Dabel, Jane E. *A Respectable Woman: The Public Roles of African American Women in 19th-Century New York*. New York: New York University Press, 2008.

Dailey, Jane E. *Before Jim Crow: The Politics of Race in Postemancipation Virginia*. Chapel Hill: University of North Carolina Press, 2000.

Davis, David Brion. *The Problem of Slavery in the Age of Emancipation*. New York: Vintage, 2015.

Davis, Hugh. "The Pennsylvania State Equal Rights League and the Northern Black Struggle for Legal Equality, 1864–1877." *Pennsylvania Magazine of History and Biography* 126 (2002): 611–34.

———. *We Will Be Satisfied with Nothing Less: The African-American Struggle for Equal Rights in the North during Reconstruction*. Ithaca: Cornell University Press, 2011.

Deyle, Steven. *Carry Me Back: The Domestic Slave Trade in American Life*. Oxford: Oxford University Press, 2005.

Dick, Robert C. *Black Protest: Issues and Tactics*. Westport, Conn: Greenwood, 1974.

Diemer, Andrew. "Reconstructing Philadelphia: African Americans and Politics in the Post–Civil War North." *Pennsylvania Magazine of History and Biography* 133, no. 1 (2009): 29–58.

Dittmer, John. "The Education of Henry McNeal Turner." In *Black Leaders of the Nineteenth Century*, edited by Leon F. Litwack and August Meier, 253–72. Urbana: University of Illinois Press, 1991.

Dobak, William A., and Thomas D. Phillips. *The Black Regulars, 1866–1898*. Norman: University of Oklahoma Press, 2006.

Donald, David Herbert. *Lincoln*. New York: Simon and Schuster, 1995.

Douglas, Davison M. *Jim Crow Moves North: The Battle over School Segregation in the North, 1865–1954*. New York: Cambridge University Press, 2005.

DuBois, Ellen Carol. *Feminism and Suffrage: The Emergence of an Independent Women's Movement in America, 1848–1869*. Ithaca: Cornell University Press, 1978.

———. "Outgrowing the Compact of the Fathers: Equal Rights, Woman Suffrage, and the United States Constitution." *Journal of American History* 74, no. 3 (December 1987): 836–62.

Du Bois, W. E. B. *Black Reconstruction in America, 1860–1880*. 1935. Reprint, New York: Free Press, 1992.

———. *The Souls of Black Folk*. 1903. Reprint, Boston: Bedford Books, 1997.

Edgerton, Robert B. *Hidden Heroism: Black Soldiers in America's Wars*. Boulder, Colo.: Westview Press, 2001.

Egerton, Douglas. *Thunder at the Gates: The Black Civil War Regiments That Redeemed America*. Philadelphia: Basic Books, 2016.

Emberton, Carole. "'Only Murder Makes Men': Reconsidering the Black Military Experience." *Journal of the Civil War Era* 2, no. 3 (2012): 369.

Ernest, John. *A Nation within a Nation: Organizing African-American Communities before the Civil War.* Chicago: Ivar R. Dee, 2011.

Farrison, William. *William Wells Brown: Author and Reformer.* Chicago: University of Chicago Press, 1969.

Faulkner, Carol. *Women's Radical Reconstruction: The Freedmen's Aid Movement.* Philadelphia: University of Pennsylvania Press, 2004.

Faust, Drew Gilpin. *This Republic of Suffering: Death and the American Civil War.* New York: Alfred A. Knopf, 2008.

Fehrenbacher, Don E. *The Dred Scott Case: Its Significance in American Law and Politics.* New York: Oxford University Press, 1978.

———. *The Slaveholding Republic: An Account of the United States Government's Relations to Slavery.* Oxford: Oxford University Press, 2001.

Finkelman, Paul. *Encyclopedia of African American History: From the Colonial Period to the Age of Frederick Douglass.* Oxford: Oxford University Press, 2006.

———. "Prelude to the Fourteenth Amendment: Black Legal Rights in the Antebellum North." *Rutgers Law Journal* 17 (1986): 415–82.

Fleche, Andre. "'Shoulder to Shoulder as Comrades Tried': Black and White Veterans and Civil War Memory." *Civil War History* 51 (June 2005): 175–201.

Flexner, Eleanor, and Ellen Fitzpatrick. *Century of Struggle: The Women's Rights Movement in the United States.* Enlarged edition. Cambridge, Mass.: Harvard University Press, 1996.

Foner, Eric. *The Fiery Trial: Abraham Lincoln and American Slavery.* New York: W. W. Norton, 2010.

———. "Lincoln, Colonization, and the Rights of Black Americans." In *Slavery's Ghost: The Problem of Freedom in the Age of Emancipation*, edited by Richard Follett, Eric Foner, and Walter Johnson, 31–49. Baltimore: Johns Hopkins University Press, 2011.

———. *Reconstruction: America's Unfinished Revolution, 1863–1877.* New York: Harper and Row, 1988.

Foner, Philip S. "The Battle to End Discrimination against Negroes on Philadelphia Streetcars (Part I): Background and Beginning of the Battle." *Pennsylvania History* 40, no. 3 (July 1973): 261–90

———. "The Battle to End Discrimination against Negroes on Philadelphia Streetcars (Part II): The Victory." *Pennsylvania History* 40, no. 4 (October 1973): 355–79.

———. *Blacks in the American Revolution.* Westport, Conn.: Greenwood, 1976.

Foster, A. Kristen. "'We Are Men!': Frederick Douglass and the Fault Lines of Gendered Citizenship." *Journal of the Civil War Era* 1, no. 2 (June 2011): 143.

Fredrickson, George. *The Black Image in the White Mind: The Debate on Afro-American Character and Destiny, 1817–1914.* New York: Harper and Row, 1971.

Freehling, William W. *The South vs. the South: How Anti-Confederate Southerners Shaped the Course of the Civil War.* New York: Oxford University Press, 2001.

Frey, Sylvia. *Water from the Rock: Black Resistance in a Revolutionary Age.* Princeton, N.J.: Princeton University Press, 1991.

Furstenberg, Francois. "Beyond Freedom and Slavery: Autonomy, Virtue, and Resistance in Early American Political Discourse." *Journal of American History* 89, no. 4 (2003): 1295–30.

Gallagher, Gary W. *The Union War*. Cambridge, Mass.: Harvard University Press, 2011.

Gallicchio, Marc. "Memory and the Lost Found Relationship between Black Americans and Japan." In *The Unpredictability of the Past: Memories of the Asia-Pacific War in U.S.-East Asian Relations*, edited by Marc Gallicchio, 255–86. Durham, N.C.: Duke University Press, 2007.

Gallman, J. Matthew. "In Your Hands That Musket Means Liberty: African American Soldiers and the Battle of Olustee." In *Wars within a War: Controversy and Conflict over the American Civil War*, edited by Gary W. Gallagher and Joan Waugh, 87–109. Chapel Hill: University of North Carolina Press, 2009.

Gannon, Barbara A. *The Won Cause: Black and White Comradeship in the Grand Army of the Republic*. Chapel Hill: University of North Carolina Press, 2011.

Garb, Margaret. "The Political Education of John Jones: Black Politics in a Northern City, 1845–1879." *Journal of the Historical Society* 8, no. 1 (2008): 29–60.

Gardner, Eric. *Unexpected Places: Relocating Nineteenth-Century African American Literature*. Jackson: University of Mississippi Press, 2009.

Geffert, Hannah. "They Heard His Call: The Local Black Community's Involvement in the Raid on Harpers Ferry." In *Terrible Swift Sword: The Legacy of John Brown*, edited by Paul Finkelman and Peggy A. Russo, 23–45. Athens: Ohio University Press, 2005.

Geffert, Hannah, and Jean Libby. "Regional Black Involvement in John Brown's Raid on Harpers Ferry." In *Prophets of Protest: Reconsidering the History of American Abolitionism*, edited by Timothy Patrick McCarthy and John Stauffer, 165–82. New York: New Press, 2006.

Gerber, David A. "Peter Humphries Clark." In *Black Leaders of the Nineteenth Century*, edited by Leon F. Litwack and August Meier, 73–83. Urbana: University of Illinois Press, 1991.

Giesberg, Judith. *Army at Home: Women and the Civil War on the Northern Home Front*. Chapel Hill: University of North Carolina Press, 2009.

Gilbert, Alan. *Black Patriots and Loyalists: Fighting for Emancipation in the War for Independence*. Chicago: University of Chicago Press, 2012.

Glatthaar, Joseph T. "Black Glory: The African-American Role in Union Victory." In *Why the Confederacy Lost*, edited by Gabor S. Boritt, 133–62. New York: Oxford University Press, 1992.

———. *Forged in Battle: The Civil War Alliance between Black Soldiers and White Officers*. New York: Free Press, 1990.

Glenn, Evelyn Nakano. *Unequal Freedom: How Race and Gender Shaped American Citizenship and Labor*. Cambridge, Mass.: Harvard University Press, 2002.

Gosse, Van. "'As a Nation, the English Are Our Friends': The Emergence of an African American Politics in the British Atlantic World, 1772–1861." *American Historical Review* 113, no. 4 (2008): 1003–28.

Grant, Susan-Mary. "Fighting for Freedom: African American Soldiers in the Civil War." In *The American Civil War: Explorations and Reconsiderations*, edited by Susan-Mary Grant and Brian Holden Reid, 185–208. Harlow, England: Pearson Education, 2000.

Grimsley, Mark. *The Hard Hand of War: Union Military Policy toward Southern Civilians*. Cambridge: Cambridge University Press, 1995.

Grover, Kathryn. *The Fugitive's Gibraltar: Escaping Slaves and Abolitionism in New Bedford, Massachusetts*. Amherst: University of Massachusetts Press, 2003.

Guelzo, Allen C. *Lincoln's Emancipation Proclamation: The End of Slavery in America*. New York: Simon and Schuster, 2004.

Hahn, Stephen. *A Nation under Our Feet: Black Struggles in the Rural South, from Slavery to the Great Migration*. Cambridge: Cambridge University Press, 2003.

———. *The Political Worlds of Slavery and Freedom*. Cambridge, Mass.: Harvard University Press, 2009.

Hargrove, Hondon B. *Black Union Soldiers in the Civil War*. Jefferson, N.C.: McFarland, 1988.

Heller, Charles E. *Portrait of an Abolitionist: George Luther Stearns, 1809–1867*. Westport, Conn.: Greenwood, 1996.

Henkin, Louis. "The Constitution and United States Sovereignty: A Century of Chinese Exclusion and Its Progeny." *Harvard Law Review* 100 (1986–87): 853–86.

Higham, John. *Strangers in the Land: Patterns of American Nativism, 1860–1925*. New York: Atheneum, 1963.

Hinks, Peter. *To Awaken My Afflicted Brethren: David Walker and the Problem of Antebellum Slave Resistance*. University Park: Pennsylvania State University Press, 1997.

Hofstadter, Richard. *The American Political Tradition and the Men Who Made It*. New York: A. A. Knopf, 1948.

Hogue, James K. *Uncivil War: Five New Orleans Street Battles and the Rise and Fall of Radical Reconstruction*. Baton Rouge: Louisiana State University Press, 2011.

Hollandsworth, James G., Jr. *The Louisiana Native Guards: The Black Military Experience during the Civil War*. Baton Rouge: Louisiana State University Press, 1995.

Holton, Woody. *Forced Founders: Indians, Debtors, Slaves and the Making of the American Revolution in Virginia*. Chapel Hill: University of North Carolina Press, 1999.

———. "'Rebel against Rebel': Enslaved Virginians and the Coming of the American Revolution." *Virginia Magazine of History and Biography* 105, no. 2 (1997): 157–92.

Horton, James O., and Lois E. Horton. "The Affirmation of Manhood: Black Garrisonians in Antebellum Boston." In *Courage and Conscience: Black and White Abolitionists in Boston*, edited by Donald M. Jacobs, 127–54. Bloomington: Indiana University Press, 1993.

———. *In Hope of Liberty: Culture, Community and Protest among Northern Free Blacks, 1700–1860*. New York: Oxford University Press, 1997.

Howard-Pitney, David. *The Afro-American Jeremiad: Appeals for Justice in America*. Philadelphia: Temple University Press, 1990.

Humphreys, Margaret A. *Intensely Human: The Health of the Black Soldier in the American Civil War*. Baltimore: Johns Hopkins University Press, 2008.

Hunter, Carol. *To Set the Captives Free: Reverend Jermain Wesley Loguen and the Struggle for Freedom in Central New York, 1835-1872.* New York: Hyrax, 2013.

Isenberg, Nancy. *Sex and Citizenship in Antebellum America.* Chapel Hill: University of North Carolina Press, 1998.

Izeksohn, Vitor. *Slavery and War in the Americas: Race, Citizenship and State Building in the United States and Brazil, 1861-1870.* Charlottesville: University of Virginia Press, 2014.

Jackson, Debra. "A Cultural Stronghold: The *Anglo-African* Newspaper and the Black Community in New York." *New York History* 85 (Fall 2004): 331-57.

Jacobson, Matthew Frye. *Whiteness of a Different Color: European Immigrants and the Alchemy of Race.* Cambridge, Mass.: Harvard University Press, 1998.

James, Rawn, Jr. *The Double V: How Wars, Protest and Harry Truman Desegregated America's Military.* New York: Bloomsbury, 2013.

Johnson, Charles. *African American Soldiers in the National Guard: Recruitment and Deployment during Peacetime and War.* Westport, Conn.: Greenwood, 1992.

Jones, Charles K. *Francis Johnson (1792-1844): Chronicle of a Black Musician in Early Nineteenth-Century Philadelphia.* Bethlehem, Pa.: Lehigh University Press, 2006.

Jones, Martha S. *All Bound Up Together: The Woman Question in African American Public Culture, 1830-1900.* Chapel Hill: University of North Carolina Press, 2007.

———. *Birthright Citizens: A History of Race and Rights in Antebellum America.* Cambridge: Cambridge University Press, 2018.

Jordan, William. "'The Damnable Dilemma': African-American Accommodation and Protest during World War I." *Journal of American History* 81, no. 4 (March 1995): 1562-83.

Kachun, Mitchell A. *Festivals of Freedom: Memory and Meaning in African American Emancipation Celebrations, 1808-1915.* Amherst: University of Massachusetts Press, 2003.

Kantrowitz, Stephen. *More than Freedom: Fighting for Black Citizenship in a White Republic, 1829-1889.* New York: Penguin, 2012.

———. "The Other Thirteenth Amendment: Free African Americans and the Constitution That Wasn't." *Marquette University Law Review* 93 (2010): 1367-74.

Kauffman, Michael W. *American Brutus: John Wilkes Booth and the Lincoln Conspiracies.* New York: Random House, 2004.

Kenner, Charles L. *Buffalo Soldiers and the Officers of the Ninth Cavalry, 1867-1898.* Norman: University of Oklahoma Press, 1999.

Kerber, Linda K. *No Constitutional Right to Be Ladies: Women and the Obligations of Citizenship.* New York: Hill and Wang, 1998.

Kettner, James H. *The Development of American Citizenship, 1608-1870.* Chapel Hill: University of North Carolina Press, 1978.

Keysaar, Alexander. *The Right to Vote: The Contested History of Democracy in the United States.* New York: Basic Books, 2000.

King, Desmond. *Immigration, Race, and the Origins of the Diverse Democracy.* Cambridge, Mass.: Harvard University Press, 2000.

Klarman, Michael J. *Unfinished Business: Racial Equality in American History.* New York: Oxford University Press, 2007.

Klinker, Philip A., and Rogers Smith. *The Unsteady March: The Rise and Decline of Racial Equality in America*. Chicago: University of Chicago Press, 1999.

Knauer, Christine. *Let Us Fight as Free Men: Black Soldiers and Civil Rights*. Philadelphia: University of Pennsylvania Press, 2014.

Koschnik, Albrecht. *"Let a Common Interest Tie Us Together": Associations, Partisanship and Culture in Philadelphia, 1775–1840*. Charlottesville: University of Virginia Press, 2007.

Kugler, Israel. *From Ladies to Women: The Organized Struggle for Women's Rights in the Reconstruction Era*. Westport, Conn.: Greenwood, 1988.

Kynoch, Gary. "Terrible Dilemmas: Black Enlistment in the Union Army during the American Civil War." *Slavery and Abolition* 18 (1997): 104–27.

Lang, Andrew. *In the Wake of War: Military Occupation, Emancipation and Civil War America*. Baton Rouge: Louisiana State University Press, 2017.

Lapp, Rudolph M. *Blacks in Gold Rush California*. New Haven, Conn.: Yale University Press, 1977.

Lawson, Melinda. *Patriot Fires: Forging a New American Nationalism in the Civil War North*. Lawrence: University of Kansas Press, 2002.

Lebsock, Suzanne. "Radical Reconstruction and the Property Rights of Southern Women." *Journal of Southern History* 43 (May 1977): 195–216.

Leckie, Shirley A., and William H. Leckie. *The Buffalo Soldiers: A Narrative of the Black Cavalry in the West*. Norman: University of Oklahoma Press, 2003.

Leiker, James N. *Racial Borders: Black Soldiers along the Rio Grande*. College Station: Texas A&M University Press, 2002.

Lentz-Smith, Adrienne. *Freedom Struggles: African Americans and World War I*. Cambridge, Mass.: Harvard University Press, 2009.

Leonard, Elizabeth D. *Men of Color to Arms!: Black Soldiers, Indian Wars, and the Quest for Equality*. New York: W. W. Norton, 2010.

Levin, Kevin M. *Remembering the Battle of the Crater: War as Murder*. Lexington: University Press of Kentucky, 2012.

Levine, Bruce. *Confederate Emancipation: Southern Plans to Free and Arm Slaves during the Civil War*. Oxford: Oxford University Press, 2006.

———. "In Search of a Usable Past: Neo-Confederates and Black Confederates." In *Slavery and Public History: The Tough Stuff of American Memory*, edited by James Oliver Horton and Lois E. Horton, 187–212. New York: New Press, 2006.

Linebaugh, Peter, and Marcus Rediker. "The Many-Headed Hydra: Sailors, Slaves and the Atlantic Working Class in the Eighteenth Century." *Journal of Historical Sociology* 3, no. 3 (September 1990): 191–214.

Litwack, Leon. *North of Slavery: The Negro in the Free States*. Chicago: University of Chicago Press, 1961.

Litwack, Leon, and August Meier, eds. *Black Leaders of the Nineteenth Century*. Urbana: University of Illinois Press, 1988.

Lorini, Alessandra. "Class, Race, Gender and Public Rituals: The New York African-American Community in the Civil War Era." *Storia Nordamericana* 7, no. 2 (1990): 17.

Manning, Chandra M. *Troubled Refuge: Struggling for Freedom in the Civil War*. New York: Alfred A. Knopf, 2016.

———. *What This Cruel War Was Over: Soldiers, Slavery and the Civil War*. New York: Random House, 2007.

Martin, Sandy Dwayne. "Black Churches and the Civil War: Theological and Ecclesiastical Significance of Black Methodist Involvement, 1861–1865." *Methodist History* 32 (1994): 174.

Masur, Kate. "The African-American Delegation to President Lincoln: A Reappraisal." *Civil War History* 56 (2010): 117.

———. *An Example for All the Land: Emancipation and the Struggle over Equality in Washington, D.C.* Chapel Hill: University of North Carolina Press, 1988.

Mays, Joe H. *Black Americans and Their Contributions to Union Victory*. Lanham, Md.: University Press of America, 1984.

McCarthy, Kathleen D. *American Creed: Philanthropy and the Rise of Civil Society, 1700–1865*. Chicago: University of Chicago Press, 2003.

McClure, James P., Leigh Johnsen, Kathleen Norman, and James Vanderlan, eds. "Circumventing the *Dred Scott* Decision: Edward Bates, Salmon P. Chase and the Citizenship of African Americans." *Civil War History* 43, no. 4 (December 1997): 279–309.

McConnell, Stuart. *Glorious Contentment: The Grand Army of the Republic, 1865–1900*. Chapel Hill: University of North Carolina Press, 1992.

McCurry, Stephanie. *Confederate Reckoning: Power and Politics in the Civil War South*. Cambridge, Mass.: Harvard University Press, 2010.

McDaniel, W. Caleb. *The Problem of Democracy in the Age of Slavery: Garrisonian Abolitionists and Transatlantic Reform*. Baton Rouge: Louisiana State University Press, 2013.

McFeely, William S. *Frederick Douglass*. New York: Norton, 1991.

McPherson, James M. *Battle Cry of Freedom: The Civil War Era*. New York: Oxford University Press, 1988.

———. *For Cause and Comrades: Why Men Fought in the Civil War*. New York: Oxford University Press, 1997.

———. "The *Glory* Story." *New Republic* 202, no. 2/3 (1990): 22.

———. *The Negro's Civil War: How American Negroes Felt and Acted during the War for the Union*. New York: Pantheon Books, 1965.

———. *The Struggle for Equality: Abolitionists and the Negro in the Civil War and Reconstruction*. Princeton, N.J.: Princeton University Press, 1964.

Miller, Stuart Creighton. *The Unwelcome Immigrant: The American Image of the Chinese, 1785–1882*. Berkeley: University of California Press, 1969.

Morgan, Edmund. *American Slavery, American Freedom: The Ordeal of Colonial Virginia*. New York: Norton, 1975.

Mullen, Robert W. *Blacks in America's Wars: The Shift in Attitudes from the Revolutionary War to Vietnam*. New York: Monad, 1973.

Nash, Gary B. *Forging Freedom: The Formation of Philadelphia's Black Community, 1720–1840*. Cambridge, Mass.: Harvard University Press, 1988.

———. *Red, White, and Black: The Peoples of Early North America*. 4th ed. Upper Saddle River, N.J.: Prentice Hall, 2000.

Neem, Johann N. *Creating a Nation of Joiners: Democracy and Civil Society in Early National Massachusetts*. Cambridge, Mass.: Harvard University Press, 2008.

Nelson, William Edward. *The Fourteenth Amendment: From Political Principle to Judicial Doctrine*. Cambridge, Mass.: Harvard University Press, 1988.

Newman, Richard S. *Freedom's Prophet: Bishop Richard Allen, the AME Church, and the Black Founding Fathers*. New York: New York University Press, 2008.

———. *The Transformation of American Abolitionism: Fighting Slavery in the American Republic*. Chapel Hill: University of North Carolina Press, 2002.

Novak, William J. "The Legal Transformation of Citizenship in Nineteenth-Century America." In *The Democratic Experiment: New Directions in American Political History*, edited by Meg Jacobs, William J. Novak, and Julian Zelizer, 85–119. Princeton, N.J.: Princeton University Press, 2003.

Oakes, James. "'The Compromising Expedient': Justifying a Proslavery Constitution." *Cardozo Law Review* 17 (1995–1996): 2023–56.

———. *Freedom National: The Destruction of Slavery in the United States, 1861–1865*. New York: W. W. Norton, 2013.

———. "Natural Rights, Citizenship Rights, States' Rights, and Black Rights: Another Look at Lincoln and Race." In *Our Lincoln: New Perspectives on Lincoln and His World*, edited by Eric Foner, 109–34. New York: W. W. Norton, 2008.

Packard, Jerrold. *American Nightmare: The History of Jim Crow*. New York: St. Martin's, 2002.

Park, John S. W. *Elusive Citizenship: Immigration, Asian Americans, and the Paradox of Civil Rights*. New York: New York University Press, 2004.

Pease, Jane H., and William H. Pease. "Negro Conventions and the Problem of Black Leadership." *Journal of Black Studies* 2 (September 1972): 29.

———. *They Who Would Be Free: Blacks' Search for Freedom, 1831–1861*. New York: Atheneum, 1974.

Perman, Michael. *The Road to Redemption: Southern Politics, 1869–1879*. Chapel Hill: University of North Carolina Press, 1984.

Phillips, Kimberly L. *War! What Is It Good For? Black Freedom Struggles and the U.S. Military from World War II to Iraq*. Chapel Hill: University of North Carolina Press, 2012.

Polgar, Paul. "'To Raise Them to an Equal Participation:' Early National Abolitionism, Gradual Emancipation, and the Promise of African American Citizenship." *Journal of the Early Republic* 31, no. 2 (2011): 229.

Potter, David. *The Impending Crisis: America before the Civil War, 1848–1861*. New York: Harper and Row, 1976.

Pybus, Cassandra. *Epic Journeys of Freedom: Runaway Slaves of the American Revolution and Their Global Quest for Liberty*. Boston: Beacon, 2006.

Quarles, Benjamin. *Allies for Freedom: Blacks and John Brown*. New York: Oxford University Press, 1974.

———. *Black Abolitionists*. New York: Oxford University Press, 1969.

———. "Black History's Antebellum Origins." In *African-American Activism before the Civil War: The Freedom Struggle in the Antebellum North*, edited by Patrick Rael, 78–100. New York: Routledge, 2008.

———. *The Negro in the Civil War*. Boston: Little and Brown, 1953.

Rael, Patrick. *Black Identity and Protest in the Antebellum North*. Chapel Hill: University of North Carolina Press, 2002.

———. "The Market Revolution and Market Values in Black Antebellum Protest Thought." In *African-American Activism before the Civil War: The Freedom Struggle in the Antebellum North*, edited by Patrick Rael, 272–94. New York: Routledge, 2008.

Ramold, Steven J. *Slaves, Sailors, Citizens: African Americans in the Union Navy.* DeKalb: Northern Illinois University Press, 2002.

Reed, Harry A. *Platform for Change: The Foundations of the Northern Free Black Community, 1775–1865.* East Lansing: Michigan State University Press, 1994.

Reidy, Joseph P. "The African American Struggle for Citizenship Rights in the Northern United States during the Civil War." In *Civil War Citizens: Race, Ethnicity and Identity in America's Bloodiest Conflict*, edited by Susannah J. Ural, 213–36. New York: New York University Press, 2010.

———. "Broadening Both the Letter and Spirit of the Law: Black Assertions of the Rights of Citizenship during the Civil War and Reconstruction." *Journal of the Afro-American Historical and Genealogical Society* 8 (1987): 148.

Richardson, Heather Cox. *The Death of Reconstruction: Race, Labor and Politics in the Post–Civil War North, 1865–1901.* Cambridge, Mass.: Harvard University Press, 2001.

———. *West from Appomattox: The Reconstruction of America after the Civil War.* New Haven, Conn.: Yale University Press, 2007.

Robertson, Craig. *The Passport in America: The History of a Document.* New York: Oxford University Press, 2010.

Rodrigue, John C. *Reconstruction in the Cane Fields: From Slavery to Free Labor in Louisiana's Sugar Parishes, 1862–1880.* Baton Rouge: Louisiana State University Press, 2001.

Rosen, Hannah. *Terror in the Heart of Freedom: Citizenship, Sexual Violence, and the Meaning of Race in the Postemancipation South.* Chapel Hill: University of North Carolina Press, 2009.

Rothman, Adam. *Slave Country: American Expansion and the Origins of the Deep South.* Cambridge, Mass.: Harvard University Press, 2005.

———. "The 'Slave Power' in the United States, 1783–1865." In *Ruling America: A History of Wealth and Power in a Democracy*, edited by Steve Fraser and Gary Gerstle, 64–91. Cambridge, Mass.: Harvard University Press, 2005.

Royster, Charles. *A Revolutionary People at War: The Continental Army and American Character, 1775–1783.* New York: W. W. Norton, 1979.

Sachs, Albie, and Joan Hoff Wilson. *Sexism and the Law: A Study of Male Beliefs and Legal Bias in Britain and the United States.* New York: Free Press, 1979.

Salyer, Lucy. *Laws as Harsh as Tigers: Chinese Immigrants and the Shaping of Modern Immigration Law.* Chapel Hill: University of North Carolina Press, 1995.

Samito, Christian G. *Becoming American under Fire: Irish Americans, African Americans and the Politics of Citizenship during the Civil War Era.* Ithaca, N.Y.: Cornell University Press, 2009.

Saville, Julie. *The Work of Reconstruction: From Slave to Wage Laborer in South Carolina, 1860–1870.* Cambridge: Cambridge University Press, 1996.

Schor, Joel. *Henry Highland Garnet: A Voice of Black Radicalism in the Nineteenth Century.* Westport, Conn.: Greenwood, 1977.

Schubert, Frank N. *Buffalo Soldiers, Braves and the Brass: The Story of Fort Robin-son, Nebraska*. Shippensburg, Pa.: White Mane, 1993.

Schwalm, Leslie A. *A Hard Fight for We: Women's Transition from Slavery to Free-dom in South Carolina*. Urbana: University of Illinois Press, 1997.

Shaffer, Donald. *After the Glory: The Struggles of Black Civil War Veterans*. Law-rence: University of Kansas Press, 2004.

———. "'I Do Not Suppose That Uncle Sam Looks at the Skin': African Americans and the Civil War Pension System, 1865–1934." *Civil War History* 46, no. 2 (June 2000): 132–47.

Shklar, Judith N. *American Citizenship: The Quest for Inclusion*. Cambridge, Mass.: Harvard University Press, 1991.

Sinha, Manisha. "Allies for Emancipation?: Lincoln and Black Abolitionists." In *Our Lincoln: New Perspectives on Lincoln and His World*, edited by Eric Foner, 167–96. New York: W. W. Norton, 2008.

———. "Coming of Age: The Historiography of Black Abolitionism." In *Prophets of Protest: Reconsidering the History of American Abolitionism*, edited by Timothy Patrick McCarthy and John Stauffer, 23–40. New York: New Press, 2006.

Slap, Andrew. *The Doom of Reconstruction: The Liberal Republicans in the Civil War Era*. New York: Fordham University Press, 2006.

Smith, Jessie Carney. "Mary Ann Campbell." In *Notable Black American Women: Book II*, edited by Jessie Carney Smith, 80–81. Detroit: Gale, 1996.

Smith, John David. "Let Us All Be Grateful That We Have Colored Troops That Will Fight." In *Black Soldiers in Blue: African American Troops in the Civil War Era*, edited by John David Smith, 1–77. Chapel Hill: University of North Carolina Press, 2002.

———. *Lincoln and the U.S. Colored Troops*. Carbondale: Southern Illinois University Press, 2013.

Smith, Rogers M. *Civic Ideals: Conflicting Visions of Citizenship in U.S. History*. New Haven, Conn.: Yale University Press, 1997.

———. "'One United People': Second-Class Female Citizenship and the American Quest for Community." *Yale Journal of Law and the Humanities* 1 (1988–89): 229–93.

Smith, Stacy L. *Freedom's Frontier: California and the Struggles over Unfree Labor, Emancipation and Reconstruction*. Chapel Hill: University of North Carolina Press, 2013.

Stampp, Kenneth. *The Era of Reconstruction, 1865–1877*. New York: Vintage, 1965.

Stancliff, Michael. *Frances Ellen Watkins Harper: African American Reform Rheto-ric and the Rise of a Modern Nation State*. New York: Routledge, 2011.

Stauffer, John. *The Black Hearts of Men: Radical Abolitionists and the Transforma-tion of Race*. Cambridge, Mass.: Harvard University Press, 2002.

Stearns, Francis Preston. *Cambridge Sketches*. 1905. Reprint, New York: Freeport, 1968.

Stewart, James Brewer. *Holy Warriors: The Abolitionists and American Slavery*. New York: Hill and Wang, 1976.

Stone, Frank A. *African American Connecticut: African Origins, New England Roots*. Storrs, Conn.: Isaac N. Thut World Education Center, 1991.

Summers, Mark W. *A Dangerous Stir: Fear, Paranoia, and the Making of Reconstruction*. Chapel Hill: University of North Carolina Press, 2009.

Tate, Gayle T. "How Antebellum Black Communities Became Mobilized: The Role of Church, Benevolent Society, and Press." *National Political Science Review* 4 (1993): 16.

Taylor, Alan. *Internal Enemy: Slavery and War in Virginia, 1772–1832*. New York: W. W. Norton, 2014.

Taylor, Amy Murrell. *Embattled Freedom: Journeys through the Civil War's Slave Refugee Camps*. Chapel Hill: University of North Carolina, Press 2018.

Taylor, Brian. "A Politics of Service: Black Northerners' Debate over Enlistment in the American Civil War." *Civil War History* 58 (2012): 451.

Taylor, Quintard. *In Search of the Racial Frontier: African Americans in the West, 1528–1990*. New York: Norton, 1990.

Teters, Kristopher A. *Practical Liberators: Union Officers in the Western Theater during the Civil War*. Chapel Hill: University of North Carolina Press, 2018.

Tomblin, Barbara. *Bluejackets and Contrabands: African Americans and the Union Navy*. Lexington: University of Kentucky, 2009.

Toppin, Edgar A. "Humbly They Served: The Black Brigade in the Defence of Cincinnati." *Journal of Negro History* 48 (1963): 75.

Trefousse, Hans L. *Thaddeus Stevens: Nineteenth-Century Egalitarian*. Chapel Hill: University of North Carolina Press, 1997.

Trotter, Joe William. *African American Urban Life in the Ohio Valley*. Lexington: University of Kentucky Press, 1998.

Trudeau, Noah Andre. *Like Men of War: Black Troops in the Civil War, 1862–1865*. Boston: Little, Brown, 1998.

Urwin, Gregory J. W. *Black Flag over Dixie: Racial Atrocities and Reprisals in the Civil War*. Carbondale: Southern Illinois University Press, 2014.

Varon, Elizabeth. *Appomattox: Victory, Defeat and Freedom at the End of the Civil War*. Oxford: Oxford University Press, 2014.

Voegeli, V. Jacque. *Free but Not Equal: The Midwest and the Negro during the Civil War*. Chicago: University of Chicago Press, 1967.

Vorenberg, Michael. "Citizenship and the Thirteenth Amendment: Understanding the Deafening Silence." In *The Promises of Liberty: The History and Contemporary Relevance of the Thirteenth Amendment*, edited by Alexander Tsesis, 58–77. New York: Columbia University Press, 2010.

———. *Final Freedom: The Civil War, the Abolition of Slavery, and the Thirteenth Amendment*. Cambridge: Cambridge University Press, 2001.

Waldstreicher, David. *In the Midst of Perpetual Fetes: The Making of American Nationalism, 1776–1820*. Chapel Hill: University of North Carolina Press, 1997.

Walker, Clarence E. *A Rock in a Weary Land: The African Methodist Episcopal Church during the Civil War and Reconstruction*. Baton Rouge: Louisiana State University Press, 1982.

Wang, Xi. *The Trial of Democracy: Black Suffrage and Northern Republicans, 1860–1910*. Athens: University of Georgia Press, 1997.

Wayman, A. W. *Cyclopaedia of African Methodism*. Baltimore: Methodist Episcopal Book Depository, 1882.

Weigley, Russell F. *The American Way of War: A History of United States Strategy and Military Policy.* Bloomington: Indiana University Press, 1973.

Wellman, Judith. *Brooklyn's Promised Land: The Free Black Community of Weeksville, New York.* New York: New York University Press, 2014.

Westwood, Howard C. *Black Troops, White Commanders, and Freedmen during the Civil War.* Carbondale: Southern Illinois University Press, 1992.

Wilentz, Sean. *The Rise of American Democracy: Jefferson to Lincoln.* New York: W. W. Norton, 2005.

Williams, Chad Louis. *Torchbearers of Democracy: African American Soldiers in the World War I Era.* Chapel Hill: University of North Carolina Press, 2010.

Williams, George Washington. *A History of the Negro Troops in the War of the Rebellion, 1861–1865.* New York: Kraus, 1969.

Williams, Gilbert Anthony. *"Christian Recorder," Newspaper of the African Methodist Episcopal Church: History of a Forum for Ideas.* Jefferson, N.C.: McFarland, 1996.

Wills, Garry. *Lincoln at Gettysburg: The Words That Remade America.* New York: Simon and Schuster, 1992.

Wilson, Carol. *Freedom at Risk: The Kidnapping of Free Blacks in America, 1780–1865.* Lexington: University of Kentucky Press, 1994.

Wilson, Douglas L. *Lincoln's Sword: The Presidency and the Power of Words.* New York: Alfred A. Knopf, 2006.

Wilson, Joseph T. *The Black Phalanx: A History of the Negro Soldiers of the United States in the Wars of 1775–1812, 1861–'65.* Hartford, Conn.: American, 1890.

Wilson, Keith P. *Campfires of Freedom: The Camp Life of Black Soldiers during the Civil War.* Kent, Ohio: Kent State University Press, 2002.

Winch, Julie. *A Gentleman of Color: The Life of James Forten.* New York: Oxford University Press, 2002.

———. *Philadelphia's Black Elite: Activism, Accommodation, and the Struggle for Autonomy, 1787–1848.* Philadelphia: Temple University Press, 1988.

Winkle, Kenneth. *Lincoln's Citadel: The Civil War in Washington, D.C.* New York: W. W. Norton, 2013.

Wynn, Neil A. *The African American Experience during World War II.* Lanham, Md.: Rowman and Littlefield, 2010.

Young, Alfred F. "George Robert Twelves Hewes (1742–1840): A Boston Shoemaker and the Memory of the American Revolution." *William and Mary Quarterly* 38, no. 4 (1981): 561.

Zuczek, Richard. *State of Rebellion: Reconstruction in South Carolina.* Columbia: University of South Carolina Press, 1996.

FILM

Glory. Produced by Pieter Jan Brugge et al. McDonough, Ga.: Columbia TriStar Home Video. 2 DVDs, 1989. 122 minutes.

INDEX

abolition, 59, 159

abolitionist movement, 5, 54, 84; activities of, 16, 21, 30, 31, 60, 98, 131, 138; Garrisonian wing of, 28, 30, 32–33; tensions within, 27–28

African American citizenship: new historical perspectives on, 9–10; pre–Civil War developments related to, 16, 19, 21–22; *Dred Scott* decision and, 29–30; black Northerners' thinking about, 33, 35, 48, 85, 102; African Americans' demands for, 62, 131–34, 138; Edward Bates's December 1862 decision and, 76–77, 87, 123, 186–87n33; black enlistment and, 79; protest over Union pay policy and, 112–13; black women and children's contributions to, 115; postwar campaign for, 131–34; "buffalo soldiers" and, 151–52; Civil War–era changes to, 141, 143, 145, 147, 149, 154–56, 158

African American military service, 23; prewar debate about, 15–16, 33–36; pre–Civil War history of, 17–19; as rhetorical touchstone for black protest, 24–25; as justification for black rights and citizenship, 134–35; Republicans' rhetorical use of, 142; impact of, 143, 148, 153–56

African American press, 5, 76, 102, 107

African American protest culture, 23–24; centrality of military service to, 24–25; acceptance of American principles in, 25–26; appeal to Declaration of Independence in, 26–27; and question of blacks' allegiance to United States, 31–36

African American women, 6, 28, 30, 113–15, 118

African Methodist Episcopal (AME) Church, 5, 43, 57

Ali, Muhammad, 160–61, 162

Aliened American, 146

Allen, Richard, 21, 23, 26, 83–84

Allen, W. P., 133

Alston, William Johnson, 117

American Anti-Slavery Society, 28, 32

Anderson, Peter, 58

Andrew, John, 8, 73–74, 80, 83, 87, 89, 92, 108, 188–89n53

Anglo-African Magazine, 137, 139

Antietam, Battle of, 65

Appomattox, 137, 150, 158

Appropriations Act, 122

Army of Northern Virginia, 60

Army of the Potomac, 121

Articles of Confederation, 19, 136

Attucks, Crispus, 17–18

Atwood, A., 137–38

Augusta, Alexander, 96

Banneker, Benjamin, 26

Banneker Institute, 50

Bannister, Carteaux, 121

Bates, Edward, and December 1862 opinion, 76–77, 79, 85, 87, 102, 104, 113, 121, 128–29, 131–32, 133, 147, 186–87n33; and definition of citizenship, 103, 107, 112, 123, 131–32; and black soldiers' pay, 122

CPSIA information can be obtained
at www.ICGtesting.com
Printed in the USA
LVHW092024110920
665720LV00009B/904